Royal Naval Missiles
The Royal Marines

Chapter 3 - The British Ar
British Army Major Units
British Army Equipment Sur
The Army Board
Chief of The General Staff

C000260379

Chain of Command	73
HQ Land Command	74
The Structure of Land Command	74
Ready Divisions	74
Composition of 1(UK) Armoured Division	75
Composition of 3 (UK) Division	76
The Battlegroup	77
Regenerative Divisions	78
Northern Ireland	79
Military Districts	80
16 Air Assault Brigade	81
The Cavalry	81
The Infantry	83
The Royal Artillery	88
Army Air Corps	91
Corps of Royal Engineers	93
The Royal Corps of Signals	95
The Royal Logistic Corps	96
Royal Electrical & Mechanical Engineers	98
Army Medical Services	99
The Adjutant General's Corps	100
Smaller Corps	101
The Regular Army Reserve	102

AS 90	
227 mm MLRS	115
Starstreak	116
Rapier	116
Lynx AH - Mark 7/9	117
Longbow Apache	118
BR90 Family of Bridges	119

Chapter 4 - The Royal Air Force

Squadron Listing	120
Air Force Board	126
Chief of The Air Staff	126
Chain of Command	128
Strike Command	128
No 1 Group	129
Air Warfare Centre (AWC)	129
No 2 Group	130
No 3 Group	131
Joint Helicopter Command	132
ASACS	133
Personnel & Training Command	135
RAF Logistics	139
Equipment Repair	140
Overseas Bases	141
RAF Station Organisation	142
Flying Squadron Organisation	142
Administration Wing Organisation	143

Operations Wing Organisation	143
Engineering Wing	144
Tornado GR-4	144
Tornado GR4A	146
Tornado F3	146
Jaguar	147
Harrier	148
Eurofighter Typhoon	149
Future Joint Combat Aircraft	150
Sentry AEW1	151
Nimrod	152
ASTOR	153
Tucano	154
C-130 Hercules	156
C-17 Globemaster	157
A-400	157
Chinook	158
Puma	159

Sea King HAR3	160
EH101 (Merlin)	160
RAF Weapons	161
RAF Regiment	166
RAF Reserves	168

Chapter 5 - Miscellaneous

The MoD's Civilian Staff	170
QinetiQ	171
The UK Defence Industry	172
Major Contractors Listing	173
The Services Hierarchy	174
Pay Scales	175
Codewords and Nicknames	177
Dates and Timings	177
Phonetic Alphabet	178
Useful Quotations	179
Abbreviations	182

Chapter 1 – THE MANAGEMENT OF DEFENCE

General Information

Populations - European Union - Top Five Nations

Germany	82.2 million
United Kingdom	58.7 million
France	59.5 million
Italy	57.5 million
Spain	39.0 million

Finance - European Union - Top Five Nations (2002 Figures)

	GDP	Per Capita Income
Germany	Euro 2,234 bn (US$2,128 bn)	US$25,900
United Kingdom	£983 bn (US$1,525 bn)	US$25,500
France	Euro 1,498 (US$1,427 bn)	US$24,600
Italy	Euro 1,295 (US$1,234 bn)	US$21,300
Spain	Euro 691 bn (US$659 bn)	US$16,600

UK Population - 58.7
(2001 census)

England -	49.1 million	Wales	-	2.9 million
Scotland -	5.06 million	Northern Ireland	-	1.68 million

UK Population Breakdown - Military Service Groups
(2003 estimate - figures rounded up)

Age Group	Total	Males	Females
15-19	3.6 million	1.8 million	1.7 million
20-24	3.5 million	1.7 million	1.7 million
25-29	3.8 million	1.8 million	1.9 million
30-34	4.4 million	2.1 million	2.3 million
35-39	4.6 million	2.2 million	2.3 million
40-44	4.1 million	2.0 million	2.0 million
45-49	3.7 million	1.8 million	1.8 million

UK Area (in square kilometres)

England	-	130,423
Wales	-	20,766
Scotland	-	78,133
Northern Ireland	-	14,160
Total	-	243,482

Government

The executive government of the United Kingdom is vested nominally in the Crown, but for practical purposes in a committee of Ministers that is known as the Cabinet. The head of the ministry and leader of the Cabinet is the Prime Minister and for the implementation of policy, the Cabinet is dependent upon the support of a majority of the Members of Parliament in the House of Commons. Within the Cabinet, defence matters are the responsibility of the Secretary of State for Defence. The Secretary of State for Defence has three principal deputies; the Minister for the Armed Forces; Minister for Defence Procurement and the Minister for Veterans.

The Missions of the Armed Forces

The MoD mission statement for the armed forces reads as follows "Defence policy requires the provision of forces with a high degree of military effectiveness, at sufficient readiness and with a clear sense of purpose, for conflict prevention, crisis management and combat operations. Their demonstrable capability, conventional and nuclear, is intended to act as an effective deterrent to a potential aggressor, both in peacetime and during a crisis. They must be able to undertake a range of Military Tasks to fulfil the missions set out below, matched to changing strategic circumstances." These missions are not listed in any order of priority:

A: Peacetime Security: To provide forces needed in peacetime to ensure the protection and security of the Untied Kingdom, to assist as required with the evacuation of British nationals overseas, to afford Military Aid to the Civil Authorities in the United Kingdom, including Military Aid to the Civil Power, Military Aid to Other Government Departments and Military Aid to the Civil Community.

B: Security of the Overseas Territories: To provide forces to meet any challenges to the external security of a British Overseas Territory (including overseas possession and the Sovereign Base Areas) or to assist the civil authorities in meeting a challenge to internal security. (An amendment to legislation in due course will formalise the change of title from "Department Territories" to "Overseas Territories").

C: Defence Diplomacy: To provide forces to meet the varied activities undertaken by the Ministry of Defence to dispel hostility, build and maintain trust, and assist in the development of democratically accountable armed forces (thereby making a significant contribution to conflict prevention and resolution).

D: Support to Wider British Interests: To provide forces to conduct activities to promote British interests, influence and standing abroad.

E: Peace Support and Humanitarian Operations: To contribute forces to operations other than war in support of British interests and international order and humanitarian principles, the latter most likely under UN auspices.

F: Regional Conflict Outside the NATO Area: To contribute forces for a regional conflict (but on an attack on NATO or one of its members) which, if unchecked, could adversely affect European security, or which could pose a serious threat to British interests elsewhere, or to international security. Operations are usually under UN or Organisation for Security Co-operation in Europe auspices.

G: Regional Conflict Inside the NATO Area: To provide forces needed to respond to a regional crisis or conflict involving a NATO ally who calls for assistance under Article 5 of the Washington Treaty.

H: Strategic Attack on NATO: To provide, within the expected warning and readiness preparation times, the forces required to counter a strategic attack against NATO.

This mission statement is further sub-divided into a number of Military Tasks (MT) which accurately define the way in which the missions are actually accomplished.

Total British Armed Forces – Overview (as at 1 June 2003)

Regular: 206,420; Locally Entered 4,000; Regular Reserves 240,000; Volunteer Reserves 50,000; Cadet Forces 130,000; MoD Civilians 115,000 (includes 14,000 locally entered civilians).

Regular Army 111,780; Royal Navy 41,370; Royal Air Force 53,270; (figures include all trained and untrained personnel). Royal Naval figure includes some 5,900 Royal Marines.

Strategic Forces

4 x Vanguard Class submarines each with 16 x Trident (D5) Submarine Launched Ballistic Missiles (SLBM) deploying with 48 x warheads per submarine. If necessary a D5 missile could deploy with 12 MIRV (multiple independently targetable re-entry vehicles). Future plans appear to be for a stockpile of 200 operationally available warheads and 58 missile bodies. Strategic Forces are provided by the Royal Navy.

Royal Navy

41,370: 12 x Tactical Submarines; 3 x Aircraft Carriers; 32 x Destroyers and Frigates; 22 x Mine Counter Measures Vessels; 2 x Assault Ships; 23 x Patrol Craft; 1 x Harrier Squadron; 9 x Helicopter Squadrons; 3 x Commando Groups and 1 x Logistic Unit (Royal Marines). Royal Fleet Auxiliary - 7 x Tankers; 4 x Fleet Replenishment Ships; 1 x Aviation Training Ship; 5 x Landing Ships; 1 x Forward Repair Ship; 2 x Roll-on Roll-off vessel; 1 x Ice Patrol Ship; 3 x Survey Ships.

Merchant Naval Vessels Registered in the UK, Crown Dependencies and Overseas Territories: 125 x Tankers; 144 x General Cargo Ships; 59 x Refrigerated Cargo Ships; 93 x Cellular Container Ships; 41 x Ro-Ro Ships; 19 x Passenger (Cruise) Ships; 11 x Large Tugs.

Royal Air Force

53,270: 5 x Strike/Attack Squadrons (includes 1 x reserve squadron); 3 x Offensive Support Squadrons; 6 x Air Defence Squadrons (includes 1 x reserve squadron); 4 x Maritime Patrol Squadrons (includes 1 x reserve squadron); 5 x Reconnaissance Squadrons; 2 x Airborne Early Warning Squadrons; 10 x Transport and Tankers Squadrons (includes 1 x reserve squadron); 12 x Helicopter Squadrons (including 8 x Helicopter Squadrons now part of the Joint Helicopter Command); 4 x Surface to Air Missile Squadrons; 6 x Ground (Field) Defence Squadrons.

Army

111,780 (excluding some 3,669 Gurkhas; 1 x Corps Headquarters in Germany (ARRC); 1 x Armoured Divisional HQ in Germany; 1 x Mechanised Divisional HQ in UK; Germany: 3 x Armoured Brigade Headquarters and 1 x Logistics Brigade HQ; UK: 3 x Deployable Combat Brigade HQ and 1 x Logistics Brigade HQ; 10 x Regional Brigade HQ; 3 x Northern Ireland Brigade HQ.

National Police Forces: England and Wales 125,000 Scotland 14,000, Northern Ireland 11,000.

Ministry of Defence (MoD)

In 1963, the three independent service ministries were merged to form the present Ministry of Defence (MoD). This large organisation which directly affects the lives of about half a million servicemen, reservists and MoD employed civilians, is controlled by The Secretary of State for Defence and his two deputies.

The Secretary of State for Defence chairs The Defence Council. This Defence Council is the body making the policy decisions that ensure the three services are run efficiently, and in accordance with the wishes of the government of the day.

Defence Council

The composition of The Defence Council is as follows:

The Secretary of State for Defence
Minister for the Armed Forces
Minister for Defence Procurement
Parliamentary Under-Secretary of State for Defence
Chief of the Defence Staff
Vice-Chief of the Defence Staff
Chief of the Naval Staff and First Sea Lord
Chief of the Air Staff
Chief of the General Staff
Permanent Under-Secretary of State
Chief of Defence Procurement
Chief Scientific Adviser
Second Permanent Under Secretary of State

Chief of The Defence Staff

The Chief of the Defence Staff (CDS) is the officer responsible to the Secretary of State for Defence for the co-ordinated effort of all three fighting services. He has his own Central Staff Organisation and a Vice Chief of the Defence Staff who ranks as number four in the services hierarchy, following the three single service commanders.
The current Chief of the Defence Staff is:

General Sir Michael Walker KCB CMG CBE ADC Gen

General Sir Michael Walker was born on 7 July 1944 in Salisbury, Southern Rhodesia. He was educated partly in Rhodesia and partly in Yorkshire. On leaving school he taught at a preparatory school for 18 months before attending the Royal Military Academy, Sandhurst. He was commissioned into the Royal Anglian Regiment in 1966 and served with the 1st Battalion as a platoon commander in Celle and Catterick. In 1969 he was posted to Cyprus as an ADC to the GOC Near East Land Forces. He returned to his battalion in 1971 and during the course of the next five years served in Northern Ireland, Cyprus and Tidworth variously as Operations Officer, Regimental Signals Officer and Adjutant. In 1975 he was posted to the Ministry of Defence as a Staff Officer.

He attended the Army Staff Course at Shrivenham and Camberly, returning to his battalion in Tidworth as a Company Commander. At the end of 1979 he was posted back to the Ministry of Defence to the Directorate of Military Operations. On promotion to Lieutenant Colonel he was appointed Military Assistant to the CGS from 1982 to 1985. He then commanded his battalion in Londonderry and Gibraltar. He commanded 20 Armoured Brigade in Detmold from December 1987 and after three years in command was appointed Chief of Staff 1 (British Corps) in Bielefeld (Germany). General Walker assumed the appointment of GOC North East District and Command 2 Infantry Division on 30

September 1991 and then GOC Eastern District on 1 April 1992. In December 1992 he returned to the Ministry of Defence as Assistant Chief of the General Staff.

In December 1994, as a Lieutenant General, he assumed command of the ARRC in Rheindahlen, Germany, and deployed with HQ ARRC to Bosnia Herzegovina from December 1995 to November 1996 to command the multinational land component of IFOR. On relinquishing command of the ARRC he became the Commander-in-Chief Land Command, based at Wilton in Wiltshire and became Chief of the General Staff on 14 April 2000. In April 2003 he became the Chief of the Defence Staff following the retirement of Admiral Sir Michael Boyce.

General Walker

Chain of Command

The Chief of the Defence Staff (CDS) commands and co-ordinates the activities of the three services through the following chain of command

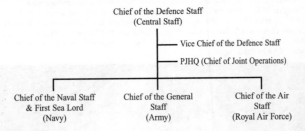

Chief of the Defence Staff
(Central Staff)

— Vice Chief of the Defence Staff

— PJHQ (Chief of Joint Operations)

Chief of the Naval Staff
& First Sea Lord
(Navy)

Chief of the General
Staff
(Army)

Chief of the Air
Staff
(Royal Air Force)

The three single service commanders exercise command of their services through their respective headquarters. However, the complex inter-service nature of the majority of modern military operations, where military, air and naval support must be co-ordinated, has led to the establishment of a permanent Tri-Service Joint Headquarters (PJHQ).

Permanent Joint Headquarters (PJHQ)

The UK MoD established a Permanent Joint Headquarters (PJHQ) at Northwood in Middlesex for joint military operations on 1 April 1996. This headquarters brought together on a permanent basis, intelligence, planning, operational and logistics staffs. It contains elements of a rapidly deployable in-theatre Joint Force Headquarters that has the capability of commanding rapid deployment front line forces.

The UK MoD Defence Costs Study of January 1994 identified a number of shortcomings with the command and control of UK military operations overseas. The establishment of PJHQ was an attempt to provide a truly joint force headquarters that would remedy the problems of disruption, duplication and the somewhat 'ad hoc' way in which previous operations had been organised

MOD officials have described the primary role of PJHQ as 'Working proactively to anticipate crises and monitoring developments in areas of interest to the UK'. The establishment of PJHQ has set in place a proper, clear and unambiguous connection between policy and the strategic direction and conduct of operations. Because it exists on a permanent basis rather than being established for a particular operation, PJHQ is involved from the very start of planning for possible operations. Where necessary, PJHQ then takes responsibility for the subsequent execution of these plans.

PJHQ, commanded by the Chief of Joint Operations (CJO), (currently a three star officer) occupies existing accommodation above and below ground at Northwood in Middlesex. PJHQ is responsible for planning all UK-led joint, potentially joint, combined and multinational operations and works in close partnership with MoD Head Office in the planning of operations and policy formulation, thus ensuring PJHQ is well placed to implement policy. Having planned the operation, and contributed advice to Ministers, PJHQ will then conduct such operations. The most recent example of PJHQ operational planning is the UK involvement in coalition operations in Afghanistan during 2001 and the the UK's involvement with the International Security Assistance Force (ISAF)in Kabul during 2002.

When another nation is in the lead, PJHQ exercises operational command of UK forces deployed on the operation.

Being a permanent joint Headquarters, PJHQ provides continuity of experience from the planning phase to the execution of the operation, and on to post-operation evaluation and learning of lessons.

Principal Additional Tasks of PJHQ Include:
Monitoring designated areas of operational interest
Preparing contingency plans
Contributions to the UK MoD's decision making process
Exercise of operational control of Overseas Commands (Falklands, Cyprus and Gibraltar)
Managing its own budget
Formulation of joint warfare doctrine at operational and tactical levels
Conducting joint force exercises
Focus for Joint Rapid Reaction Force planning and exercising

Overview Of International Operations.
From 1 Aug 1996 PJHQ assumed responsibility for current operations in the Middle East and the Former Yugoslavia. Non-core functions, such as the day-to-day management of the Overseas Commands in Cyprus, Falkland Islands, and Gibraltar, are also delegated by MoD Head Office to the PJHQ. This allows MoD Head Office to concentrate in particular on policy formulation and strategic direction. As of July 2003 PJHQ has been involved with UK commitments in the following areas:

Afghanistan, Albania, Algeria, Angola, Bosnia, Burundi, East Timor, Eritrea, Honduras, Iraq (including operations during 2003), Kosovo, Montenegro, Montserrat, Mozambique, Sierra Leone, East Zaire, West Zaire (Democratic Republic of the Congo).

Headquarters Structure.
PJHQ, brings together at Northwood some 420 civilian, specialist and tri-service military staff from across the MoD. The headquarters structure resembles the normal Divisional organisation, but staff operate within multidisciplinary groups which draw from across the headquarters. The headquarters must have the capability of supporting a number of operations simultaneously on behalf of the UK MoD.

PJHQ in the MoD Chain of Command

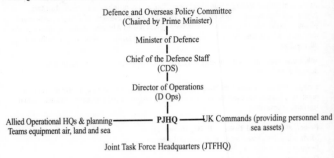

PJHQ Headquarters Structure

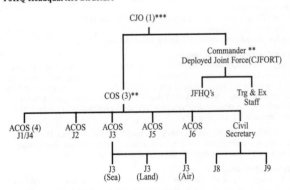

Notes:
(1) CJO - Chief of Joint Operations; (2) *** Denotes the rank of the incumbent (3) COS - Chief of Staff; (4) ACOS - Assistant Chief of Staff.

J1 Personnel and Admin	J6 Communication and Information Systems
J2 Intelligence	J7 Doctrine and Training
J3 Operations	J8 Plans
J4 Logistics	J9 Finance
J5 Policy	

The annual PJHQ budget is in the region of UK£381 million (2003). The annual running costs of the Headquarters is estimated at approximately UK£38 million.

Included in the overall PJHQ budget are the costs of the UK forces in the Falkland Islands, Cyprus and Gibraltar. Major operations such as the 1999 Kosovo commitment, Afghanistan and the 2003 operation in Iraq are funded separately by way of a supplementary budget, and in almost all cases this requires government- level approval. Small operations and the cost of reconnaissance parties are funded from the standard PJHQ budget.

Joint Rapid Reaction Force (JRRF)

The JRRF is essentially the fighting force that PJHQ has immediately available. The JRRF provides a force for rapid deployment operations using a core operational group of the Army's 16th Air Assault Brigade and the Royal Navy's 3rd Commando Brigade, supported by a wide range of air and maritime assets including the Joint Force Harrier and the Joint Helicopter Command.

The force uses what the MoD has described as a 'golfbag' approach with a wide range of units available for specific operations. For example, if the operational situation demands assets such as heavy armour, long range artillery and attack helicopters, these assets can easily be assigned to the force. This approach means that the JRRF can be tailored for specific operations, ranging from support for a humanitarian crisis to missions including high intensity operations.

The 'reach' of the JRRF will be enhanced by the Royal Navy's new amphibious vessels HMS Albion and HMS Bulwark, currently entering service. Both of these ships will be able to carry 650 troops plus a range of armoured vehicles including main battle tanks. A flight deck will allow ship-to-shore helicopter operations.

Responsibility for providing units to the JRRF remains with the single service commands who ensure that units assigned are at an extremely high state of readiness. JRRF units remain committed to NATO and a JRRF-assigned battalion group provides the UK commitment to the Allied Command Europe Mobile Force (Land).

The force commander is the CJRRFO (Chief of the Joint Rapid Reaction Force) who is responsible to the Chief of Joint Operations (CJO) at PJHQ. CJRRFO is supported by the Joint Force Operations Staff at PJHQ which would provide the deployable staff element of the JRRF when the force is deployed on operations.

Joint Force Logistics Component

The Joint Force Logistics Component (JFLogC) provides a joint logistic headquarters with force logistics under the command of PJHQ. It delivers co-ordinated logistic support to the deployed Joint Force in accordance with the commander's priorities. The composition of the JFLogC will be determined by PJHQ during the mission planning stage. Two logistic brigades have been assigned to JFLogC, one of these brigades was operational from March 2001 and the second available from March 2003.

Staff Branches

The Staff Branches that you would expect to find at every level in a headquarters from the Ministry of Defence down to garrison/station/port level are as follows:

Commander - The senior officer of the formation who in a large headquarters could be an Admiral, General or Air Marshal. The Army often refers to the commander as the GOC (General Officer Commanding), the Royal Air Force to the AOC (Air Officer Commanding) while the Royal Navy uses the term Flag Officer.

Chief of Staff - The officer who runs the headquarters on a day-to-day basis and who often acts as a second-in-command.

Gl Branch - Responsible for personnel matters including manning, discipline and personal services.
G2 Branch - Responsible for intelligence and security
G3 Branch - Responsible for operations including staff duties, exercise planning, training, requirements, combat development & tactical doctrine.
G4 Branch - Logistics and quartering.
G5 Branch - Civil and military co-operation.

An operational headquarters in the field will almost certainly be a tri-service organisation with branches from the Army, Navy and Air Force represented. The Staff Branches are the same for all three services.

Defence Logistics Organisation (DLO)

Following the establishment of PJHQ at Northwood it became important to combine the separate logistics functions of the three Armed Forces. As a result, in 2000 the three distinct separate service logistic functions were fused into one and the DLO was formed.
With its mission 'to sustain UK capability, current and future', the DLO spends approximately £9 billion a year to support front line operations. The DLO is responsible for keeping the services fully equipped and ready to act at any time, in war or peace. As the main logistics provider to the Armed Forces the DLO's responsibilities include:

Logistics planning, resource management, contractual support and policy
Global fleet management of land-based equipment
Support of the naval fleet and all naval systems
Communication and Information Systems
Transport and movements
Food and ration packs
Ammunition
Fuel, Oil and Lubricants
Postal services
Clothing and tentage
Storage for all equipment and material

At its inception it had been charged with reducing stock levels by £2.2 billion or 20 per cent of its stores. By 2003 the DLO had exceeded this target and delivered £2.8 billion in stock savings.

With approximately 28,000 personnel, the DLO is one of the largest organisations within the MoD. At the core of the DLO are its Integrated Project Teams (IPT's) which concentrate on supplying and supporting the armed forces. These teams fall into the five business units of Equipment Support (Land), Equipment Support (Air), The Warship Support Agency, the

Defence Communication Services Agency and the Defence Supply Chain. While each of these divisions is charged with a distinct task, together they keep the armed forces moving. The sixth unit that makes up the DLO is the Deputy Chief of Defence Logistics (DCDL). This area includes the DLO HQ, charged with setting policy and guidance for the DLO as a whole and providing briefing to the Chief of Defence Logistics (CDL).

The DLO needs to keep on track to achieve its Strategic Goal (to reduce output costs by 20 per cent before March 2006), whilst maintaining a first-class service to the personnel and units engaged in training and operations.

NATO Command Structure

The United Kingdom is a member of NATO (North Atlantic Treaty Organisation) and the majority of military operations are conducted in concert with the forces of NATO allies. In 1993, NATO was reorganised from three into two major Commands with a further re-organisation of these two commands in 2003. The first is ACT (Allied Command Transformation) with headquarters at Norfolk, Virginia (USA) and the second is ACO (Allied Command Operations), with its headquarters at Mons in Belgium.

NATO operations in which the United Kingdom was a participant would almost certainly be as part of a NATO force under the command and control of Allied Command Operations (ACO). The current Supreme Allied Commander is General James L Jones.

SACEUR - General James L Jones

General Jones is the Supreme Allied Commander, Europe (SACEUR) and the Commander of the United States European Command (COMUSEUCOM). From the Supreme Headquarters Allied Powers Europe, Mons, Belgium, General Jones leads Allied Command Europe (ACE), comprising NATO's military forces in Europe. The mission of ACE is to preserve the peace, security, and territorial integrity of the NATO member nations in Europe. As COMUSEUCOM, General Jones commands five US components: US Army, Europe; US Navy, Europe; US Air Forces in Europe; US Marine Forces; Europe and Special Operations Command, Europe. The European Command's mission is to support and achieve US interests and objectives throughout 93 countries in Central and Eastern Europe, Africa and portions of the Middle East. The command performs a variety of functions including planning for and conducting contingency operations such as noncombatant evacuations and humanitarian relief operations; providing combat-ready forces to both Allied Command Europe and other US unified commands; and conducting intelligence activities and security assistance.

General Jones spent his formative years in France, returning to the United States to attend the Georgetown University School of Foreign Service, from which he earned a Bachelor of Science degree in 1966. He was commissioned a Second Lieutenant in the Marine Corps in January 1967. Upon completion of The Basic School, Quantico, Virginia, in October 1967, he was ordered to the Republic of Vietnam, where he served as a Platoon and Company Commander with Company G, 2nd Battalion, 3rd Marines. While overseas, he was promoted to First Lieutenant in June 1968.

Returning to the United States in December 1968, General Jones was assigned to Camp Pendleton, California, where he served as a Company Commander until May 1970. He then received orders to Marine Barracks, Washington, DC, for duties as a Company Commander, serving in this assignment until July 1973. He was promoted to Captain in December 1970. From July 1973 until June 1974, he was a student at the Amphibious Warfare School, Quantico, Virginia.

In November 1974, he received orders to report to the 3rd Marine Division on Okinawa, where he served as the Company Commander of Company H, 2nd Battalion, 9th Marines, until December 1975. From January 1976 to August 1979, General Jones served in the Officer Assignments Section at Headquarters Marine Corps, Washington, DC. During this assignment, he was promoted to Major in July 1977. Remaining in Washington, his next assignment was as the Marine Corps Liaison Officer to the United States Senate, where he served until July 1984. He was promoted to Lieutenant Colonel in September 1982. He was then selected to attend the National War College in Washington, DC. Following graduation in June 1985, he was assigned to command the 3rd Battalion, 9th Marines, 1st Marine Division, Camp Pendleton, California., from July 1985 to July 1987.

In August 1987, General Jones returned to Headquarters Marine Corps, where he served as Senior Aide to the Commandant of the Marine Corps. He was promoted to Colonel in April 1988, and became the Military Secretary to the Commandant of the Marine Corps in February 1989. During August 1990, General Jones was assigned as the Commanding Officer, 24th Marine Expeditionary Unit at Camp Lejeune, North Carolina. During his tour with the 24th MEU, he participated in Operation Provide Comfort in Northern Iraq and Turkey. He was advanced to Brigadier General on April 23, 1992. General Jones was assigned to duties as Deputy Director, J-3, US European Command, Stuttgart, Germany, on July 15, 1992. During this tour of duty, he was reassigned as Chief of Staff, Joint Task Force Provide Promise, for operations in Bosnia-Herzegovina and Macedonia.
Returning to the United States, he was advanced to the rank of Major General in July 1994, and was assigned as Commanding General, 2nd Marine Division, Marine Forces Atlantic, Camp Lejeune, North Carolina. General Jones next served as Director, Expeditionary Warfare Division (N85), Office of the Chief of Naval Operations, during 1996, then as the Deputy Chief of Staff for Plans, Policies and Operations, Headquarters Marine Corps, Washington, DC. He was advanced to Lieutenant General on July 18, 1996.

His next assignment was as the Military Assistant to the Secretary of Defence. He was promoted to General on June 30, 1999, and became the 32nd Commandant of the United States Marine Corps on July 1, 1999. General Jones assumed duties as the Commander of US European Command on 16 January 2003 and Supreme Allied Commander Europe on 17 January 2003.

General Jones' personal decorations include: the Defense Distinguished Service Medal with two oak leaf clusters, Silver Star Medal, Legion of Merit with four gold stars, Bronze Star Medal with Combat "V", and the Combat Action Ribbon.

General Jones

Allied Command Operations (ACO)

Allied Command Operations, with its headquarters, SHAPE, near Mons, Belgium, will be responsible for all Alliance operations. The levels beneath SHAPE will be significantly streamlined, with a reduction in the number of headquarters. The operational level will consist of two standing Joint Force Commands (JFCs) one in Brunssum, the Netherlands, and one in Naples, Italy - which can conduct operations from their static locations or provide a land-based Combined Joint Task Force (CJTF) headquarters and a robust but more limited standing Joint Headquarters (JHQ), in Lisbon, Portugal, from which a deployable sea-based CJTF HQ capability can be drawn.

The current organisation of Allied Command Operations is as follows:

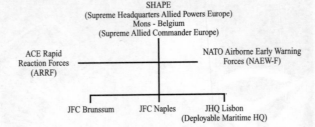

Component Headquarters at the tactical level

The component or tactical level will consist of six Joint Force Component Commands (JFCCs), which will provide service-specific - land, maritime, or air - expertise to the operational level. Although these component commands will be available for use in any operation, they will be subordinated to one of the Joint Force Commanders.

Joint Forces Command - Brunssum

Joint Forces Command - Naples

Static Air Operations Centres (CAOC)

In addition to the above component commands there will be a four static Combines Air Operations Centres with two more deployable as follows:

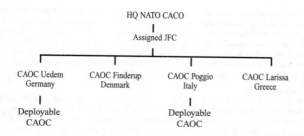

As the deployable CAOCs will need to exercise their capability to mobilise and deploy, the current facilities at Torrejon Air Base in Spain will probably be the primary site for training and exercising in that region. A small NATO air facility support staff would be stationed at Torrejon to support this capability.

Allied Command Transformation (ACT)

Allied Command Transformation, with its headquarters in Norfolk, US, will oversee the transformation of NATO's military capabilities. In doing so, it will enhance training, improve capabilities, test and develop doctrines and conduct experiments to assess new concepts. It will also facilitate the dissemination and introduction of new concepts and promote interoperability. There will be an ACT Staff Element in Belgium primarily for resource and defence planning issues.

ACT will command the Joint Warfare Centre in Norway, a new Joint Force Training Centre in Poland and the Joint Analysis and Lessons Learned Centre in Portugal. ACT Headquarters will also supervise the Undersea Research Centre in La Spezia, Italy. There will be direct linkages between ACT, Alliance schools and NATO agencies, as well as the US Joint Forces Command. A NATO Maritime Interdiction Operational Training Centre in Greece, associated with ACT, is also envisaged. In addition, a number of nationally- or multinationally-sponsored Centres of Excellence focused on transformation in specific military fields will support the command.

The new (2003) NATO concept

Under the new concept, NATO forces should be able to rapidly deploy to crisis areas and remain sustainable, be it within or outside NATO's territory, in support of both Article 5 and Non-Article 5 operations. The successful deployments of the Allied Command Europe Rapid Reaction Corps (ARRC) to two NATO-led Balkan operations (the Implementation Force (IFOR) to Bosnia Herzegovina in 1995 and Kosovo Force (KFOR) to Kosovo in 1999) are early examples of non-Article 5 crisis response operations outside NATO territory.

The new concept will have its largest impact on land forces. Maritime and air forces are by nature already highly mobile and deployable and often have a high state of readiness. Most of NATO's land based assets, however, have been rather static and have had limited

19

(strategic) mobility. In the new structure, land forces should also become highly deployable and should have tactical and strategic mobility. The mobility requirements will have great impact on the Alliance's transport and logistic resources (sea, land and air based). The need for quick reaction requires a certain amount of highly trained forces that are readily available. Further, interoperability (the possibility of forces to co-operate together with other units) and sustainability (the possibility to continue an operation for an extended period of time) are essential in the new force structure.

Multinationality

To express the Alliance's solidarity and its political cohesiveness and to enhance flexibility, there is also a need for multinationality, not only with regard to member countries, but further still. In the case of NATO-led crisis response operations there should be room for the participation of Partner countries or other non-NATO countries. Last but not least, adequate co-ordination mechanisms with international organisations must be ensured in these operations.

High Readiness Forces and Forces of Lower Readiness

There will be forces of two different kinds of readiness posture. First, forces with a higher state of readiness and availability, the so-called High Readiness Forces (HRF) to react on short notice. Second, forces with a lower state of readiness (FLR) to reinforce and sustain. Graduated Readiness Headquarters will be developed to provide these forces with command and control facilities.

- **Land forces:** Their deployable headquarters will be able to command and control assigned forces up to the corps-size level. Also a wide range of options will be available to command and control land forces at the brigade and division size to operate as stand-alone formation or subordinated to a higher HQ.
- **Maritime forces:** Their deployable headquarters will be able to command and control assigned forces up to the NATO Task Force Level. Also a wide range of options will be available to command and control maritime forces at NATO Task Unit level to operate as stand-alone formation or subordinated to a higher HQ.
- **Air forces:** The air forces will use the air command and control facilities of the present NATO Command Structure.

Implementation

At the level of the NATO Supreme Commanders programmes are underway to evaluate and certify the candidate HQ's according to the new standards and requirements. The High Readiness Forces (Land) Headquarters have already been certified and the Headquarters of Forces with Lower Readiness (Land) will follow in the coming years. The certification of the High Readiness Forces (Maritime) Headquarters will be finalised in 2004.

High Readiness Forces (Land) Headquarters candidates:

- The Allied Command Europe Rapid Reaction Corps (ARRC) HQ in Rheindalen (Germany) with the United Kingdom as framework nation;
- The Rapid Deployable German-Netherlands Corps HQ, based on the 1st German-Netherlands Corps HQ in Munster (Germany);
- The Rapid Deployable Italian Corps HQ based on the Italian Rapid Reaction Corps HQ in Solbiate Olona close to Milan (Italy);

- The Rapid Deployable Spanish Corps HQ based on the Spanish Corps HQ in Valencia (Spain);
- The Rapid Deployable Turkish Corps HQ based on the 3rd Turkish Corps HQ near Istanbul (Turkey);
- The EUROCORPS HQ in Strasbourg (France) sponsored by Belgium, France, Germany, Luxembourg and Spain.

Note: The EUROCORPS Headquarters which has a different international military status based on the Strasbourg Treaty, has signed a technical arrangement with SACEUR and can also be committed to NATO missions.

Forces of Lower Readiness (Land) Headquarters candidates:

The Multinational Corps HQ North-East in Szczecin (Poland) sponsored by Denmark, Germany and Poland;

The Greek "C" Corps HQ near Thessaloniki (Greece).

High Readiness Forces (Maritime) Headquarters:

Headquarters Commander Italian Maritime Forces on board of Italy's GARIBALDI;

Headquarters Commander Spanish Maritime Forces (HQ COMSPMARFOR) on board of LPD CASTILLA;

Headquarters Commander United Kingdom Maritime Forces (HQ COMUKMARFOR) on board of HMS ARK ROYAL.

The Allied Rapid Reaction Corps (ARRC)

The concept of the Allied Rapid Reaction Corps was initiated by the NATO Defence Planning Committee in May 1991 and confirmed during November 1991. The concept called for the creation of Rapid Reaction Forces to meet the requirements of future challenges within the alliance. The ARRC provides the Supreme Allied Commander Europe with a multinational corps in which forward elements can be ready to deploy in Western Europe within 14 days.

Currently the ARRC trains for missions across the spectrum of operations from deterrence and crisis management to regional conflict. The formation has to be prepared to undertake Peace Support Operations - both peacekeeping and peacemaking. Belgium, Canada, Denmark, Germany, Greece, Italy, The Netherlands, Norway, Portugal, Spain, Turkey, the United Kingdom and the United States all contribute to the Corps. Ten divisions are assigned to the ARRC and up to four of them could be placed under command for any specific operation. These divisions range from heavily armoured formations to lighter air-portable units more suited to mountainous or difficult terrain. Some of these formations are National Divisions, some are Framework Divisions, where one nation takes the lead and another contributes, and two are Multinational Divisions where the member nations provide an equal share of the command, staff and combat forces.

Headquarters ARRC is located in Rheindahlen, Germany with a peace-time establishment of 400 personnel. It comprises staff from all the contributing nations. A French liaison officer is officially accredited to the Headquarters. As the Framework Nation, the UK provides the infrastructure, administrative support, communications and 60% of the staff.

The Commander (COMARRC) and Chief of Staff are UK 3 Star and 2 Star generals and the Deputy Commander is an Italian 2 Star general. The other appointments, as with the training and exercise costs, are shared among the contributing nations.

During early 1996, HQ ARRC deployed to Sarajevo in the Former Yugoslavia to command the NATO Implementation Force (IFOR). In 1999 HQ ARRC was responsible for operations in Kosovo and in 2002 in Afghanistan.

Outline Composition of the ARRC (ACE Rapid Reaction Corps)

The assigned divisions fall into three categories:
National Divisions. National divisions are provided from: Greece, the 2nd (GR) Mechanised Division (Edessa, Greece) and Turkey, 1st (TU) Mechanised Division (Ankara, Turkey). Spain will also provide a divisional sized force (the Spanish Rapid Reaction Division - RRD) based in Madrid, Spain under special bi-lateral co-ordination agreements with NATO.
Framework Divisions. Framework divisions fall under the lead of one nation but have other nation's forces assigned for ARRC operations. The 7th (GE) Armoured Division (Düsseldorf, Germany) has assigned a Polish Brigade; The 3rd (IT) Mechanised Division (Milan, Italy) has assigned a Portuguese Parachute Brigade; the 1st (UK) Armoured Division (Herford, Germany) has assigned the Danish Reaction Brigade and the Czech Rapid Reaction Brigade; the 3rd (UK) Mechanised Division (Bulford, England) has assigned the Italian 132 Ariete Brigade; and the 1st (US) Armoured Division (Bad Kreuznach, Germany) has assigned a Hungarian Mechanised Brigade.

COMARRC has no command authority over these divisions in peace. However, he exercises co-ordinating authority over them which enables him and his staff to maintain a continual liaison with divisional commanders and their staffs. HQ ARRC and the assigned divisions train regularly together and hold joint seminars and study days. Common procedures have been established and headquarters work in a single language (English) so that the Corps can be operationally effective from the outset.

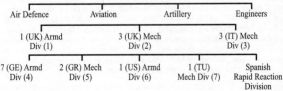

HQ ARRC
|
Corps Troops (including 7 Air Defence Bde)
Corps Combat Support Cell

Air Defence   Aviation   Artillery   Engineers

1 (UK) Armd Div (1)   3 (UK) Mech Div (2)   3 (IT) Mech Div (3)

7 (GE) Armd Div (4)   2 (GR) Mech Div (5)   1 (US) Armd Div (6)   1 (TU) Mech Div (7)   Spanish Rapid Reaction Division

Notes: (1) Resident in Germany (2) Resident in the UK (3) IT - Italy (4) GE - Germany (5) GR - Greece (6) US - United States (7) TU - Turkish.

The operational organisation, composition and size of the ARRC would depend on the type of crisis, area of crisis, its political significance, and the capabilities and availability of lift assets, the distances to be covered and the infrastructure capabilities of the nation receiving assistance. It is considered that a four-division ARRC would be the maximum employment structure.

The main British contribution to the ARRC is 1 (UK) Armoured Division that is stationed in Germany and there is also a considerable number of British personnel in both the ARRC Corps HQ and Corps Troops. In addition, in times of tension 3(UK) Mechanised Division and 16 Air Assault Brigade will move to the European mainland to take their place in the ARRC's order of battle. In total, we believe that if the need arises some 50,000 British soldiers could be assigned to the ARRC (20,000+ resident in Germany) together with substantial numbers of Regular Army Reservists and formed TA Units.

The Finances of Defence

"You need three things to win a war,
Money, money and more money".
Trivulzio (1441-1518)

In general terms defence is related to money, and a nation's ability to pay for its defence is linked to its GDP (Gross Domestic Product) as measured by the sum of all economic activity within a country. Estimates for the world's top six GDP rankings for 2002 (in billions of US$ and the latest year for which accurate figures are available) are as follows:

United States	-	$10,708 billion
Japan	-	$4,055 billion
Germany	-	$2,128 billion
United Kingdom	-	$1,525 billion
France	-	$1,472 billion
Italy	-	$1,1234 billion

In the 2002-2003 Financial Year (FY) the UK Government planned to spend £24.597 billion on defence.

For comparison purposes defence expenditure is often expressed as a percentage of GDP. Expenditure in FY 2000-2001 represented about 2.6 per cent of GDP and fell to around 2.4 per cent of GDP in FY 2001-02. It remains close to that level. In 1985 UK defence expenditure represented 5.2 per cent of GDP.

The total Central Government Expenditure plans for the FY 2002-2003 were budgeted at £306.58 billion and for comparison purposes the Government's major expenditure programmes during that period are as follows:

Central Government Expenditure 2002-2003

(In thousands of millions of pounds - one thousand million pounds is generally referred to as one billion)

Education and Skills	16,240
Health	52,603
Transport and Regions	8,674
Local Government	242
Home Office	6,001
Lord Chancellor's Departments	2,531
Attorney General's Departments	442
Defence	24,543
Foreign and Commonwealth Office	1,435
International Development	3,340
Trade and Industry	4,453
Environment, Food and Rural Affairs	2,165
Culture, Media and Sport	1,143
Work and Pensions	6,540
Scotland	11,735
Wales	5,576
Northern Ireland Executive	5,894
Northern Ireland Office	1,152
Chancellor's Departments	4,280
Cabinet Office	1,579
Social Security	109,170
Civil Service Pensions	5,050
Other	85,792
Total central government expenditure	360,580

Defence Budgets - NATO Comparison

The nations of the North Atlantic Treaty Organisation (NATO), spent some US$508 billion on defence during 2002. Of this total the European members of NATO spent US$149.92 billion. For ease of conversions from national currencies, amounts are shown in US$.

Country	2000 Budget
United States	$291.2 billion
Canada	$7.6 billion
Czech Republic	$1.153 billion
Denmark	$2.3 billion
France	$27.0 billion
Germany	$23.3 billion
Greece	$3.3 billion
Hungary	$791 million
Iceland	No defence budget
Italy	$16.0 billion
Luxembourg	$100 million
Netherlands	$6.2 billion
Norway	$2.9 billion
Poland	$3.2 billion
Portugal	$1.6 billion
Spain	$7.0 billion
Turkey	$7.7 billion
United Kingdom	$34.5 billion
TOTAL	**$438.144 billion**

Note: Iceland has no military expenditure although it remains a member of NATO.

An interesting comparison is made by the total national defence budget divided by the total number of full time personnel in all three services. 2002 figures for the top five world defence spending nations are as follows:-

Ranking	Nation	2000 Defence Budget	Total Service Personnel	Cost per Serviceman
1	USA	US$350.7 billion	1,414,000	US$248,000
2	Japan	US$42.6 billion	239,000	US$178,000
3	UK	US$38.4 billion	204,700	US$187,000
4	France	US$29.5 billion	260,000	US$113,461
5	Germany	US$24.9 billion	296,000	US$84,121

UK Defence Budget - Top Level Budget Holders

Under the early 1990s "New Management Strategy" the UK defence budget was allocated to a series of "Top Level Budget Holders" each of whom were allocated a budget with which to run their departments. The money allocated to these Top Level Budgets (TLBs) constitutes the building bricks upon which the whole of the defence budget is based.

Top Level Budgets 2002-2003

Naval Operational Areas (C-in-C Fleet)	£1,268 million
Army Operational Areas (C-in-C Land Command)	£3,740 million
General Officer Commanding (Northern Ireland)	£526 million
Air Force Operational Areas (AOC RAF Strike Command)	£1,851 million
Chief of Joint Operations	£381 million
Chief of Defence Logistics	£5,253 million
Second Sea Lord/Naval Home Command	£612 million
Adjutant General (Army) Personnel & Training Commanding	£1,425 million
Air Officer Commanding RAF Personnel & Training Command	£790 million
Second Permanent Under Secretary of State (Central)	£2,124 million
Defence Procurement Agency (1)	£5,813 million
Major Customers Research Budgets	£413 million
Conflict Prevention (following requests for extra resources)	£400 million
Total:	£24,597 million

Equipment Expenditure

From the 2000-2001 equipment budget the MoD Procurement Executive's business units were allocated money under the following headings:

Sea Equipment	-	£1,800 million
Land Equipment	-	£1,363 million
Air Equipment	-	£3,964 million
General Support	-	£1,031 million

Some of the more interesting equipment expenditure figures for the 2000-2001 Financial Year (the latest year for which the figures are available) are amongst the following:

Navy

Ships, hulls and machinery	-	£484 million
Naval weapon systems	-	£216 million
Ship equipment & support services	-	£113 million
Ship/weapon maintenance stores & equip	-	£600 million
Dockyard services	-	£386 million

Army

Guns, small arms and NBC defence stores	-	£15 million
Ammunition, mines and explosives	-	£27 million
Fighting vehicles	-	£103 million
Load carrying vehicles	-	£67 million
Engineering equipment	-	£76 million
Guided weapons	-	£165 million
Communications	-	£276 million
Surveillance equipment	-	£51 million
Maintenance	-	£583 million

Air Force

Aircraft, engines & aircraft equipment	-	£2,480 million
Guided weapons & electronic equipment	-	£1,485 million

Defence Personnel Totals
Total Service and Civilian Personnel Strength (1 April 2002)

UK service personnel	-	204,700
UK civilian personnel	-	89,300
Gurkhas	-	3,800
Locally entered/engaged service personnel	-	400
Locally entered/engaged civilian personnel	-	14,100
Royal Irish (Home Service)	-	3,600
		317,800

For comparison: Total Service and Civilian Personnel Strength (1 April 1990)

UK service personnel	305,700
UK civilian personnel	141,400
Locally entered/engaged service personnel	9,000
Locally entered/engaged civilian personnel	30,900
	487,000

Note: In 1990, the figures for the then Ulster Defence Regiment (full time personnel) were included in the UK service personnel total.

Strength of UK Regular Forces (1 April 2002)

Royal Navy	Officers	Other Ranks
Trained	6,500	30,300
Untrained	1,300	3,600
Army	Officers	Other Ranks
Trained	12,900	83,600
Untrained	1,200	12,400
Royal Air Force	Officers	Other Ranks
Trained	9,600	39,300
Untrained	1,300	2,800

Deployment in Budgetary Areas (1 April 2002)

	Officers	Other Ranks
Naval Operational Areas Consolidated Figure (1)	2,800	19,700

Royal Fleet Auxiliary total personnel 2,400

Note: (1) Consolidated figures are for: Naval Aviation, Fleet Infrastructure, Surface Fleet, Submarines and Royal Marines.

Army Operational Areas	Officers	Other Ranks
Joint Helicopter Command	1,300	10,500
1st (UK) Armoured Division	1,300	15,700
2nd Division	400	2,800
3rd UK Division	1,300	15,700
4th Division	300	1,100
5th Division	200	1,600
UK Support Command (Germany)	200	400

GOC Northern Ireland	600	6,500
Command and Training	1,800	15,400
Land Support	500	2,600
	7,700	**72,300**

Air Force Operational Areas	Officers	Other Ranks
1 Group	1,000	8,600
2 Group	1,600	8,700
3 Group	700	4,600
Chief of Staff	1,200	3,100
	4,600	**25,000**

Deployment Locations(1 April 2002)

United Kingdom

Royal Navy/Royal Marines	37,890
Army	78,600
Royal Air Force	47,230
Civilians	83,230

Balkans

Royal Navy/Royal Marines	-
Army	4,170
Royal Air Force	210
Civilians	-

Elsewhere in Mainland Europe

Royal Navy/Royal Marines	600
Army	18,700
Royal Air Force	1,150
Civilians	1,310

Gibraltar

Royal Navy/Royal Marines	220
Army	80
Royal Air Force	100
Civilians	60

Cyprus

Royal Navy/Royal Marines	10
Army	2,260
Royal Air Force	1,200
Civilians	300

Other Mediterranean

Royal Navy/Royal Marines	300 (On RN ships at sea)
Army	-
Royal Air Force	-
Civilians	-

Middle East

Royal Navy/Royal Marines	1,190
Army	2,090
Royal Air Force	1,910
Civilians	40

Far East/Asia

Royal Navy/Royal Marines	60
Army	280
Royal Air Force	40
Civilians	20

Sierra Leone

Royal Navy/Royal Marines	-
Army	240
Royal Air Force	10
Civilians	-

Elsewhere in Africa

Royal Navy/Royal Marines	-
Army	970
Royal Air Force	130
Civilians	-

USA

Royal Navy/Royal Marines	240
Army	200
Royal Air Force	160
Civilians	90

Canada

Royal Navy/Royal Marines	180
Army	860
Royal Air Force	110
Civilians	10

Central and South America

Royal Navy/Royal Marines	-
Army	390
Royal Air Force	-
Civilians	-

Falkland Islands

Royal Navy/Royal Marines	40
Army	640
Royal Air Force	670
Civilians	50

Other Locations

Royal Navy/Royal Marines	630

Army	120
Royal Air Force	80
Civilians	2,420

Unallocated

Royal Navy/Royal Marines	280
Army	310
Royal Air Force	-
Civilians	1,760

Note: These tables include personnel on detachment from units in the UK.

Recruitment of UK Regular Forces (2001-2002)

	Officers	Other Ranks
Royal Navy	410 (665)	4,600 (4,704)
Army	820 (1,525)	13,960 (18,743)
Royal Air Force	450 (936)	3,340 (6,078)

For Comparison - 1985-86 figures are in brackets.

Outflow of UK Regular Forces (2001-2002)

	Officers	Other Ranks
Royal Navy	530 (771)	5,220 (7,232)
Army	1,070 (1,985)	13,240 (19,316)
Royal Air Force	670 (983)	3,860 (6,234)

For Comparison - 1985-86 figures are in brackets.

Reserve Forces

In an emergency the UK MoD could call upon a tri-service reserve component of some 270,000 personnel (early-2003 figure). This figure is composed of Regular Reserves and Volunteer Forces as follows:

Naval Regular Reserves	- 23,500
Naval Volunteer Reserves	- 4,100
Regular Army Reserves	- 160,800
Territorial Army & Others	- 35,500
Royal Air Force Regular Reserves	- 40,300
Royal Air Force Volunteer Reserves	- 1,600

Regular Reserves (224,600) comprise ex-service personnel who have completed regular service and have a reserve liability in civilian life. The Volunteer Forces (41,200) comprise volunteers who may not have had prior regular service and train on a part time basis, generally at establishments close to their home.

Cadet Forces

In mid 2002 there were 129,300 in the cadet forces of the three services. Single service cadet force numbers (including Combined Cadet Force but excluding officers and administrative staff) are as follows:

Royal Navy	- 18,900

Army   - 66,800

Royal Air Force   - 43,500

Outline 2003 Figures - Regular Forces Personnel Strengths as at 1 June 2003

Notes: (1) Figures are for UK Regular Forces (including both Trained and Untrained personnel), and do not include Gurkhas, Full Time Reserve Service personnel, the Home Service battalions of the Royal Irish Regiment, mobilised reservists and Naval Activated Reservists. (2) Figures are taken from DASA information published in July 2003.

	Strength At 1 May 2003	Intake during May 2003	Outflow during May 2003	Strength at 1 June 2002	Intake 1 Apr 03 to 1 Jun 03	Outflow 1 April 03 to 1 Jun 03
All Services	**206,420**	**1,970**	**1,940**	**206,440**	**3,600**	**4,030**
Officers	33,110	260	150	33,280	380	380
Males	29,750	210	140	29,880	300	350
Females	3,360	40	10	3,400	70	30
Other Ranks	173,310	1,710	1,790	173,160	3,230	3,650
Males	158,770	1,530	1,640	158,600	2,890	3,320
Females	14,540	180	160	14,560	340	320
Royal Navy	**41,370**	**460**	**440**	**41,380**	**650**	**810**
Officers	7,760	50	40	7,780	60	90
Males	7,140	40	40	7,160	40	90
Females	610	10	-	630	20	-
Other Ranks	33,610	410	400	33,600	600	720
Males	30,530	340	360	30,500	490	640
Females	3,090	60	50	3,100	100	80
Army	**111,780**	**1,160**	**1,150**	**111,780**	**2,130**	**2,420**
Officers	14,360	180	60	14,520	190	150
Males	12,900	160	60	13,040	170	130
Females	1,460	20	10	1,480	20	20
Other Ranks	97,410	980	1,090	97,260	1,930	2,270
Males	90,630	930	1,020	90,500	1,820	2,100
Females	6,780	60	80	6,760	120	160
Royal Air Force	**53,270**	**340**	**350**	**53,270**	**820**	**800**
Officers	10,980	20	50	10,980	130	140
Males	9,700	20	50	9,680	100	120
Females	1,290	10	-	1,300	30	20
Other Ranks	42,280	320	300	42,300	700	660
Males	37,620	260	260	37,600	580	580
Females	4,670	60	30	4,690	120	80

Chapter 2 – THE ROYAL NAVY

Personnel Summary (at 1 June 2003)

	Strength at 1 June 2003
Royal Navy	**41,380**
Officers	7,780
Males	7,160
Females	630
Other Ranks	33,600
Males	30,500
Females	3,100

Note: The above figures include some 5,900 Royal Marines but do not include the approximate figure of 1,600 from the Army attached to 3 Commando Brigade. There are approximately 2,300 civilian personnel manning support ships operated by the Royal Fleet Auxiliary (RFA).

Estimated Fleet Strength

Submarines
In Service:
4 x Nuclear Powered Ballistic Missile firing (UK Strategic Deterrent) type. Displace 16,000 tons (three operational),
12 x Nuclear Powered Attack type. Displace 5,000 tons. Missile/torpedo armed (six operational).
New Construction:
3 x Nuclear Powered Attack type. Will displace 7,200 tons. Expected to enter service from 2008.

Major Surface Ships For Worldwide Operations
In Service:
3 x Aircraft Carriers. Displace 20,600 tons. Mix of fixed wing Harriers and helicopters (two operational).
1 x Helicopter Carrier. Displaces 22,000 tons. Helicopter Assault (one operational).
1 x Assault Ship. Displaces 19,500 tons. Amphibious Assault (one operational).
5 x Landing Ships. Displace 6,000 tons. Amphibious and Support Operations (four operational).
2 x Ro-Ro Ships. Displace 12,500 tons. Vehicle and Stores Carriers (two operational).
3 x new Ro-Ro Ships. Displace 15,000 tons. Strategic Sealift (Civil management - two operational).
1 x Forward Support Ship. Displaces 11,000 tons. Maintenance/Repair in operational area (one operational).
New Construction:
1 x Assault Ship. Will displace 19,500 tons. Second of class enters service 2004.
4 x Landing Ships. Will displace 16,000 tons. Expected to enter service from 2004.
3 x Ro-Ro Ships. Expected to enter service under civil management from late 2003.
Projected:

2 x Aircraft Carriers. Will displace 40,000 tons plus. Air Group of 40 plus fixed wing aircraft. Planned to enter service from 2012.

Destroyers And Frigates

In Service:
11 x Destroyers. Displace 4,500 tons. Missile and gun armed (six operational).
20 x Frigates. Displace 4,200 tons. Missile and gun armed (fifteen operational).
New Construction:
6 x Destroyers. Will displace 7,300 tons. Expected to enter service from 2008.

Minewarfare Vessels

In Service:
22 x Minehunters and Minesweepers. Deployable worldwide (fifteen operational).

Fleet Support Ships

(Manned by Royal Fleet Auxiliary personnel. Supply fuel, stores and ammunition at sea to fleet units).
In Service:
2 x Large Support Ships. Displace 36,500 tons. Supply fuel and stores (two operational).
1 x Large Fleet Tanker. Displaces 31,000 tons. Supplies fuel and some stores (one operational).
3 x Fleet Tankers. Displace 11,500 tons. Supply fuel (two operational).
2 x Large Stores Ships. Displace 23,400 tons. Supply ammunition and stores (two operational).
4 x Large Support Tankers. Displace 38,000 tons (three operational).
New Construction:
1 x Large Fleet Tanker displaces 31,000 tons. Supplies fuel and some stores. Enters service 2004.

Survey Ships

In Service:
1 x Ocean Survey Ship. Displaces 13,500 tons (one operational).
1 x Ocean Survey Ship. Displaces 3,700 tons (one operational).
1 x Small Survey Ship. Displaces 1,500 tons (one operational).
1 x Inshore Survey Craft. Displaces 26 tons. UK coastal waters only (one operational).
New Construction:
1 x Survey Ship. Displaces 3,700 tons. Enters service 2004.

Training And Patrol Ships And Craft

In Service:
1 x Aviation Training Ship. Displaces 26,000 tons. Helicopter training in home waters. Deployable overseas (one operational).
1 x Antartic Patrol Ship. Displaces 6.500 tons (one operational).
6 x Patrol Vessels. Displace 1,500 tons. Fishery Protection and patrol duties (five operational).
16 x Patrol Craft. Displace 50 tons. Training and Patrol duties (fourteen operational).
New Construction:
2 x Patrol Vessels. Displace 1,700 tons. Enter service from late 2003.

Naval Aircraft

28 x Sea Harrier. Air Defence and Recce/Attack.
38 x Sea King and Merlin Helicopters. Anti-submarine warfare.
48 x Lynx Helicopters. Anti-submarine warfare and missile armed for surface ship attack.
8 x AEW Sea King Helicopters. Provide radar airborne early warning to fleet.
29 x Sea King Commando Helicopters. Royal Marine Commando operations.
6 x Lynx Helicopters. Anti Tank attack role. Part of Commando Force.
9 x Gazelle Helicopters. Reconnaissance duties.

Composition of the Fleet

Submarines			Home Base
Trident	4	Vanguard, Victorious, Vigilant, Vengeance	Faslane
Fleet	7	Tireless, Torbay, Trafalgar Turbulent, Trenchant, Talent, Triumph	Devonport
	5	Sceptre, Spartan, Splendid, Superb, Sovereign.	Faslane
Carriers	3	Invincible, Illustrious, Ark Royal	Portsmouth
Destroyers (Type 42)	11	Cardiff, Exeter, Manchester Newcastle, Nottingham, Southampton Glasgow, Liverpool, York, Gloucester, Edinburgh	Portsmouth
Frigates (Type 23)	16	Norfolk, Sutherland, Monmouth Northumberland, Somerset, Argyll, Montrose, Richmond, Lancaster, Iron Duke, Westminster, Grafton, Marlborough, Kent, Portland, St Albans	Devonport/ Portsmouth
(Type 22)	4	Campbeltown, Chatham, Cornwall, Cumberland	Devonport
Assault Ships	1	Albion	Portsmouth
Helicopter Carrier	1	Ocean	Devonport
Offshore Patrol (Castle Class)	2	Dumbarton Castle, Leeds Castle	Portsmouth
(Island Class)	3	Anglesey, Guernsey, Lindisfarne	Portsmouth
(River Class)	1	Tyne	Portsmouth
Minehunters (Hunt Class)	11	Brocklesby, Chiddingford, Dulverton, Ledbury, Middleton, Atherstone, Cattistock, Cottesmore, Quorn, Hurworth, Brecon	Portsmouth
(Sandown Class)	11	Inverness, Sandown, Walney, Bridport, Penzance, Pembroke,	Faslane/Portsmouth

		Grimsby, Bangor, Ramsay, Blythe, Shoreham	
Coastal Training Craft	16	Biter, Blazer, Archer, Charger, Dasher, Smiter, Puncher, Pursuer, Example, Explorer, Express, Exploit, Tracker, Raider, Ranger, Trumpeter	

Two of these craft (Ranger and Trumpeteer) act as Gibraltar Guardships for Search & Rescue. The remaining 14 are employed as Universtity Naval Units (URNU) for training.

Ice Patrol	1	Endurance	Portsmouth
Survey Ships	5	Beagle, Herald, Scott Bulldog, Roebuck	Devonport
	1	Gleaner	Portsmouth

Note: Note: Numbers of surface ships and submarines worked up and fully operational can vary greatly, due to refit, repair or other problems. For example, at one point within the last few years the whole of the flotilla of 12 Fleet Submarines (SSNs) had to be checked out as a result of a serious reactor problem that developed in Tireless. See the 'Estimated Fleet Strength' section above for our estimate of current numbers operational of all types. The Royal Navy has very high standards of both operational efficiency and safety. The Fleet is worked hard.

Royal Fleet Auxiliary

Large Fleet Tankers	1	Wave Knight
Small Fleet Tankers	3	Black Rover, Gold Rover, Grey Rover
Support Tankers	4	Bayleaf, Brambleleaf, Oakleaf, Orangeleaf
Replenishment Ships	4	Fort George, Fort Austin, Fort Rosalie, Fort Victoria.
Aviation Training Ship	1	Argus
Landing Ship	5	Sir Galahad, Sir Geraint, Sir Bedivere, Sir Percivale, Sir Tristram
Forward Repair Ship	1	Diligence
Ro-Ro Cargo Ship	1	Sea Crusader

Civilian Managed Strategic Sealift Ships

Ro-Ro Cargo Ships	3	Hurst Point, Eddystone, Longstone

Fleet Air Arm

Role	Number	Type
Sea Harrier Force (See Note 1 below)		
Air Defence / Attack	14	Sea Harrier FA-2
Operational Conversion	12	Sea Harrier FA-2/T Mk8

Note 1. The Joint Force Harrier (JFH) was established on 1 April 2000 and

brought together the Sea Harrier FA.2 squadrons, previously under Naval Air Command, with the RAF's Harrier GR.7 squadrons in a new command within RAF Strike Command. See 'Fleet Air Arm' section later for more details.

Naval Helicopters

Anti-Submarine	20	Merlin HM Mk1
Anti-Submarine	22	Sea King HAS 5/6
Anti-Submarine / Anti-Ship	48	Lynx HAS 3, HMA 8
Airborne Early Warning	8	Sea King AEW 2

Commando Helicopter Force (See Note 2 below)

Commando Assault	29	Sea King HC4
Ground Attack	6	Lynx AH7
Reconnaissance	9	Gazelle

Note 2. As from 1 October 1999 the Commando Helicopter Force joined with the support and battlefield helicopters of the Army Air Corps and the Royal Air Force in the new Joint Helicopter Command (JHC). See 'Fleet Air Arm' section later for more details.

Aircrew Training

Observer Training	9	Jetstream T2 /T3
Search & Rescue Training	5	Sea King HAS Mk5
Fleet Training & Support	12	Hawk

Royal Marines Summary

1 x Commando Brigade Headquarters

3 x Royal Marine Commando (Battalion Size)

3 x Commando Assault Helicopter Squadrons

1 x Commando Light Helicopter Squadron

1 x Commando Regiment Royal Artillery

1 x Commando Squadron Royal Engineers

1 x Commando Logistic Regiment

1 x Special Boat Service Squadron

2 x Assault Squadrons (Landing-Craft)

1 x Security Unit for National Strategic Deterrent

Reserve Units

Higher Management of the Royal Navy

The Ministry of Defence (MoD) is a Department of State, headed by the Secretary of State for Defence (SofS) who creates Defence Policy and plans the spending of the Defence Budget. The MoD is the highest level of headquarters for the Armed Forces, both Administrative and Operational. All major issues of policy are referred to the SofS or to one of his three Ministerial colleagues:

- Minister for the Armed Forces Min(AF) responsible for Operational and Policy Issues
- Minister for Defence Procurement Min(DP) responsible for all Procurement Matters

- Under Secretary of State for Defence (USofS) responsible for Personnel, Estate Matters and Veterans Issues.

Under the Defence Council management of the Services is the responsibility of the Service Boards, in the case of the Royal Navy the Admiralty Board.

The Admiralty Board

The routine management of the Royal Navy is the responsibility of The Admiralty Board, the composition of which is as follows:

The Secretary of State for Defence

Minister of State (Armed Forces)

Minister of State (Defence Procurement)

Parliamentary Under-Secretary of State for Defence

Chief of the Naval Staff and First Sea Lord

Commander-in-Chief Fleet

Second Sea Lord and Commander-In-Chief Naval Home Command

Naval Member for Logistics

Controller of the Navy

Second Permanent Under-Secretary of State and Secretary of the Admiralty Board

Assistant Chief of Naval Staff

The Admiralty Board meets formally twice a year

The Navy Board

The First Sea Lord's responsibilities (delivery of naval capabilities, maintaining the strategic deterrent, planning and operational advice, management, overall efficiency and morale of the service) are exercised through the Service Executive Committee of the Admiralty Board, known as the Navy Board (NAVB). The First Sea Lord is the chairman of NAVB; its membership is the same as the Admiralty Board, but without Ministers. NAVB meets formally on a regular basis.

Sub Navy Board Committee

Many pan Navy decisions are taken by the Sub Navy Board Committee (SNBC) which is chaired by the Assistant Chief of Naval Staff (ACNS) with the NAVB members' deputies; Deputy Commander in Chief Fleet (DCINCFLEET), COS/2SL/CNH, Chief of the Strategic Systems Executive (CSSE), Capability Manager (Strategic Deterrent CM(SD) and Director General Resources and Plans (DGRP).

First Sea Lord and Chief of the Naval Staff
Admiral Sir Alan West KCB DSC ADC

Born in 1948, Admiral Sir Alan West joined the Navy in 1965. He has spent the majority of his career at sea serving in fourteen different ships and commanding three of them. He qualified as a Principal Warfare Officer in 1975 and Advanced Warfare Officer (Above Water Weapons) in 1978 and is also a Fighter Controller. He is a graduate of the Royal

Naval Staff Course, the Higher Command and Staff Course and the Royal College of Defence Studies.

In 1980 promoted to Commander, he took command of the frigate HMS Ardent taking the ship south to the Falkland Islands in 1982 where she was sunk in the successful retaking of the Islands. He was subsequently awarded the Distinguished Service Cross for his part in the action and led the Victory Parade through the City of London.

He has held several appointments in the Ministry of Defence and played a prominent role in the re-organisation of the MoD, the initiation of a new budgetary system (NMS) within the Services and he headed the study into women's integration and their service at sea.

Admiral Sir Alan West

Promoted to Rear Admiral in February 1994 he was responsible for naval manning, numbers and structures as well as career management and deployment. He moved the department from London to Portsmouth, set up the new organisation and prepared it for agency status. In February 1996 he became Commander United Kingdom Task Group and was almost permanently deployed in one of the CVSs leading the two largest and longest UK deployments since the Gulf and Falkland wars. The only European seaborne principal subordinate commander in NATO he was also a UK designated Joint Force Commander. He was promoted to Vice Admiral in October 1997 and appointed as Chief of Defence Intelligence.

He was created KCB in the Millennium New Years Honours List and promoted to Admiral in November 2000 when he took up his position as Commander-in-Chief Fleet, NATO Commander-in-Chief East Atlantic and NATO Commander Allied Naval Forces North. During this period as CinC he reorganised the Fleet Headquarters and moved the bulk of it to Portsmouth. He was also responsible for organising the Fleet response to "September 11th" which involved major maritime deployments in the northern Indian Ocean and the Royal Marines into Afghanistan.

He was appointed as First Sea Lord and Chief of the Naval Staff in September 2002 and this carries membership of the Defence Council and Admiralty Board. He is also the First and Principal Naval Aide-de-Camp to Her Majesty The Queen.

Management changes in the Royal Navy

Recent developments

Changes in the way that the Navy operates, is manned, supported and trained are proceeding currently. Though fleet strength has fallen by over 30% in the past 10 years the level of demand on the fleet remains undiminished. Therefore, a variety of measures are being undertaken to make best use of the ships in service and to streamline the command and HQ system. The chain of command diagrams of recent years have now been overtaken by fundamental changes and this is explained below.

Examples of changes are everywhere, not least the fact that the system of Squadrons of ships and submarines, each commanded by a Captain (F), (D) or (SM), has gone. Previously, the Commanding Officer of an individual ship would know that his Captain (F) was the person to whom he was responsible for the operational performance of his ship as a fleet unit. The Squadron staff, mostly based in Captain (F)'s ship, was there to advise the less experienced specialists in individual ships. However, a shrinking but busy fleet, deployed worldwide, has meant that individual ships rarely met up with their Captain (F)'s ship. A more supportive and efficient command/management system was needed and now it is being put in place.

Next, there is the question of sea training and in the past ships went to Flag Officer Sea Training (FOST) at Portland to be mercilessly chased for six weeks before emerging hopefully with a 'Sat', not to return for perhaps two years. That has all changed and FOST is now responsible for training at sea on a continuing basis for all surface ships and submarines - 'from cradle to grave'. These are examples of two of many changes.

Fleet First

A decision for change was made in 1999 and the Fleet Future Integrated and Rationalised Study Team (Fleet First) was set up to make proposals and then implement them. The first decision to be implemented was to co-locate the majority of shore staff in one building. Whale Island, Portsmouth was selected and the main Fleet Staff is now in situ. CinC Fleet and the deployment staff who manage day-to-day fleet operations remain at Northwood, together with the NATO Staff and the Permanent Joint Headquarters (PJHQ). Next, the previous organisation by type (i.e. submarines, aircraft, surface ships, Marines) has changed to one based on function - operations, capability, support. The seven destroyer, submarine and frigate squadrons have been replaced by 'Fleet Waterfront Organisations' at Portsmouth, Devonport and Faslane - each is commanded by a Commodore. These organisations are very much part of the Fleet HQ, though geographically dispersed and they exist to provide guidance and support to the units under their command. On return from a task or deployment the individual ship will be welcomed and supported in its home base by a shore staff familiar with the ship and its possible problems. A similar 'Waterfront' scheme has been established for the Royal Marines, Fleet Air Arm and the ships of the Royal Fleet Auxiliary.

Fleet Command and Organisation

The three simplified diagrams below provide the broad picture of the new command and management system for the fleet.

Overall Fleet Command Organisation

For clarity, this diagram and those below are simnplified. Many Commanders have two 'hats', e.g. COM (Ops) is also Rear Admiral Submarines.

Ranks of Commanders

Four Star is Admiral, Three Star is Vice Admiral, Two Star is a Rear Admiral (or Major General RM), One Star is a Commodore (or Brigadier RM).

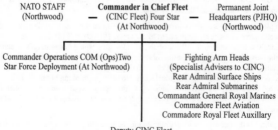

NATO STAFF
(Northwood)
— **Commander in Chief Fleet**
(CINC Fleet) Four Star
(At Northwood)
— Permanent Joint
Headquarters (PJHQ)
(Northwood)

Commander Operations COM (Ops) Two
Star Force Deployment (At Northwood)

Fighting Arm Heads
(Specialist Advisers to CINC)
Rear Admiral Surface Ships
Rear Admiral Submarines
Commandant General Royal Marines
Commodore Fleet Aviation
Commodore Royal Fleet Auxiliary

Deputy CINC Fleet
Three Star.
(At Portsmouth)
Main Fleet Staff
Force Provision
(See next)

Outline Fleet Staff Organisation

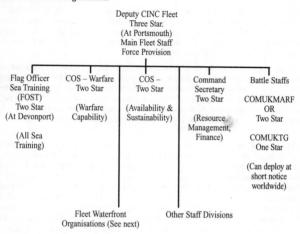

Deputy CINC Fleet
Three Star.
(At Portsmouth)
Main Fleet Staff
Force Provision

| Flag Officer Sea Training (FOST) Two Star (At Devonport) (All Sea Training) | COS – Warfare Two Star (Warfare Capability) | COS – Two Star (Availability & Sustainability) | Command Secretary Two Star (Resource Management, Finance) | Battle Staffs COMUKMARF OR Two Star COMUKTG One Star (Can deploy at short notice worldwide) |

Fleet Waterfront Organisations (See next)

Other Staff Divisions

Fleet Waterfront Organisations

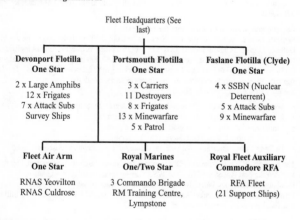

Fleet Headquarters (See last)

Devonport Flotilla One Star	**Portsmouth Flotilla One Star**	**Faslane Flotilla (Clyde) One Star**
2 x Large Amphibs	3 x Carriers	4 x SSBN (Nuclear Deterrent)
12 x Frigates	11 Destroyers	5 x Attack Subs
7 x Attack Subs	8 x Frigates	9 x Minewarfare
Survey Ships	13 x Minewarfare	
	5 x Patrol	

Fleet Air Arm One Star	**Royal Marines One/Two Star**	**Royal Fleet Auxiliary Commodore RFA**
RNAS Yeovilton	3 Commando Brigade	RFA Fleet
RNAS Culdrose	RM Training Centre, Lympstone	(21 Support Ships)

Naval Personnel

The Navy's 'Second Sea Lord and CINC Naval Home Command' is responsible for all naval manpower matters. With a nation having no serious current unemployment problems, the Royal Navy is competing for high grade people against attractive other careers. The key word is 'quality' as highly intelligent officers and ratings are essential to man the ships - and the same applies to the Royal Marines and RFA.

'Stretch' (long periods away from UK) is a matter of some importance as, though sailors and marines will respond to good leadership, they can be pushed (stretched) too far - good pay or even Financial Retention Incentives (FRIs is the slogan) are not enough. The Fleet has been stretched for many years and has continued to perform satisfactorily but personnel numbers have been falling. As mentioned above, the size of the Fleet has also been reducing following the end of the Cold War but it is now needs to stabilise at its present level in support of UK government policy.

Over a similar period as the 'Fleet First' initiative discussed previously the Second Sea Lord's department has been undertaking a fundamental study of today's and tomorrow's personnel problems. The long term vehicle for strategic management change in the Naval Service is called 'Tomorrow's Personnel Management System - Topmast' and the aim has been to look very carefully into the future using a team drawn from all levels of officers and ratings. One initiative already underway in surface ships is to group junior ratings of the three main branches (Warfare, Engineering, Supply) into 'Squads' in individual ships. For example, a Warfare Squad will have about 1.3 times the number of personnel to fill the posts in the complement, allowing the margin to be sent on leave, do courses ashore or undertake advancement training without affecting the fighting efficiency of the ship. The system is managed by the ship's officers, so that all involved are treated as valuable individuals.

Logistic and Maintenance Support for the Fleet

Separate logistic support for the three Services ended in 2000 with the establishment of the Defence Logistics Organisation (DLO). The DLO's mission is to provide joint logistic support to the UK Armed Services and employs about 30,000 personnel, of whom about 7,250 are uniformed (45% of uniformed personnel are R.N. officers and ratings). The DLO supports all equipments, systems and platforms in service with the Navy and its five agencies all support the Fleet. These agencies are:

- Warship Support Agency. This is the principal agency that supports the Fleet
- Equipment Support (Land). Support for Royal Marines
- Equipment Support (Air). Support for Fleet Air Arm
- Defence Supply Chain. Food, Stores and Ammunition
- Defence Communications. All voice and data services, including Satcom

The majority of RN personnel in DLO work in the Naval Bases and are managed by the Warship Support Agency (WSA). The WSA was set up in April 2001 and has its Headquarters in Abbey Wood, Bristol with other elements at Bath, Rosyth, Exeter, Pembroke Dock and the three Naval Bases. The WSA's annual budget is about £2 billion and fixed assets are valued at over £7 billion.

The support of modern warships as different and complex as nuclear submarines, carriers and minesweepers is a vast subject and is outside the scope of this brief summary. However, an example of a major operational problem with huge implications was the discovery of a serious nuclear plant defect in HMS Tireless. Every UK nuclear submarine (16 of them) had to be checked and this involved close co-operation between a wide variety of authorities both service and civilian. The highly successful repair programme was managed by WSA.

Royal Navy Shore Establishment and Reserve Units

Base	Function	Other functions
HM Naval Base, Portsmouth	Home base to surface ships, notably Carriers, Type 42 Destroyers and Type 23 Frigates.	Comander-in-Chief Home Command organisation
HM Naval Base, Devonport	Largest naval base in Western Europe. Home port for nuclear Attack submarines (SSNs), Large Assault Ships, Type 42 Destroyers, Type 23 Frigates, Hydrographic Ships.	Flag Officer Sea Training R.N. Hydrographic School
HM Naval Base, Clyde	Home base to UK's nuclear deterrent ballistic missile submarines (SSBNs). Also base to SSNs and minewarfare vessels.	HMS Caledonia at Rosyth provides support for naval personnel standing by ships and submarines in refit.
RN Air Station, Yeovilton	Home base to RN Sea Harriers, naval helicopter squadrons and other fixed wing aircraft. Yeovilton operates over 100 aircraft of different types. Nearly 4,000 uniformed and civilian personnel work at RNAS Yeovilton.	Training of aircrew and engineers of resident aircraft types. RN Fighter Controller School trains ground and airborne AEW controllers.
RN Air Station, Culdrose	RNAS Culdrose supports the Anti-Submarine Warfare and Airborne Early Warning helicopter squadrons of the Royal Navy. Eight Naval Air Squadrons are based at RNAS Culdrose, both front line and training Squadrons.	Responsible for the Operational and Advanced Flying Training of helicopter pilots, observers and aircrewmen.

Training Establishments

Establishment	Function	Other Functions
BRNC Dartmouth	The principal function of the College is the training of young officers for service in the Royal Navy. A large number of students from friendly Navies are also trained here.	A variety of other course are undertaken including Leadership & Teambuilding Programmes, seamanship, navigation and other naval subjects.
HMS Collingwood	HMS Collingwood is the Royal Navy's School of Communications and Weapon Engineering and is one of the largest training establishments in Europe. Collingwood is in the process of taking over the functions of H.M.S. Dryad and is becoming the new centre for all Maritime Warfare Training.	Training is currently split into 3 faculties - Communications, Engineering Principles and Weapon Engineering. The Maritime Warfare function is being rapidly developed. The training is carried out by both civilian and uniformed personnel.
HMS Dryad	The School of Maritime Operations (SMOPS) trains Warfare personnel appropriately for their individual tasks. Much of the training is in the process of being moved to H.M.S. Collingwood and Dryad is expected to be closed by the end of 2007.	Training of UK and foreign students in both above and under water warfare is the principal task. H.M.S. Dryad is also the specialist navigation school of the Royal Navy.
HMS Excellent	HMS Excellent has proud and important traditions but is also one of the newest establishments, having been recommissioned in 1994 to deliver a wide range of different training functions. These include damage control and firefighting and harbour training on board HMS Bristol for RNR personnel, cadet forces and youth organisations.	HMS Excellent provides support for a number of lodger units, most notably the Headquarters of Commander in Chief Fleet, and the UK's Operational Battle Staffs.
HMS Raleigh	HMS Raleigh is the new entry training establishment for all junior ratings entering the Royal Navy and the Royal Naval Reserve. About 2,500 people work in the Establishment and a New Entry of up to some 100 ratings joins almost every week of the year. The Artificer Apprentice Part 1 Training course takes place at Fisgard. Squadron within HMS Raleigh.	Also houses the Royal Naval Supply School, the Royal Naval Submarine School, the Royal Naval Seamanship School and schools for Firefighting and Nuclear Biological Chemical Defence.
HMS Sultan	HMS Sultan is the school of Marine and Air Engineering for the R.N. Training of Marine and Air Engineers of Foreign and Commonwealth Navies is also undertaken. Large numbers of officer and rating students are trained annually e.g. the Ship Systems Group alone has a throughput of some 1400 students per year. There are five other similar training groups	Also home to the Admiralty Interview Board, and other lodger units including the Central Air and Admiralty Medical Board.

Training Establishments
Royal Naval Reserve (RNR) Units

RNR Units are located at:

HMS Calliope	Gateshead
HMS Cambria	Penarth
HMS Caroline	Northern Ireland
HMS Dalriada	Greenock
HMS Eaglet	Liverpool
HMS Ferret	Chicksands
HMS Flying Fox	Bristol
HMS Forward	Birmingham
HMS King Alfred	Portsmouth
HMS President	London
HMS Scotia	Pitreavie
HMS Sherwood	Nottingham
HMS Vivid	Devonport
HMS Wildfire	Northwood

The 1998 Strategic Defence Review (SDR) announced that the size of the Royal Naval Reserve would be increased to 3,850. Current numbers are estimated at 3,000 (1,000 officers).

The RNR is a part time organisation, which complements the Royal Navy in times of war, conflict and in peacetime when there is a requirement. Entry into the RNR is the same as for the regular service. Training takes place on evenings and at weekends at the units listed above.

Principal Warships of the Royal Navy

In the following paragraphs we comment briefly on the significant classes of warship currently in service with the Royal Navy, together with those under construction and projected. The most important units are those with which we open our remarks, the four units which provide the UK's strategic nuclear deterrent.

Strategic Deterrent

The United Kingdom's Strategic Deterrent is undertaken by the Royal Navy and submarine launched ballistic missiles (SLBM) have been installed in Royal Naval submarines since the late 1960s. Operational patrols commenced in 1969 with US Polaris missiles embarked. The first class of UK SSBN (Nuclear Powered Ballistic Missile Submarine) was the Resolution Class with four boats - this class has now been replaced by the larger Vanguard class armed with 16 x US Trident II D5 missiles. Each missile has the capability of carrying up to 12 x MIRV (Multiple Independently Targeted Re-entry Vehicles) warheads, making a possible total of 192 warheads per submarine. The UK is believed to have purchased 58 x Trident 2D-5 missile bodies from the United States and the range of the missile is believed to be in excess of 9,000 km with a CEP (Circular Error of Probability) of about 100 metres. It is believed that in UK service the Trident II D5 carry eight warheads per missile.

These large submarines displace over 16,000 tonnes and have a length of 150 metres. The three decks offer accommodation for the crew of 130 which is unusually spacious for a submarine. Good domestic facilities are provided for the crew and the air purification system enables them to remain submerged for long periods without any outside support. Each submarine has two crews known as Port and Starboard - when one crew is away on patrol the other crew is training or taking leave.

Following the 1998 Strategic Defence Review (SDR), the UK MoD revealed that it was no longer necessary to have a stockpile of 300 warheads and that the stockpile was being reduced to 200 operationally available warheads. In addition, the 58 missile bodies already purchased would be sufficient to maintain a credible deterrent. The MoD confirmed that there would be one SSBN on patrol at any one time but carrying a reduced load of 48 warheads. In order to ensure one ship of a class to be available for operations, it is normally reckoned that three should be in service - one in repair or refit, one preparing for operations or working up and one fully operational. Four submarines provide a guarantee of one operational at all times. The four submarines of the Vanguard class are as follows:

- HMS Vanguard   1993
- HMS Victorious   1995
- HMS Vigilant   1996
- HMS Vengeance   1999

Fleet Submarines

The Royal Navy operates a total of 12 Nuclear Powered Attack Submarines (SSNs) in two classes - the Swiftsure and Trafalgar classes. Both classes are capable of continuous patrols at high underwater speed, independent of base support, and can circumnavigate the globe without surfacing. Under plans set out in the 1998 Strategic Defence Review, overall SSN force levels will drop to 10 boats by 2006, although all of these are to be configured to fire the Tomahawk Land Attack Cruise missile. The first of an initial three new Astute class SSNs was planned to enter service in mid-2005, with the second and third boats following in 2007 and 2009 respectively. However, budget and build problems indicate an in-service date of 2008 for the first of class, HMS Astute.

Armament

The boats of the Swiftsure and Trafalgar classes are armed with a mix of the following:
Submarine Launched Cruise Missiles (SLCM). Tomahawk Block IIIC, range 1,700 km
Anti-Ship Missiles. UGM-84B Sub Harpoon Block 1C; range 130 km
Wire-guided Anti-ship/submarine torpedoes. Range to 30 kms.

Swiftsure Class

Key specifications are as follows:
Length 82.9 m
Displacement 4,200 tons surfaced and 4,500 tons dived
Max Speed 20 knots surfaced and over 30 knots dived
Diving depth 400m (operational) and 600m maximum
Complement 12 officers and 85 ratings

Dates of Service Entry:

- Sovereign   1973
- Superb   1974
- Sceptre   1976
- Spartan   1978
- Splendid   1979

Trafalgar Class

Key specifications are as follows:

Length 85.4 m

Displacement 4,700 tons surfaced and 5,200 tons dived

Max Speed 20 knots surfaced and 32 knots dived

Diving depth 400m (operational) and 600m maximum

Complement 12 officers and 85 ratings

Dates of Service Entry:

- Trafalgar   1981
- Turbulent   1982
- Tireless   1984
- Torbay   1985
- Trenchant   1986
- Talent   1988
- Triumph   1991

Astute Class

Likely key specifications are as follows:

Length 97.0m

Displacement 6,500 tons surfaced and 7,200 tons dived

Max Speed 29 knots dived

Complement 12 officers and 84 ratings

Armament likely to be as for Swiftsure and Trafalgar classes.

Possible Dates of Service Entry for first three projected vessels:

- Astute   2008
- Ambush   2010
- Artful   2012

Aircraft Carriers

Invincible Class

The primary task of this class of ship is to act as the command ship for a small task force and provide organic air power against limited opposition. Since entering service in the early 1970s, the ships of this class have proved vital in protecting UK interests overseas from the Falklands (Malvinas) conflict of 1982 through to the amphibious assault on Iraq in the spring of 2003. Lessons have been learned over the years and the vital importance of 'an eye in the sky' has been recognised by developing the AEW Sea King helicopters. The problem with the ships is, of course, their small size for air operations at sea and the typical

Air Group below has been augmented by adding additional RAF Harriers and helicopters for specific operations.

Key specifications are as follows:
Length: 209.1m
Displacement: 20,600 tons full load
Max Speed: 28 knots. Range 7,000
n.miles at 19 knots.

Complement: 685 (60 officers) plus 366 (80 officers) air group plus up to 600 marines

Armament:
Aircraft. A typical embarked air group could consist of: 6 x Sea Harriers, 6 x Sea King HAS.6 (Anti-Submarine), 3 x Sea King HAS.2 (Airborne Early Warning).
Guns: 3 x Close-in Weapon Systems (Goalkeeper or Vulcan Phalanx) anti-aircraft or anti-missile.

Dates of Service Entry:

- Invincible   1977
- Illustrious   1978
- Ark Royal   1981

The Future Carrier (CVF)
Following the 1998 Strategic Defence Review (SDR), the UK MoD announced its intention to replace the Royal Navy's current carrier force with two larger vessels once the current vessels have reached the end of their planned lives. The intention was to acquire two CVFs, with the first unit entering service in 2012. Each would be capable of operating up to 50 aircraft (implying a displacement of at least 40,000 tonnes) and would have a crew of about 1,000 officers and ratings, including the Air Group. In addition to strike aircraft belonging to the RN/Royal Air Force Joint Force 2000 organization, the CVF will be required to support helicopter and UAV (unmanned aerial vehicle) operations. The short take-off and vertical landing (STOVL) variant of the US JSF (Joint Strike Fighter) is the UK's preferred choice for its Future Carrier Borne Aircraft requirement, to replace the Sea Harrier FA2 and Harrier GR7. The ships are to be built in UK but as yet no really serious money has been committed. "Build Decision Time" seems set for the spring of 2004 and, whatever happens, the programme cost will be high. Though the UK is much stronger economically than when a new carrier was debated in the late 1960s, budgetary problems are bound to be a problem.

Assault Ships.

Ocean (LPH)
HMS Ocean, an LPH (Landing Platform Helicopter) was built by Kvaerner Govan, on the Clyde, taking advantage of commercial build methods and facilities, before sailing for Barrow-in-Furness for fitting out prior to acceptance into service with the Royal Navy. The hull of the ship was built to Merchant Navy standards at a cost of some £170 million. The ship is capable of carrying an air group of 12 x Sea King troop lift helicopters and 6 x Lynx attack helicopters. In her relatively short service life Ocean has proved most valuable in undertaking varied "expeditionary" type activities worldwide.
Key specifications are as follows:

Length: 203.4 m
Displacement: 21,758 tons full load
Max Speed: 19 knots. Range 8,000 n.miles at 15 knots.
Complement: 285, 206 Air Group, plus up to 830 marines (Marine Commando Group)
Military lift: 4 LCVP Mk 5 (on davits); 2 Griffon hovercraft; 40 vehicles
Armament.
Aircraft. Helicopters: 12 Sea King HC Mk 4/Merlin plus 6 Lynx (or navalised variants of
WAH-64 Apache).
Guns: 8 Oerlikon/BMARC 20 mm GAM-B03 (4 twin). 3 Vulcan Phalanx Mk 15 Close-in
Weapon Systems

Date of Service Entry:

- Ocean   1998

Albion Class (LPD)

The contract (worth £449 million) to build the two LPDs (Landing Platform Docks) was
awarded on 18 July 1996 and first steel was cut 17 November 1997. There are two
helicopter landing spots and the configuration includes a well dock and stern gate together
with side ramp access. Substantial command and control facilities are included within a
large combined Operations Room. The ships are being built to military damage control
standards. Though conceived under the previous Conservative government this class fits in
well with the government's current concept of expeditionary activities worldwide. The UK
is developing a useful amphibious capability with the new Assault ships and other new
Landing Ships coming along.

Key specifications are as follows:
Length: 203.4 m
Displacement: 19,560 tons full load
Max Speed: 20 knots. Range 8,000 n.miles at 15 knots.
Complement: 325. Military lift: 305 troops; overload 710 troops; 67 support vehicles; 4
LCU Mk 10 or 2 LCAC (dock); 4 LCVP Mk 5 (davits)
Armament.
Guns: 2-20 mm (twin). 2 Goalkeeper Close-in Weapon Systems (CIWS)
Helicopters: Platform for 3 Merlin EH 101. Chinook capable.

Date of Service Entry:

- Albion   2003
- Bulwark   2004

Destroyers

Type 42 Class

The ships of this class are armed with the ageing Sea Dart medium-range air defence
missile system, which also has a limited anti-ship capability. In addition they have a useful
gun armament. They have been useful work horses of the fleet for many years and are
equipped with the latest communication and sensor equipments. HMS Nottingham was
very severely damaged by grounding on a charted reef off Lord Howe Island in 2002 and
will be non-operational for some years. She might have been scrapped but the fact that she

had just completed a costly update and that the Type 45s are delayed probably tipped the balance in favour of repair.

Key specifications are as follows:
Length:125.0 m
Displacement: 4,100 tons full load
Max Speed: 29 knots. Range 4,000 n.miles at 18 knots.
Complement: 253 (24 officers)
Armament:
Missiles: SAM: British Aerospace Sea Dart twin launcher, radar/semi-active radar guidance to 40 km; limited anti-ship capability.
Guns: 1 x 4.5 in (25 rounds/min. Range 22 km). 2 or 4 x 20 mm (Range 2kms). 2 x 20 mm Phalanx Close-in Weapon Systems (Range 1.5kms).
Modern above and under water sensors and decoys.
Helicopter: Lynx (Missile and torpedo armed).

Date of Service Entry
Batch 1

Cardiff	1979
Newcastle	1978
Glasgow	1979

Batch 2

Exeter	1980
Southampton	1981
Nottingham	1982 (See remarks above)
Liverpool	1982

Batch 3

Manchester	1982
Gloucester	1985
Edinburgh	1985
York	1985

Type 45 - Daring Class
This project has gone through many stages, resulting in slippage of the originally envisaged in-service date of first of class from 2000 to 2007. The lives of the Type 42 class ships have, therefore, had to be extended. The contract for the design and build of the first three ships was placed in December 2000. Following extensive consultation this was amended in late 2001 to reflect a new procurement strategy in which commitment was made to the first six ships. An order for a further batch of three may be placed in 2004.

Plans are believed to include 12 x Type 45 Destroyers that are needed in service by 2015, with the entire programme budgeted at about £6 billion. The Type 45, displacing around 7,200 tons, will be equipped with the UK variant of the Principal Anti-Air Missile System (PAAMS). Design and construction of the first ships is to be split between BAE Systems and Vosper Thornycroft. Overall project management is the responsibility of BAE Systems, with two of the ships being assembled at Scotstoun, by BAE Systems and the other by Vosper Thornycroft at a new shipbuilding facility at Portsmouth Naval Yard.

Key specifications are as follows:
Length:152.4 m
Displacement: 7,350 tons full load
Max Speed: 29 knots. Range 7,000 n.miles at 18 knots.
Complement: 187
Armament (Estimated).
Missiles: SSM: 8 Harpoon (2 quad)
Surface to Air (SAM): 6 DCN Sylver A 50 VLS PAAMS (principal anti-air missile system); 16 Aster 15 and 32 Aster 30 weapons or combination.
Guns: 1 Vickers 4.5 in (114 mm)/55 Mk 8 Mod 1. 2 x 20 mm Vulcan Phalanx Close-in Weapon Systems.
Helicopters: Lynx or Merlin.

Date of Service Entry (Projected):

Daring	2007
Dauntless	2008
Diamond	2010
Dragon	2011
Defender	2012
Duncan	2012

Frigates

Type 23 (Duke Class)

The first of class was ordered from Yarrows on 29 October 1984 at the height of the Cold War. Further batches of three were ordered in September 1986, July 1988, December 1989, January 1992 and February 1996. The class is now completed. There were some early problems, e.g. the Command System was not operational as quickly as had been planned, but these have been overcome and the RN has made steady improvements to weapons and sensors in the ships over the years since first introduction. From 1999, the Lynx helicopter was replaced on some of the vessels by the EH 101 Merlin helicopter. These ships are powered by a CODLAG system (Combined diesel-electric and gas-turbine propulsion) and the diesel-electric is used for minimum underwater noise during ASW operations.

Key specifications are as follows:
Length:133.0 m
Displacement: 4,200 tons full load
Max Speed: 28 knots. Range 7,800 n.knots.

Complement: 181 (13 officers)
Armament:
Missiles:Surface-to-Surface (SSM). 8 x Harpoon (130km range). Surface-to-Air (SAM). Sea Wolf (Range 6 kms)
Guns: 1 x 4.5 in (25 rounds/min. Range 22kms). 2 x 30mm twins (Range 10kms)
Date of Service Entry:

Norfolk	1987
Argyll	1989
Marlborough	1989
Lancaster	1990
Iron Duke	1991
Monmouth	1991
Montrose	1992
Westminster	1992
Northumberland	1992
Richmond	1993
Somerset	1994
Grafton	1994
Sutherland	1996
Kent	1998
St Albans	2000
Portland	1999

Type 22 (Broadsword) Class

The remaining four ships of this class have a useful armament and sensor fit and, by the standards of some Navies, are still quite youthful. The above water armament reflects the lessons of the Falklands conflict - plenty of guns and missiles. The earlier ships have either been sold to Brazil (the Batch 1 frigates) or scrapped.

Key specifications are as follows:

Length:148.0 m
Displacement: 4,500 tons full load
Max Speed: 30 knots (18 knots on Tynes). Range 4,500 n.miles at 18 knots.
Complement: 250 (31 officers)
Armament:
Missiles:Surface-to-Surface (SSM). 8 x Harpoon (130km range). Surface-to-Air (SAM). Sea Wolf (Range 6 kms)
Guns: 1 x 4.5 in (25 rounds/min. Range 22kms). 1 x Goalkeeper 30mm Close-in Weapon System. 2 x 30mm twins (Range 10kms)
Modern above and underwater sensors and decoys.
Helicopter: 2 Westland Lynx HMA 3/8; or 1 Westland Sea King HAS 5 (Missile and Torpedo armed)

Date of Service Entry:

Cornwall	1988
Cumberland	1988
Campbeltown	1989
Chatham	1989

Mine Warfare Vessels.

Hunt Class (Minesweepers/Minehunters - Coastal)

The first of this advanced class of GRP-built mine countermeasures vessels, HMS Brecon, entered service in 1979. The Royal Navy has a small but highly efficient mine warfare force and the Hunts were regarded as very costly when first entering service. However they have proved their value repeatedly and modernisation proceeds. There are upgrade plans for a new minehunting sonar and command system. When deployed operationally they are fitted with additional weapon systems and communications. Also used for Fishery Protection duties.

Key specifications are as follows:

Length: 57.0 m
Displacement: 750 tons full load
Max Speed: 15 knots. Range 1,500 n.miles at 12 knots.
Complement: 45 (5 officers)
Armament: 1 x 30 mm (650 rounds/min. Range 10 km). For operational deployments also fitted with 2 x 20 mm (900 rounds/min to 2 km) and 2 x 7.62 mm MGs.
Full range of sensors and systems for dealing with all types of ground and moored mines.

Date of Service Entry:

Brecon	1979
Ledbury	1979
Cattistock	1981
Cottesmore	1982
Brocklesby	1982
Middleton	1983
Dulverton	1982
Chiddingfold	1983
Hurworth	1984
Atherstone	1986
Quorn	1988

Sandown Class (Minehunters)

HMS Sandown, the first of the new Single-Role Minehunter class, entered service in 1988, and HMS Blythe, the latest, entered service in January 2001. Of Glass Reinforced Plastic (GRP) construction, they are capable of operating in deep and exposed waters, e.g. the approaches to the Clyde where the ballistic missile armed submarines are based. Sandown Class vessels are equipped with a mine-hunting sonar and mine-disposal equipment, making them capable of dealing with mines at depths of up to 200 m.

Key specifications are as follows:

Length: 52.2 m
Displacement: 450 tons full load
Max Speed: 13 knots. Range 2,500 n.miles at 12 knots.
Complement: 34 (5 officers)
Armament: 1 x 30 mm (650 rounds/min. Range 10 km).
Full range of sensors and systems for undertaking any minehunting task.

Date of Service Entry:

Sandown	1988
Inverness	1990
Walney	1991
Bridport	1992
Penzance	1997
Pembroke	1997
Grimsby	1998
Bangor	1999
Ramsey	1999
Blythe	2001
Shoreham	2001

Antartic Patrol Ship

Endurance

HMS Endurance (previously MV Polar Circle) entered service with the Royal Navy in 1991 and supports British interests in the South Atlantic and Antarctic waters. The ship works alongside members of the British Antarctic Survey Team, carrying out hydrographic surveying, meteorological work and research programmes. The hull is painted red for easy recognition in ice and the vessel has importance as a political presence in the Southern Ocean and Antartica

Key specifications are as follows:

Length: 57.0 m
Displacement: 6,500 tons full load
Max Speed: 15 knots. Range 6,500 n.miles at 12 knots.
Complement: 112 (15 officers) plus 14 Royal Marines
Helicopters: 2 Westland Lynx HAS 3.
Range of Sensors.

Date of Service Entry
Endurance   1991

Survey Ships

HMS Scott

This ship was ordered in January 1995 and entered service in June 1997. She is equipped with an integrated navigation suite for surveying operations, together with a Sonar Array Sounding System (SASS) and data processing equipment. She also has gravimeters, a towed proton magnetometer and the Sonar 2090 ocean environment sensor. The ship is planned to remain at sea for 300 days per year with a crew of 42, with 20 personnel being rotated from shore to allow leave and recreation.

Key specifications are as follows:

Length: 131.1m
Displacement: 13,500 tons full load
Max Speed: 17.5 knots.
Complement: 62 (12 officers)

Hydrographic sensor fit (See above).
Helicopters: Platform for 1 light helicopter.

HMS Scott entered service in 1997.

Echo Class

An order was placed with Vosper Thornycroft in 2000 for two new Hydrographic Vessels. This is a 'through life contract' covering support for 25 years. The ships will work with the fleet worldwide, supporting mine warfare and amphibious tasks besides carrying out specialist hydrographic activities. As with Scott (see previous entry) the ships are planned to work over 300 days per year at sea.

Displacement, tons: 3,470 full load
Dimensions, feet (metres): 295.3 x 55.1 x 18 (90 x 16.8 x 5.5)
Main machinery: Diesel electric; 4 MW; 2 azimuth thrusters
Speed, knots: 15. Range, 9,000 miles at 12 kt
Complement: 46 with accommodation for 81
Hydrographic Sensor fit.

Date of Service Entry:

Echo	2003.
Enterprise	2004.

Patrol Vessels

Patrol Vessels are used for fishery protection and patrolling Britain's offshore gas and oilfield installations. In addition these useful ships can be used further afield, e.g. Castle class are used in the Falklands patrol role.

Island Class

The original order for ships of this class was placed in July 1975. The earlier ships were retrofitted and the remainder built with enlarged bilge keels to damp down their motion in heavy weather. Stabilisers fitted. Generally used in the Fishery Protection Squadron. Can carry small RM detachment and two Avon Sea Rider semi-rigid craft with 85 hp motor, for boarding. Being replaced by the River Class, now entering service.

Key specifications are as follows:
Length: 59.0m
Displacement: 1,260 tons full load
Max Speed: 16.5 knots. Range 7,000 n.miles at 12 knots.
Complement: 35 (5 officers)
Armament: 1 x 20mm
Sensors and Combat Data System

Date of Service Entry:

Guernsey	1977	
Lindisfarne	1978	
Anglesey	1979	

Castle Class

Ships were started as a private venture and ordered in August 1980. The design includes an ability to lay mines. Inmarsat commercial communications terminals are fitted. Two Avon Sea Rider high-speed craft are embarked. HMS Leeds Castle is based in the Falklands.

Key specifications are as follows:
Length: 81.0 m
Displacement: 1,427 tons full load
Max Speed: 19.5 knots. Range 10,000 n.miles at 12 knots.
Complement: 45 (6 officers) plus austerity accommodation for 25 Royal Marines
Armament: 1 x 30 mm, range 10 kms
Sensors and Combat Data System
Helicopters: Platform for operating Sea King or Lynx.

Date of Service Entry

Leeds Castle	1981
Dumbarton Castle	1982

River Class

Vosper Thornycroft contracted in May 2001 for the construction, lease and support of three vessels over an initial five-year period to replace the ships of the Island Class (see previous entry). HMS Tyne was launched on 27 April 2002.

Key specifications are as follows:
Length: 79.75 m
Displacement: 1,700 tons full load
Max Speed: 20 knots. Range 5,500 n.miles at 15 knots.
Complement: 30 (plus 18 Boarding Party)
Armament: 1 x 20 mm
Sensors and Combat Data System
Small helicopter deck

Date of Service Entry:

Tyne	2003
Severn	2004
Mersey	2004

The Royal Fleet Auxiliary Service

The Royal Fleet Auxiliary Service (RFA) is a civilian manned fleet, owned by the Ministry of Defence. Its main task is replenish the warships of the Royal Navy at sea with fuel, food, stores and ammunition. Thus it fills a vital role that is becoming increasingly important as the current UK government has worldwide ambitions which demand the services of the Royal Navy. Other RFA tasks include amphibious support and sea transport for the Army. The RFA is managed by the Commodore RFA who is directly responsible to Commander in Chief Fleet for the administration and operation of the organisation.

The RFA employs over 2,000 civilian officers and ratings, and is one of the biggest employers in the UK shipping industry. Replenishment of warships at sea requires specialist knowledge and training, and RFA personnel are on terms of service that take account of both of these activities and of being directed to possible operational areas. Many RFA ships carry naval or military parties for tasks such as the operation and maintenance of helicopters.

The RFA boasts a significant number of large ships, especially in comparison with the warships it supports. The largest ship in the present Royal Navy is HMS Ocean, displacing 21,758 tons full load. In the RFA there are 10 vessels (the largest at 49,000 tons) that are larger. Though many of these ships are ageing, the UK MoD has made fair provision for realistic support of a global reach for the Royal Navy.

Tankers

Wave Class (Large Fleet Tankers)

Following a tendering process, contracts to build two ships were placed with VSEL (BAE Systems) on 12 March 1997. There have been many delays in the construction of the two vessels but at last the first, Wave Knight, entered service in March 2003, two years later than originally planned. We are forecasting Wave Ruler to enter service early in 2004. The ships have a one spot flight deck with full hangar facilities for a Merlin helicopter. There are three Replenishment rigs and one crane.

Key specifications are as follows:
Length: 181.7 m
Displacement: 30,300 tons full load
Max Speed: 18 knots. Range 10,000 n.miles at 15 knots.
Complement: 80 plus 22 helicopter personnel
Cargo capacity 16,000 metric tons
Helicopters: 1 x Merlin helicopter.
Guns: Fitted for (but not with) 2 x Phalanx Close-in Weapon Systems..

Date of Service Entry:

Wave Knight	2003
Wave Ruler	2004

Appleleaf Class (Support Tankers)

Support Tankers have the dual role of both replenishing warships and fleet tankers at sea and undertaking the bulk movement of fuels between naval supply depots. Specifications for each ship differ somewhat, therefore figures below are illustrative.

Key specifications are as follows:
Length: 170.0m
Displacement: 38,000 tons full load
Speed: 15.5 knots.
Complement: 56 (19 officers)
Cargo capacity 25,000 metric tons
Guns: 2 x 20 mm Oerlikon. 4 x 7.62 mm MGs.

Date of Service Entry:

Brambleleaf	1980
Orangeleaf	1982
Bayleaf	1982
Oakleaf	1981

Rover Class (Small Fleet Tankers)

These small tankers have proved most valuable over many years in supplying HM ships at sea with fuel, fresh water, limited dry cargo and refrigerated stores in all parts of the world. There is no hangar but a helicopter platform is served by a stores lift, to enable stores to be transferred at sea. Two of the class have been sold on, one to Portugal and one to Indonesia.

Key specifications are as follows:
Length: 140.6m
Displacement: 11,522 tons full load
Speed: 19 knots. Range 15,000 at 15 knots.
Complement: 50 (17 officers)
Cargo capacity 6,600 metric tons
Guns: 2 x 20 mm Oerlikon. 4 x 7.62 mm MGs.

Date of Service Entry:

Grey Rover	1970
Gold Rover	1974
Black Rover	1974

Fleet Replenishment Ships

Fort Victoria Class (Fleet Replenishment Ships)

These ships provide fuel and stores support to the Fleet at sea. The original plan was to build six of the class but the diminishing requirement and undoubted budget problems has meant that only two of these large and excellent ships have been constructed. There are four dual-purpose abeam replenishment rigs for simultaneous transfer of liquids and solids, besides stern refuelling. There are repair facilities for Merlin helicopters.

Key specifications are as follows:
Length: 203.5 m
Displacement: 36,580 tons full load
Speed: 20 knots
Complement: Ships crew 134 (95 RFA plus 15 RN plus 24 civilian stores staff). Embarked Air Group up to 150 personnel (includes 28 officer air crew).
Cargo capacity 12,500 metric tons liquids. 6,200 metric tons solids
Helicopters: 5 x Sea King or Merlin helicopters.
Guns: 2 x 30 mm. 2 x Phalanx Close-in Weapon Systems.
Sensor fit appropriate for aircraft control.

Date of Service Entry:

| Fort Victoria | 1994 |
| Fort George | 1993 |

Fort Grange Class (Fleet Replenishment Ships)

These ships were ordered in 1971 and after valuable service are approaching 25 years old. Usually a single helicopter is embarked and ASW armaments for helicopters are carried on board. There are six cranes, three of 10 tons lift and three of 5 tons. They have been used at Split as support ships for UK forces in the Balkans from 1997 to 2000.

Key specifications are as follows:
Length: 183.9m
Displacement: 23,384 tons full load
Speed: 22 knots. Range 10,000 miles at 20 knots
Complement: 114 (31 officers) plus 36 RNSTS (civilian supply staff) plus 45 RN aircrew
Cargo capacity 3,500 tons ammuntiion and stores.
Helicopters: Up to 4 x Sea King.
Guns: 2 x 20 mm.

Date of Service Entry:
Fort Rosalie	1978
Fort Austin	1979

Landing Ships
Sir Bedivere Class (Landing Ships Logistic)

These vessels are very old but still useful units. Fitted for bow and stern loading with drive-through facilities and deck-to-deck ramps. Facilities provided for onboard maintenance of vehicles and for laying out pontoon equipment. Mexeflote self-propelled floating platforms can be strapped one on each side. Sir Tristram was severely damaged off the Falkland Islands in June 1982 and Tyne Ship repairers were given a contract to repair and modify her. This included lengthening by 29 ft, an enlarged flight deck capable of taking Chinook helicopters, a new bridge and twin masts. The aluminium superstructure was replaced by steel and new communications, SATCOM, navigation systems and helicopter control radar were installed. Sir Bedivere had a similar SLEP (Service Life Extension Programme) contract in Rosyth from December 1994 to January 1998, including new main engines, a new bridge, and the helicopter platform lowered by one deck, which has reduced the size of the stern ramp. Plans to SLEP Sir Percival were abandoned and she will be one of the first to be replaced by Lyme Bay and Largs Bay when they enter service in 2004/05. Sir Tristram will be replaced by one of the follow-on ships and the future of Sir Bedivere is under consideration.

Key specifications are as follows:
Length: 125.6 m
Displacement: 6,700 tons full load (After Service Life Extension Programme - SLEP)
Speed: 17 knots. Range 8,000 n.mile at 15 knots
Complement: 51 (18 officers); 49 (15 officers) (SLEP)
Military Lift: 340 troops (534 hard lying); 17 or 18 (SLEP) MBTs; 34 mixed vehicles; 120 tons POL; 30 tons ammunition; 1-25 ton crane; 2-4.5 ton cranes. Increased capacity for 20 helicopters (11 tank deck and 9 vehicle deck) after SLEP
Guns: 2 or 4 x 20 mm. 4 x 7.62 mm MGs.
Helicopters: Platforms to operate Gazelle, Lynx, Chinook (SLEP) or Sea King.
Sensor fit appropriate for aircraft control.

Date of Service Entry:

Sir Bedivere	1967 (SLEP)
Sir Galahad	1968
Sir Percival	1968
Sir Tristram	1965 (SLEP)

Bay Class (Landing Ships Logistic)

These ships will displace over double the figure of the class they are replacing. Two ships were ordered in 2000 and contracts for two further ships of the class were placed in November 2001. The design is based on the Dutch LPD Rotterdam. These are planned to transport troops, vehicles, ammunition and stores as a follow-up to an amphibious assault. Offload is carried out by a flight deck capable of operating heavy helicopters, an amphibious dock capable of operating one LCU and mexeflotes which can be hung on the ships' sides. There is no beaching capability.

Key specifications are as follows:
Length: 176.0 m
Displacement: 16,160 tons full load
Speed: 18 knots. Range 8,000 n.mile at 15 knots
Complement: 60, plus 356 troops
Military Lift: Space for vehicles equating to 36 Challenger MBTs or 150 light trucks plus 200 tons ammunition
Helicopters: Platform capable of operating Chinook.

Projected Date of Service Entry:

Largs Bay	2004
Lyme Bay	2005
Mounts Bay	2005
Cardigan Bay	2006

Miscellaneous RFA Vessels

Argus – Aviation Training Ship

Argus was procured for a helicopter training role. This former Ro-Ro container ship was converted for her new task by Harland and Wolf, completing in 1988. The former Ro-Ro deck is used as a hangar with four sliding WT doors able to operate at a speed of 10 m/min. Argus can replenish other ships underway. There is one lift port midships and one abaft the funnel. Domestic facilities are somewhat limited if she is used in the Command support role. She was the first RFA to be fitted with a command system. Argus has a subsidiary role as a Primary Casualty Receiving Ship - facilities were improved significantly following an upgrade period completed late 2001. This included conversion of three decks into a permanent 100-bed hospital with three operating theatres.

Key specifications are as follows:
Length: 175.1m
Displacement: 26,421 tons full load
Speed: 18 knots. Range 20,000 n.mile at 15 knots
Complement: 80 (22 officers) plus 35 permanent RN plus 137 RN Aviation personnel

Military lift: 3,300 tons dieso; 1,100 tons aviation fuel; 138 x 4 ton vehicles in lieu of aircraft
Guns: 4 x 30 mm. 4 x 7.62 mm MGs.
Combat Data System and Sensor fit appropriate for aircraft control.
Fixed-wing aircraft: Provision to transport 12 BAe Sea Harrier FA-2.
Helicopters: 6 Westland Sea King HAS 5/6 or similar.

Date of Service Entry:

Argus   1988

Diligence - Forward Repair Ship

This ship was originally the Stena Inspector, designed as a Multipurpose Support Vessel for
North Sea oil operations, and completed in 1981. She was chartered on 25 May 1982 for
use as a fleet repair ship during the Falklands War and purchased from Stena (UK) Line in
October 1983. She was then converted in 1984 for use as Forward Repair Ship in the
South Atlantic (Falkland Islands). The conversion was a significant undertaking and
included:

- Workshops for hull and machinery repairs (in well-deck);
- Accommodation for naval Junior Rates (new accommodation block);
- Extensive craneage facilities;
- Overside supply of electrical power, water, fuel, steam, air to ships alongside;
- Large naval store and magazines;
- Naval Communications System.

The vessel has four 5 ton anchors for a four-point mooring system and is strengthened for
operations in ice. In addition to supporting the Royal Navy in the Falklands, she has also
been used as an MCMV support ship in the Gulf.

Key specifications are as follows:
Length: 112.0 m
Displacement: 10,765 tons full load
Speed: 12 knots. Range 5,000 n.mile at 12 knots
Complement: 38 (15 officers) plus accommodation for 147 plus 55 temporary
Cargo capacity: Long-jib crane SWL 5 tons; maximum lift, 40 tons
Guns: 4 x 20 mm. 4 x 7.62 mm MGs

Diligence entered service in 1984

Harbour Services

Historically, all waterborne harbour services and some others (e.g. Mooring and Salvage
Vessels) were operated by the personnel of the Royal Maritime Auxiliary Service (RMAS)
under the direction of the local Captain of the Port or Queen's Harbourmaster. However in
1996 the majority of harbour services, particularly in the Dockyard ports of Devonport,
Portsmouth and The Clyde, were awarded to Serco Denholm Ltd under a Government
Owned/Commercially Operated (GOCO) contract.

In December 2002 the Warship Support Agency (WSA) and Serco Denholm Limited
signed an innovative partnering agreement for the management of the ports at Devonport,
Portsmouth and The Clyde (dual site operation at Faslane and Great Harbour, Greenock).
This three-year agreement and contract is valued at up to £110 million and extends and
builds upon the Marine Services management contract awarded to Serco Denholm in 1996.

The WSA is a recently (2001) formed agency of the UK Ministry of Defence, and Serco Denholm is a joint venture formed to combine the shipping expertise of Denholm Group and the service industry knowledge of Serco. The MoD and Serco Denholm have jointly developed this new partnering agreement to progressively introduce efficiency measures and innovation in order to reduce the overall output costs of Marine Services. The long-term aim of the MoD is to prepare Marine Services for a PPP/PFI procurement programme. The agreement caters for the delivery of In-Port and Out-Of-Port Marine Services over the next three years whilst generating new and original solutions for the long-term provision of these services.

At the time of the launch of the WSA, personnel numbered 12,500, of whom 3,500 were Service personnel. In addition a tri-service project under the stewardship of the Chief Executive, the Non-Project procurement Office (NPPO) comprises a further 236 staff.

Fleet Air Arm

Joint Force Harrier

The Joint Force Harrier (JFH) was established on 1 April 2000 and brought together the Sea Harrier FA.2 squadrons, previously under Naval Air Command, with the RAF's Harrier GR.7 squadrons in a new command within No 3 Group, RAF Strike Command. That day also marked the first time that a naval officer had been given charge of an RAF Group. The previous Flag Officer Naval Aviation, became Air Officer Commanding No 3 Group, running JFH plus Nimrod maritime patrol aircraft and RAF search-and-rescue (SAR) Sea King helicopters. Significantly, he continues to head the Fleet Air Arm as Flag Officer Maritime Aviation (FOMA), with additional responsibility for overseeing all parts of embarked aviation among the three services.

However, less than two years later, it was anounced that the Sea Harrier FA.2 is to be retired early from the JFH under a development that will see JFH standardise on the RAF's Harrier GR.9. Announcing the move on 28 February 2002, UK MoD officials said the type rationalisation was in preparation for the introduction of the Future Joint Combat Aircraft and the Future Aircraft Carrier in 2012.

The MoD explained that the optimum development of the JFH is to support only one Harrier type to its end of service life, the 'more capable GR.9'. The Sea Harrier FA.2 will therefore be withdrawn from service between 2004 and 2006. In the interim, work has already begun to upgrade the GR.7 fleet to GR.9 standard, which will be flown by pilots from both services.

New Carrier-borne Fixed Wing Aircraft

Enhanced operational flexibility, an earlier in-service date and greater industrial benefits for UK industry have emerged as the key factors leading to the UK's selection of the short-take off/vertical landing (STOVL) variant of Lockheed Martin's F-35 Joint Strike Fighter (JSF) to fulfil its Future Joint Combat Aircraft (FJCA) requirement. The procurement of 150 of the Joint Combat Aircraft is currently estimated to cost about £10 billion. The Minister for Defence Procurement (Lord Bach) said in September 2002 that the STOVL variant of JSF would fully meet the UK's military needs and build on the RAF's and RN's "unique and valuable knowledge of STOVL aircraft, acquired during nearly four decades of operations of Harrier on land and sea." The initial cost of construction of the two new carriers is expected to be about £3 billion. The UK's first five JSFs will be produced in the programme's third of six low-rate initial production (LRIP) batches, which will run from early 2008 until late 2009.

Joint Helicopter Command

As from 1 October 1999 the Commando Helicopter Force joined with the support and battlefield helicopters of the Army Air Corps and the Royal Air Force in a new Joint Helicopter Command (JHC). The JHC is a single authority under Commander-in-Chief Land. The RN contribution consisted of all the aircraft (plus about 1,000 personnel) of 845, 846, 847 and 848 Naval Air Squadrons plus 9 further aircraft from an attrition reserve.

Current Naval Aircraft Inventory

Role	Number	Type	Squadron
Sea Harrier Forec - See remarks above about Joint Force Harrier (JFH)			
Air Defence / Attack	7	Sea Harrier FA-2	800 Sqn
Air Defence /Attack	7	Sea Harrier FA-2	801 Sqn
Operational Conversion	12	Sea Harrier FA-2/T Mk8	899 Sqn
Naval Helicopters			
Anti-Submarine	8	Merlin HM Mk1	814 Sqn
Anti-Submarine	9	Sea King HAS 5/6	819 Sqn
Anti-Submarine	9	Sea King HAS 5/6	820 Sqn
Anti-Submarine	4	Merlin HM Mk1	700 Sqn
Anti-Submarine	8	Merlin HM Mk1	824 Sqn
Anti-Submarine / Anti-Ship	36	Lynx HAS 3, HMA 8	815 Sqn (See Note 2)
Anti-Submarine / Anti-Ship	12	Lynx HAS 3, HMA 8	702 Sqn
Note 2.The total for 815 Squadron includes 6 aircraft with Squadron HQ. The remaining aircraft are mostly dispersed in flights of 1 or 2 aircraft amongst the ships of the Fleet.			
Airborne Early Warning	8	Sea King AEW 2	849 Sqn
Commando Helicopter Force (See remarks above about Joint Helicopter Command)			
Commando Assault	10	Sea King HC4	845 Sqn
Commando Assault	10	Sea King HC4	846 Sqn
Commando Assault	9	Sea King HC4	848 Sqn
Ground Attack	6	Lynx AH7	847 Sqn
Reconnaissance	9	Gazelle	847 Sqn
Aircrew Training			
Observer Training	9	Jetstream T2/T3	750 Sqn
Search & Rescue Training	5	Sea King HAS Mk5	771 Sqn
Fleet Training & Support	12	Hawk	

Naval Aircraft

Sea Harrier

In service with the Royal Navy since 1979, the Sea Harrier has been improved and updated to cope with the technological changes that the changing threat has posed. The aircraft remains the most advanced ship-borne Short Take Off and Vertical Landing (STOVL) aircraft in the world. The aircraft has a maritime fighter / reconnaissance / strike role and proved itself as an effective, flexible and reliable aircraft in the Falklands campaign, where 29 aircraft flew over 2,300 sorties and destroyed 22 enemy aircraft in air-to-air combat without loss.

The original version in RN service was the FRS1, with the newer F/A2 (FRS2) variant entering service in 1994. The FRS2 differs from the earlier model in that it has a Blue Vixen look-down/shoot-down radar combined with the fire-and-forget Advanced Medium-Range Air-to-Air Missile (AMRAAM) which allows the aircraft to engage targets beyond visual range. In addition, the Sea Eagle (anti-ship missile) and laser guided bombs can be carried.

The STOVL capability of the Sea Harrier enables the aircraft to operate from the flight deck of an aircraft carrier without the use of catapult-assisted take-off and arrester-wire equipment. 'Ski-jump' launching ramps that improve the aircraft's take-off performance are fitted to all three of the Royal Navy's aircraft carriers.

Since 1998, 18 new F/A2 aircraft have entered service and 31 of the remaining aircraft have received their mid-life update to bring them up to the F/A2 standard. The T4 is a two seat trainer version of the Harrier. Expect a Sea Harrier Squadron to have 9 established crews.

Principal Characteristics
F/A2 (FRS2) Crew 1
Length Overall 14.17m
Wingspan 7.70m
Height 3.71m
Max Level Speed 1185 km h
(736mph) at low level
Max Take-Off Weight approx 11,880 kg (26,200lbs)
Armament - Able to carry bombs, rockets, guns, missiles and flares attached to 4 x wing weapon pylons and 1 x under-fuselage weapon pylon; Engine 1 x Rolls-Royce Pegasus Mk 2 vectored thrust turbofan
Ferry Attack Radius 463 kms (288 miles)

Sea King

The Westland Sea King is a licence-built version of the US Sikorsky S-61. The Royal Navy's HAS Mark 1 aircraft's first flight was in 1969. Since that time, the aircraft has been extensively upgraded and passed through a series of Marks.

The current situation is that the Royal Navy operates the HAS Mk 5/6 in the anti-submarine role. The aircraft can remain on station for long periods up to 100 miles from the ship and can search for submarine targets using either its own sonar-buoys or those dropped by maritime patrol aircraft such as Nimrods. Targets that have been located are then attacked with torpedoes or depth charges.

The AEW 2 is used for airborne early-warning and is a Sea King HAS Mark 2 fitted with a Thorn EMI Search Water Radar carried in a radardome that can be swivelled down underneath the aircraft for operational searches. A detachment of 3 x AEW 2 aircraft generally deploys with each aircraft carrier.

The Sea King HC4 (Commando) is a tactical military helicopter capable of transporting 28 fully equipped troops or 6,000 lbs (2,720 kg) as an internal load. Carrying 28 troops the aircraft has a range of about 246 miles (396 km). The first HC4 deliveries were made to the Royal Navy in 1979.

The Mk 5 aircraft in service with 771 Sqn are SAR aircraft (Search & Rescue). RN SAR aircraft are stationed at Prestwick and Culdrose.

Principal Characteristics
HAS Mk 5/6
Crew 2 on flight deck and 2 in
cabin
Fuselage Length 17.01m
Width 3.78m
Height 4.72m
Weight (empty) 6201kg
Max Take-Off Weight 9525 kg
Rotor Diameter 18.9m
Cruising Speed 208 km h (129mph) at sea level
Service Ceiling 1,220m
Mission Radius (with 2 hours on station and carrying 3 x torpedoes) 231 kms (144 miles)

Lynx
Lynx aircraft are at sea with all frigates and destroyers, to provide anti-surface surveillance, anti-submarine warfare (ASW) capabilities and anti-ship attack capabilities. With the introduction into service of the first of the upgraded 44 x HAS 3, HMA 8 aircraft in late 1994, the Lynx in Royal Naval service has been turned from an anti-submarine helicopter into a dedicated maritime attack aircraft. Capable of carrying anti-submarine torpedoes (range 10km) and anti-ship Sea Skua missiles (range 20 km), the HMA 8 is capable of integrating its navigational, communications and fighting systems through a 1553B databus.

Typical combat mission profiles in the anti-submarine role could be a patrol out to 60 miles, a two-hour loiter in the search area carrying torpedoes and smoke markers etc and return.

Principal Characteristics
Crew 2 on the flight-deck and up to 2 mission crew
in the fuselage
Length Fuselage 11.92m
Height 3.2m
Rotor Diameter 12.8m
Max Speed 144mph (232km h) at sea level

Ferry Range 1,046 km (650 miles) with max internal and external fuel tanks
Weight (max take-off) 4,876kg (10,750lbs)

EH101 Merlin HM Mk1

The Royal Navy has 44 x EH 101 Merlin ASW helicopters on order in a contract worth £1.5 billion. The in-service date was 1998 and by the middle part of this decade the Merlin should have replaced the ASW Sea Kings and some of the ASW Lynx in Royal Naval service.

Extensive sea trials were held on board HMS Iron Duke in 1993 and the first production aircraft came off the production line in 1996. There are now more Merlins in service than Sea Kings.

Principal Characteristics
Service Ceiling 4,572 m
Range 550 n miles (1,019 km)
Sensors: GEC-Marconi Blue Kestrel 5000 radar, Thomson Marconi Flash AQS 960 dipping sonar, GEC-Marconi sonobuoy acoustic processor AQS-903, Racal Orange Reaper ESM
Weapons: ASW 4 x Stingray torpedoes or Mk 11 Mod 3 depth bombs plus anti-ship missiles.

Naval Missiles

Trident D-5

The UK Strategic deterrent (US Trident D-5) is deployed in the four Vanguard class Ballistic Missile Nuclear-Powered Submarines (SSBNs). The Trident D-5 missile is a three-stage, solid propellant Submarine Launched Ballistic Missile (SLBM) - it is 13.42 m long and has a body diameter of 2.11 m. It has a launch weight of 59,090 kg and a maximum range of 12,000 km. The minimum range is believed to be about 2,500 km.

It has been stated that the UK missiles will carry up to eight warheads each, but it is expected that there will be between one and four warheads fitted to most missiles. The UK plans to use some Trident D-5 missiles in a `sub-strategic' role, with a single warhead set to produce a smaller yield, believed to be around 10 kT. A statement in 1999 clarified the situation with regard to the maximum number of warheads to be carried by each of the UK's SSBNs, which will be limited to 48.

SLCM: Hughes Tomahawk Block IIIC

US-built Tomahawk is being deployed in all RN Attack submarines. In 1995, the first export order for Tomahawk missiles was announced, with the UK ordering 65 missiles, Advanced Tomahawk Weapon Control Systems for seven boats, and a shore-based mission planning system. The missiles are UGM-109C TLAM-C versions to the Block 3 build standard, to be launched from standard torpedo tubes. Two unguided test rounds and one guided flight were made from a `Swiftsure' class boat in 1998. The UK fired 20 missiles against targets in Serbia in early 1999, with more missiles fired against Afghanistan in 2001 and Iraq in 2003. Tomahawk has a range of up to 1,700kms.

Harpoon

Harpoon, manufactured by McDonnel-Douglas of the USA, is an extremely powerful anti-shipping missile that is fitted to the Type 22 and Type 23 Frigates. The Sub Harpoon (UGM-84A) is also deployed in Trafalgar and Swiftsure Class submarines. The latest versions of this missile have extremely sophisticated electronic countermeasures (ECM), and the ability to fly a sea-skimming course on a dog-leg path through three pre-programmed way points. The warhead is extremely powerful and a hit from Harpoon is almost certain to result in the destruction or disablement of a major surface vessel.

Principal Characteristics
Length 3.84 m
Diameter 0.343 m
Total Weight 526 kg
Warhead Weight 225kg
Range 110 kms

Sea Dart

Sea Dart is a surface-to-air missile system with a long range (probably in excess of 80 kms) and employs a two-stage system with a primary booster rocket powering the warhead and ramjet on their way to the target. There is a limited surface-to-surface capability out to a range of about 28 km and the guidance system is a semi-active homing radar. It is installed in Type 42 destroyers.

Principal Characteristics
Length 4.40 m
Diameter 0.42 m
Total Weight 549 kg
Range 80 km + approx

Sea Wolf

Sea Wolf is a ship-based, surface-to-air missile designed for the defence of point targets. This is a highly efficient system thought to be capable of dealing with aircraft, missiles and even artillery rounds. The guidance system is semi-automatic command to line of sight with radar and/or infra-red missile and target tracking.

Principal Characteristics
Length 1.91m
Diameter 0.18 m
Total Weight 79.8 kgs
Range 6/7,000 m
Altitude 3/4000 m

Sea Skua

Sea Skua is a short-range, anti-ship missile that has been in Royal Naval service since 1982. The missile is currently carried as the main armament of the Lynx aircraft flying from RN destroyers / frigates. The guidance system is semi-active terminal homing.

Principal Characteristics
Length 2.85 m
Diameter 0.22 m
Total Weight 147 kg
Range 20 km approx

Other Missiles

Other air-launched missiles in RN service may be found in relevant entries in the RAF Section.

The Royal Marines

The Royal Marines (RM) are an elite Corps and specialists in Amphibious Warfare - and wherever there is action, the Royal Marines are likely to be involved. They were prominent, for example, in the Falklands campaign, and they may be found wherever the UK Armed Services are actively involved e.g. Sierra Leone, Afganistan, Iraq and, of course, Northern Ireland. The Royal Marines number approximately 500 officers and 5,400 men and, since the end of the Cold War, especially in recent years, the Corps appears to have reverted to its traditional role of being ready for operations anywhere in the world.

All Royal Marines, except those in the Royal Marines Band Service, are first and foremost, commando soldiers. They are required to undergo what is recognised as one of the longest and most demanding infantry training courses in the world. This is undertaken at the Commando Training Centre Royal Marines at Lympstone in UK's West Country, not far from Dartmoor.

The titular head of the Royal Marines is always a Major General - Commandant General Royal Marines (CGRM). There have been significant recent structural changes in the higher management of the Royal Navy recently and this has added to the responsibilities and raised the profile of CGRM.

The Royal Marines have small detachments in ships at sea and other units worldwide with widely differing tasks. However, the bulk of the manpower of the Royal Marines is grouped in battalion-sized organisations known as Commandos (Cdo). There are 3 Commando Groups and they are part of a larger formation known as 3 Commando Brigade (3 Cdo Bde).

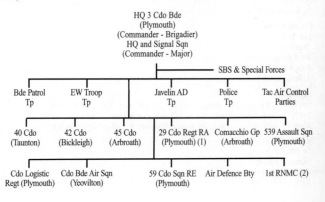

Note:
(1) 29 Cdo Regt RA has one battery stationed at Arbroath with 45 Cdo.
(2) 1st Bn The Royal Netherlands Marine Corps is part of 3 Cdo Bde for NATO assigned tasks. The Air Defence troop is equipped with Rapier. There are three regular Tactical Air Control Parties and one reserve. 539 Assault Squadron has hovercraft, landing craft and raiding craft.

Commando Organisation

Note: A troop (Tp) equates to an army platoon. Each rifle company has three troops. A Royal Marine rifle company is generally commanded by a Captain RM.

Locations

Headquarters Royal Marines Portsmouth
HQ 3 Commando Brigade Plymouth (Stonehouse)
3 Commando Bde HQ & Signal Sqn Plymouth (Stonehouse)
3 Commando Bde Air Sqn RNAS Yeovilton
40 Commando Taunton
42 Commando Plymouth (Bickleigh)
45 Commando Arbroath (Condor)
Commando Logistic Regiment Plymouth (Marsh Mills)
539 Assault Sqn Plymouth (Turnchapel)
Comacchio Group Arbroath (Condor)
Commando Training Centre Lympstone
Royal Marines Stonehouse Plymouth
Royal Marines Poole Poole
Amphibious Training & Trials Unit Bideford
There are Royal Marine Reserve Units in London, Bristol, Birkenhead, Glasgow and Newcastle Upon Tyne that form 'T' Company of the Royal Marine Reserve (RMR).

Special Boat Service

This organisation is the Naval equivalent of the Army's SAS (Special Air Service). Personnel are all volunteers from the mainstream Royal Marines and vacancies are few with competition for entry fierce.

Generally speaking only about 30 per cent of volunteers manage to complete the entry course and qualify. The SBS specialises in mounting clandestine operations against targets at sea, in rivers or harbours and against occupied coastlines.

Comacchio Company

This specialist company was formed in 1980, and has the task of guarding the UK's oil rigs and other associated installations from a variety of threats - in particular terrorist attacks.

Personnel Summary (at 1 June 2003)

	Strength at 1 June 2003
Army	111,780
Officers	14,520
Males	13,040
Females	1,480
Other Ranks	97,260
Males	90,500
Females	6,760

Note: The above figures do not include approximately 3,669 x Gurkhas, 349 x Royal Gibraltar Regiment and personnel of the Royal Irish Regiment (Home Service).

British Army Major Units

(at 1 Jan 2003)	Germany	UK	Elsewhere	TA
Armoured Regts	5	1	-	-
Armoured Recce Regts	1	3	-	-
Yeomanry Regts	-	-	-	4
Armoured Infantry Bns	6	3	-	-
Mechanised Bns	-	6	-	-
Air Assault Bns	-	4(1)	-	-
Light Role Bns	-	10	2	15
Northern Ireland Resident Bns	-	6(2)	-	-
Gurkha Bns	-	1	1	-
Land Warfare Bn	-	1(3)	-	-
Home Service Regts	-	3	1(4)	-
SAS Regts	-	1	-	2
Army Air Corps Regts (5)	1	4	-	1
Artillery Field Regts	3	4	-	2
Air Defence Regts	1	3	-	1
MLRS Regts	-	2	-	1
Commando Regt	-	1	-	-
Surveillance & Target Acquisition	-	1	-	-
HAC	-	-	-	1
Engineer Regts	4	7	-	5
Signals Regts	3	6	1	11
EW Regt	-	1	-	-
Equipment Support Bns	3	3	-	4
Equipment Support Bn (Aviation)	-	1	-	-
Logistic Regts	6	13	1	17

Medical Regts	1	4	-	-
Field Ambulances	-	-	-	4
Hospitals	-	3	-	11

(1) Includes one in-role parachute battalions.
(2) Includes one battalion stationed in either England or Scotland designated as the Provine reserve.
(3) This battalion provides the Land Warfare training battlegroup at the Combined Arms Training Centre (Warminster).
(4) Royal Gibraltar Regiment
(5) Under command of the JHC (Joint Helicopter Command)

British Army Equipment Summary

Armour: 386 x Challenger 2; 137 x Sabre (approx); 60 x Striker; 325 x Scimitar; 1,100 x FV 432; 575 x MCV 80 Warrior; 585 x Spartan; 640 x Saxon; 11 x Fuchs NBC recce vehicles; 10 x Stormer.

Artillery: 179 x AS 90; 64 x 227mm MLRS ; 48 x FH 70; 165 x 105mm Light Gun; 470 x 81mm Mortar (including 112 SP); 2,093 x 51mm Light Mortar.

Air Defence: 98 x Rapier Fire Units (24 SP); 330 x Javelin Launchers; 147 x Starstreak LML; 135 x HVM (SP).

Army Aviation: 108 x Lynx (some armed with TOW); 133 Gazelle; 7 x BN-2; 67 x Apache on order (possibly 20 in service in mid 2003); Helicopters available from RAF - 38 x Chinook; 39 x Puma; 22 x Merlin on order.

The Army Board

The routine management of the Army is the responsibility of The Army Board. The composition of which is as follows:

The Secretary of State for Defence
Minister of State (Armed Forces)
Minister of State (Defence Procurement)
Minister of State (Veterans Affairs)
Parliamentary Under-Secretary of State for the Armed Forces
Chief of the General Staff
Second Permanent Under-Secretary of State
Adjutant General
Quartermaster General
Master General of the Ordnance
Commander in Chief (Land Command)
Commander UK Support Command (Germany)
Assistant Chief of the General Staff

Decisions made by The Defence Council or the Army Board are acted upon by the military staff at the various headquarters worldwide. The Chief of the General Staff is the officer responsible for the Army's contribution to the national defence effort and he maintains control through the commander and the staff branches of each of these headquarters.

Chief of The General Staff (1 Jan 2003)
General Sir Mike Jackson MBE CBE CB KCB DSO ADC Gen

General Jackson was born in 1944, and was educated at Stamford School, The Royal Military Academy Sandhurst and Birmingham University. Commissioned from Sandhurst into the Intelligence Corps in December 1963, he studied for an in-service degree in Russian Studies from 1964 to 1967. After graduating, he spent 2 years on secondment to the Parachute Regiment and subsequently transferred from the Intelligence Corps in 1970. During the early 70s he served in Northern Ireland, and with the TA in Scotland.

He attended the Staff College in 1976, after which he spent two years as the Chief of Staff of the Berlin Infantry Brigade. He then commanded a parachute company for two years, once more in Northern Ireland.

General Jackson

After a six month course at the National Defence College at Latimer in 1981, he joined the Directing Staff at the Staff College. His two and a half year tour at Camberley included a ten week attachment to the Ministry of Defence during the Falklands conflict.

He commanded 1st Battalion The Parachute Regiment from March 1984 to September 1986. Throughout his period of command the Battalion was part of the NATO Allied Command Europe Mobile Force (Land), a role which included three winters spent in Norway on arctic training. For just over two years, until the end of 1988, he was the Senior Directing Staff (Army) at the Joint Service Defence College, Greenwich.

Following the Higher Command and Staff Course at Camberley in early 1989, he spent six months on a Service Fellowship at Cambridge writing a paper on the future of the British Army.

In 1989, he moved back to Northern Ireland to command 39 Infantry Brigade.1992 and 1993 were spent in the Ministry of Defence as Director General Personnel Services (Army). He commanded the 3rd (UK) Division from March 1994 to July 1996. In August 1995 he was selected to assume command of UNPROFOR in Bosnia at the end of that year; in the event, after the success of the Dayton talks, he spent the first half of 1996 in Bosnia commanding IFOR's Multinational Division South West.

He assumed the appointment of Commander ACE Rapid Reaction Corps in the rank of Lieutenant General in February 1997, following a brief assignment as Director General Development and Doctrine.

He deployed with ARRC HQ, as Commander Kosovo Force, to Macedonia in March 1999 and subsequently commanded Kosovo Force in Pristina from June to October 1999. He assumed the appointment of Commander in Chief Land Command on 1 March 2000 and became Chief of the General Staff in early 2003.

General Sir Mike Jackson was awarded the MBE in 1979, the CBE in 1992, the CB in 1996, the KCB in 1998, the DSO in 1999 and ADC Gen in 2001. He is married to Sarah, and has two sons, a daughter and three grandchildren. His interests include music, reading, travel, skiing and tennis.

Chain of Command

The Army is controlled from the MoD via the above three subsidiary headquarters and a number of smaller headquarters worldwide. The diagram illustrates this chain of command as at 1 Jan 2003.

Operations in Northern Ireland, Cyprus, the Balkans, Iraq, Afghanistan and the Falkland Islands are controlled directly from the MoD.

HQ Land Command

Following the MoD's "Front Line First" study, plans were drawn up to reorganise HQ United Kingdom Land Forces (HQ UKLF) in a new formation designated HQ Land Command that became operational on 1 April 1995. HQ Land Command is located at Erskine Barracks, Wilton near Salisbury and controls about 75% of the troops in the British Isles and almost 100% of its fighting capability.

Land Command's role is to deliver and sustain the Army's operational capability, whenever required throughout the world, and the Command comprises all operational troops in Great Britain, Germany, Nepal and Brunei, together with the Army Training Teams in Canada, Belize and Kenya.

Land Command has almost 70,000 trained Army personnel - the largest single Top Level Budget in Defence, with a budget of over £3.7 Billion. It contains all the Army's fighting equipment, including attack helicopters, Challenger 2 tanks, Warrior Infantry Fighting Vehicles, AS90 and the Multi-Launched Rocket System (MLRS).

Land Command is one of the three central commands in the British Army, the other two being the Adjutant General (with responsibility for administration, personnel and training) and Equipment Support (Land) responsible for supply and logistics. The Command is responsible for providing all the Army's fighting troops throughout the World. These are organised into eight formations and are commanded by Major Generals.

The Structure of Land Command

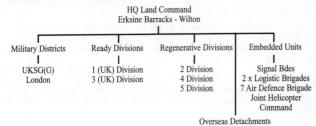

Note: Overseas Detachments include Belize, Canada, Brunei and Nepal and Kenya. Garrisons in Cyprus and the Falkland Islands are commanded from the MoD via PJHQ.

Ready Divisions

There are two "Ready" Divisions: the 1st (UK) Armoured Division, based in Germany, and the 3rd (UK) Mechanised Division in the United Kingdom. Both these divisions are earmarked to form part of the Allied Command Europe Rapid Reaction Corps (ARRC), NATO's premier strategic formation; but they also have the flexibility to be employed on rapid reaction tasks or in support of other Defence Roles.

In addition to their operational roles, they also command the Army units in specified geographic areas: in the case of the 1st Division, this area is made up of the garrisons in Germany where the Division's units are based; and in the case of the 3rd Division, the South West of England.

Composition of 1(UK) Armoured Division

1 (UK) Armoured Division has its headquarters at Herford in Germany (about 50 kms from Hanover) and the three Armoured Brigades under command are located at Osnabruck, Bergen-Hohne and Paderborn. The divisional personnel strength is 1,300 officers and 15,700 other ranks (1 January 2003) equipment totals are as follows:

> 216 x Challenger MBT
> 306 x Warrior armoured fighting vehicles
> 1,158 x Armoured personnel carriers
> 66 x 155 mm AS 90
> 19 x Armoured vehicle launched bridges
> 12 x Attack helicopters

Divisional Structure

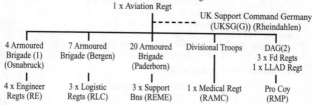

HQ 1 (UK) Armd Div
(Commander- Major General)
(Herford - Germany)
3 x Signal Regts
1 x Force Reconnaissance Regt
1 x Aviation Regt

UK Support Command Germany
(UKSG(G)) (Rheindahlen)

4 Armoured Brigade (1) (Osnabruck)	7 Armoured Brigade (Bergen)	20 Armoured Brigade (Paderborn)	Divisional Troops	DAG(2) 3 x Fd Regts 1 x LLAD Regt
4 x Engineer Regts (RE)	3 x Logistic Regts (RLC)	3 x Support Bns (REME)	1 x Medical Regt (RAMC)	Pro Coy (RMP)

Note: (1) Current plans appear to be for all three armoured brigades to have an identical organisation. (2) DAG (Divisional Artillery Group) This DAG could be reinforced by Rapier Air Defence and MLRS units from the UK as necessary. This Division could provide the Headquarters (HQs) for 9 x Battlegroups.

The 1998 SDR stated that in the future 3 of the 6 armoured regiments in 1 (UK) Division during 1998 will be returned to the UK. As a result there are now 3 armoured regiments in 1(UK) Division (one with each brigade). Each of these regiments will have 58 x MBT and 600 personnel, but will hold 30 x MBT for peacetime training. These arrangements are believed to be complete.

UKSC(G) - The United Kingdom support Command (Germany) has responsibility for British Army Troops on the Continent of Europe that are not part of 1(UK) Armoured

Division. Its headquarters replaces that of the British Army of the Rhine, whose sign it has adopted. The new headquarters is located at Rheindahlen and has 500 personnel under command.

1 (UK) Armoured Division - Armoured Brigade Organisation

The following diagram illustrates the possible composition of an Armoured Brigade in 1(UK) Armd Div on operations.

Armd Bde HQ
(Commander - Brigadier)
Signal Sqn

Armd Regt (1)	Armd Inf Bn (2)	Armd Inf Bn	Arty Regt (3)

Engr (4) Regt	RLC Sqn (5)	Pro Det RMP	Medical Sqn RAMC	REME Wksp

Totals: 58 x Challenger MBT (possibly)
104 x Warrior AIFV
350 x Armoured personel carriers
24 x AS 90 SP Gun
Approx 4,500 personnel

Notes: (1) Armoured Regiment with approx 58 x Challenger MBT; (2) Armoured Inf Battalion with approx 52 x Warrior and approx 40 x FV432; (3) Artillery Regiment with 24 x AS90 SP Guns; (4) Engineer Regiment with an HQ Sqn, Armd Engr Sqn, Mechanised Field Sqn and possibly additional resources dependent upon task; (5) Brigade Support Squadron RLC with approximately 60 -70 x trucks; (6) Depending upon task the Brigade could expect to be reinforced with Medium Reconnaissance, Aviation and Air Defence Units. This Brigade could provide the HQs for 3 Battlegroups.

Composition of 3 (UK) Mechanised Division

HQ 3 (UK) Division
(Bulford)
(Commander-Major General)

1 Mech Bde (1) (Tidworth)	(Divisional Troops)	19 Mech Bde (Catterick)	Italian Armd Bde (7)	12 Mech Bde (2) (Aldershot)

Signal Regt	Armd Recce Regt (3)	Aviation Regt (5)	MLRS Regt (4)	2 x LLAD Regts (6)	3 x Arty Fd Regts

2 x Engr Regt (RE)	Close Sp Regt (RLC)	Gen Sp Regt (RLC)	Sp Bn (REME)	1 x Medical Regt	Pro Coy (RMP)

Note: (1) 1 Mechanised Brigade; (2) 12 Mech Bde has replaced 5 Airborne Brigade which has been redesignated as 16 Air Assault Brigade and moved to Colchester; (3) Armoured Reconnaissance Regiment - now called a Force Reconnaissance Regiment (4) Artillery Regiment with Multi-Launch Rocket System; (5) Army Air Corps Regiment with Lynx &

Gazelle (provided by Joint Helicopter Command when required); (6) Air Defence Regiments with Rapier and Javelin/Starstreak missiles; (7) Under Allied Rapid Reaction Corps framework agreements this division could be reinforced by an Italian Armoured Brigade (Ariete).

3 Commando Brigade, a Royal Naval formation, is available to support 3(UK) Div if necessary. Details of the organisation of 3 Cdo Bde are given in Chapter 2 (Royal Navy). 3 Cdo Bde is not under the command of 3 (UK) Div.

During operations 3 (UK) Div equipment totals (excluding 3 Cdo Bde) could resemble the following (as at 1 Jun 2003).

Main Battle Tanks (MBT) - Approx 58 x Challenger.
Armoured Infantry Fighting Vehicles (AIFV) - Approx 156 x Warrior.
Armoured Personnel Carriers (APCs) - Approx 172 x Saxon.
Self-Propelled (SP) Artillery - Approx 66 x AS90.
Multi-Launch Rocket System (MLRS) - Approx 36 Launchers
Lynx Helicopters armed with TOW missiles - approx 24

3 (UK) Div - Mechanised Brigade Organisation

```
                              Brigade HQ
                          (Commander - Brigadier)
                              Signal Sqn

                           AAC Helicopter Det

    Armd Regt      Armd Inf Bn     Mech Bn        Mech Bn       SP Arty Regt
   (Approx 58 x   (Approx 52 x    (Approx 51 x   (Approx 51 x   (32 x AS90)
      MBT)          Warrior)        Saxon)         Saxon)

    REME          Engr            RLC            LRATGW    Fd Amb    Javelin    Pro Unit
    Wksps         Sqn             Sqn            Troop (1) Det       AD Det     RMP
```

Note: (1) Long Range Anti-Tank Guided Weapons - Currently Striker/Swingfire. (2) All three brigades have 1 x armoured infantry battalion.

The Battlegroup

A division usually consists of 3 brigades. These brigades are further sub divided into smaller formations known as battlegroups. The Battlegroup is the basic building brick of the fighting formations.

A battlegroup is commanded by a Lieutenant Colonel and the infantry battalion or armoured regiment that he commands provides the command and staff element of the formation. The battlegroup is then structured according to task, with the correct mix of infantry, armour and supporting arms.

The battlegroup organisation is very flexible and the units assigned can be quickly regrouped to cope with a change in the threat. A typical battlegroup fighting a defensive battle might be composed of one armoured squadron and two armoured infantry companies, containing about 600 men, 12 tanks and about 80 armoured personnel carriers.

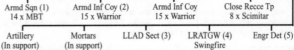

Armoured Battlegroup
BGHQ
(Commander – Lt-Col)

Armd Sqn (1)	Armd Inf Coy (2)	Armd Inf Coy	Close Recce Tp
14 x MBT	15 x Warrior	15 x Warrior	8 x Scimitar

Artillery	Mortars	LLAD Sect (3)	LRATGW (4)	Engr Det (5)
(In support)	(In support)		Swingfire	

(1) Armoured Squadron
(2) Armoured Infantry Company
(3) LLAD-Low Level Air Defence - Javelin
(4) LRATGW - Long Range Anti-Tank Guided Weapon - Swingfire.
(5) Engineer Detachment

The number of battlegroups in a division and a brigade could vary according to the task the formation has been given. As a general rule you could expect a division to have as many as 9 battlegroups and a brigade to have up to 3. The diagram shows a possible organisation for an armoured battlegroup in either 1(UK) Armd Div or 3(UK) Div.

Regenerative Divisions

There are three Regenerative Divisions, based on older UK military districts. These are the 2nd Division with its Headquarters at Edinburgh, the 4th Division with its Headquarters at Aldershot, and the 5th Division with its Headquarters at Shrewsbury. These Regenerative divisions are responsible for all Army units within their boundaries and could provide the core for three new divisions, should the Army be required to expand to meet a major international threat.

Composition of 2nd Division

The 2nd Division has responsibility for the whole of Scotland and Northern England. Though the Division was first formed in 1809 to fight in the Peninsular War, the crossed keys sign was not adopted until 1940 when it was reconstituted in England after Dunkirk. Its most famous engagement was during the Burma Campaign in 1944 when, at the battle for Kohima, the tide against the Japanese Army finally turned. The Divisional Headquarters is in Edinburgh. The 2nd Division comprises four brigades and a garrison:

15 (North East) Brigade, with its HQ in York, responsible for units in the North East of England

42 (North West) Brigade, with its HQ in Preston, responsible for units in the North West of England

51 (Scottish) Brigade, with its HQ in Perth, responsible for all units north of Stirling including Shetland and the Western Isles.

52 (Infantry) Brigade, with its HQ in Edinburgh, with light role infantry battalion at Edinburgh, Chester and Preston under command.

Catterick Garrison, including units in Ripon, Topcliffe and Dishforth. Catterick Garrison also hosts 19 (Mechanized) Brigade which is under operational command of 3rd (UK) Division.

Composition of 4th Division

The 4th Division has military responsibility for South East England, including Bedfordshire, Essex and Hertfordshire and its headquarters is in Aldershot. It was previously based in Germany until 1992 as an armoured division. The divisional symbol is the Tiger.

The division now has three brigades under command:

2 Brigade based in Shorncliffe. This is a light infantry brigade with battalions based in Chepstow, North Luffenham and Tern Hill under command.

49 (E) Brigade in Chilwell

145 Brigade in Aldershot

Composition of 5th Division

The 5th Division has responsibility for military units and establishments in Wales, the West Midlands and the North West of England and the Headquarters is in Shrewsbury. The Division emblem, inherited from Wales and Western District, depicts the Welsh Dragon, the cross of St Chad (7th Century Bishop of Mercia), and the Red Rose of Lancaster. The 5th Division fought at Waterloo and played a significant part in the endeavours of the BEF in both World Wars. The following brigades are under command:

143 Brigade based at Shrewsbury

160 Brigade based at Brecon

43 Brigade in Exeter

Northern Ireland

The military presence in Northern Ireland is commanded by HQ Northern Ireland (HQNI) situated at Lisburn just outside Belfast and there are three Brigades under command.

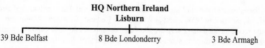

HQ Northern Ireland
Lisburn

39 Bde Belfast   8 Bde Londonderry   3 Bde Armagh

During early 2003 under the operational command of these brigades were:

> 6 x Resident Infantry Battalions(1)
> 2 x Infantry Battalions on short 6 month tours
> 1 x Engineer Regiment
> 1 x Royal Signals Regiment
> 1 x Army Air Corps Regiment
> 3 x Home Service Battalions of the Royal Irish Regiment
> 1 x RLC Logistic Support Regiment
> 1 x REME Workshop
> 1 x Military Hospital manned by the Army Medical Services

RAF: 1 x Puma Squadron
        1 x RAF Regiment Squadron (-)

Note: One of these battalions is stationed on the UK mainland ready to return to the Province if required. Due to the continuing ceasefire it is likely that many of the units listed above are not at 100% strength.

Districts

From 1 April 2000 two Districts will remain: London (although subordinated to 4th Division for budgetary purposes), and the United Kingdom Support Command (Germany). London is responsible for all Army units within the M25 boundary. The United Kingdom Support Command (Germany) with its Headquarters at Rheindahlen has similar responsibilities, but also provides essential support functions for the 1st Division and the Headquarters of the ARRC.

These divisional and district areas are further sub-divided into brigades and garrisons, which also have a varying mix of operational and infrastructure support responsibilities. As a result of the Defence Costs Studies, some brigade headquarters, which previously had purely operational functions, have been amalgamated with garrison headquarters to achieve savings and greater efficiency.

Embedded into this structure are all the other force elements which represent Land Command's operational capability. They include:

16 Air Assault Brigade, based in Colchester and under the command of the Joint Helicopter Command from 1st April 2000.

Three signal Brigades (one of which is in Germany).

Two Combat Service Support Groups (one of which is in Germany).

Various additional units which are earmarked for the ACE Rapid Reaction Corps or for National Defence tasks.

The overseas detachments in Canada, Belize, Brunei and Nepal are commanded directly from Headquarters Land Command at Wilton. The Review of the Army Command Structure recommended that the Army should be organised into three central commands and that doctrine and training should be the responsibility of the Adjutant General rather than the Command-in-Chief. Therefore Headquarters Doctrine and Training at Upavon, Wiltshire, does not form part of Land Command (although it was part of United Kingdom Land Forces until 1993).

Although Land Command is not responsible for running operations in Afghanistan, Iraq, Cyprus, Northern Ireland, Falkland Islands (a responsibility of PJHQ), it will provide the operational troops for these areas. Some 12,000 troops are involved in Northern Ireland at present, with another 12,000 in Iraq and a further 5,000 are deployed to Cyprus and the Falklands.

Some 500 troops are involved at any one time in MoD-sponsored equipment trials, demonstrations and exhibitions. Public Duties in London taking up two/three battalions at any one time. All troops not otherwise operationally committed are also available to provide Military Aid to the Civil Authorities in the United Kingdom.

16 Air Assault Brigade

Nearly 10,000 personnel are assigned to 16 Air Assault Brigade. This brigade is designed to be able to punch deep and fast into enemy territory, and radically changing Britain's ability to react rapidly to conflicts. Using everything from the latest Apache helicopter to air-mobile artillery equipment and high velocity air defence missiles, the new Brigade marks a considerable leap forward in Britain's defence capability.

The Brigade capitalises on the combat capabilities of the former 24 Airmobile Brigade and 5 Airborne Brigade, including two parachute battalions with an increase in combat service support. The introduction of the Apache Attack Helicopter, due in operational service within the next two years, will provide a new generation of weapons systems bringing major improvements in military capability.

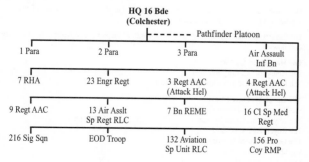

HQ 16 Bde
(Colchester)

- - - - - Pathfinder Platoon

1 Para	2 Para	3 Para	Air Assault Inf Bn
7 RHA	23 Engr Regt	3 Regt AAC (Attack Hel)	4 Regt AAC (Attack Hel)
9 Regt AAC	13 Air Asslt Sp Regt RLC	7 Bn REME	16 Cl Sp Med Regt
216 Sig Sqn	EOD Troop	132 Aviation Sp Unit RLC	156 Pro Coy RMP

Note: Parachute battalions in 16 Air Assault Brigade are now configured as Air Assault Infantry Battalions.

Support helicopters are provided by the RAF (from the Joint Helicopter Command) and the Brigade would normally expect to operate with 18 x Chinook and 18 x Puma. An airmobile infantry battalion can be moved by 20 x Chinook equivalents lifts. Each airmobile infantry battalion is equipped with 42 x Milan firing posts - a total of 84 within the Brigade.

Units of the Army (Situation at 1 August 2003)

The Cavalry

Apart from the Royal Tank Regiment, which was formed in the First World War with the specific task of fighting in armoured vehicles, tank forces in the British Army are provided by the regiments which formed the cavalry element of the pre-mechanised era. Following the "Options for Change" restructuring in January 1995 there are 11 regular armoured regiments and 4 TA Yeomanry Regiments. One of these regiments forms The Household Cavalry and the remaining regiments are known collectively as The Royal Armoured Corps (RAC).

Of the 11 regular armour roled units remaining in the British Army post SDR there are four in Germany, three MBT regiments equipped with Challenger 2 and a Force Reconnaissance Regiment. In the UK there will be the remaining three MBT regiments equipped with Challenger 2, three Force Reconnaissance Regiments and the Joint NBC Regiment.

In the UK there are three regular armoured regiments equipped with Challenger MBT, two stationed in Tidworth and one in Catterick. All three of these regiments are under the operational command of 3 (UK) Division that has a role in support of the ARRC. There are also three regular armoured reconnaissance regiments stationed in the UK one of which, based at Bovington doubles as the armoured training regiment at the RAC Training Centre. In addition to these armoured forces the Household Cavalry Mounted Regiment is stationed in London and provides mounted troops for ceremonial duties.

The Territorial Army has four Yeomanry Regiments. These units are national defence regiments with a reconnaissance role.

The Cavalry accounts for about 6% of the strength of the Army and Regimental Titles are as follows:

The Household Cavalry

The Household Cavalry Regiment	HCR
The Household Cavalry Mounted Regiment	HCMRD

The Royal Armoured Corps

1st The Queen's Dragoon Guards	QDG
The Royal Scots Dragoon Guards	SCOTS DG
The Royal Dragoon Guards	RDG
The Queen's Royal Hussars	QRH
9th/12th Royal Lancers	9/12L
The King's Royal Hussars	KRH
The Light Dragoons	LD
The Queen's Royal Lancers	QRL
1st Royal Tank Regiment	1 RTR
2nd Royal Tank Regiment	2 RTR

Armoured Regiment Wiring Diagram
Regiments equipped with Challenger 2 will in the future be equipped with 58 tanks and have 600 personnel. Armoured Regiment Diagram opposite.

Totals: 58 x MBT (Challenger 2), 8 x Scimitar, 5 x ARV, 558 men.

Notes: (1) Armoured Squadron; (2) Main Battle Tank; (3) We believe that this recce troop of 8 x Scimitar is normally held in HQ Sqn but on operations comes under the direct control of the commanding officer; (4) The basic building brick of the Tank Regiment is the Tank Troop of 12 men and three tanks. The commander of this troop will probably be a Lt or 2/Lt aged between 20 or 23 and the second-in-command will usually be a sergeant who commands his own tank. The remaining tank in the troop will be commanded by a senior corporal; (5) A Challenger tank has a crew of 4 - Commander, Driver, Gunner and Loader/Operator.

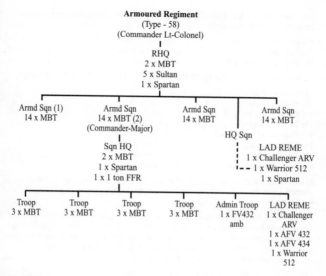

Armoured Regiment
(Type - 58)
(Commander Lt-Colonel)

RHQ
2 x MBT
5 x Sultan
1 x Spartan

Armd Sqn (1) 14 x MBT	Armd Sqn 14 x MBT (2) (Commander-Major)	Armd Sqn 14 x MBT	Armd Sqn 14 x MBT

Sqn HQ
2 x MBT
1 x Spartan
1 x 1 ton FFR

HQ Sqn

LAD REME
1 x Challenger ARV
1 x Warrior 512
1 x Spartan

Troop 3 x MBT	Troop 3 x MBT	Troop 3 x MBT	Troop 3 x MBT	Admin Troop 1 x FV432 amb	LAD REME 1 x Challenger ARV 1 x AFV 432 1 x AFV 434 1 x Warrior 512

The Infantry

The British Infantry is based on the well tried and tested Regimental System that has been justified regularly on operational deployment. It is based on battalions, which when they number more than one are grouped together to form a "large Regiment". Most Regiments now comprise one Regular and one TA Battalion and Regiments are then grouped together within Divisions, which provide a level of administrative command.

The Division of Infantry is an organisation that is responsible for all aspects of military administration, from recruiting, manning and promotions for individuals in the regiments under its wing, to the longer term planning required to ensure continuity and cohesion. Divisions of Infantry have no operational command over their regiments, and should not be confused with the operational divisions such as 1(UK) Armd Div and 3 (UK) Div.

The Divisions of Infantry are as follows:

The Guards Division	- 5 regular battalions
The Scottish Division	- 6 regular battalions
The Queen's Division	- 6 regular battalions
The King's Division	- 6 regular battalions
The Prince of Wales Division	- 7 regular battalions
The Light Division	- 4 regular battalions

Not administered by Divisions of Infantry but operating under their own administrative arrangements are the following:

The Parachute Regiment	- 3 regular battalions
The Brigade of Gurkhas	- 2 regular battalions
The Royal Irish Regiment	- 1 regular battalion

TA battalions are under the administrative command (from mid 1999) of the following:

The Guards Division	- Nil
The Scottish Division	- 2 TA battalions
The Queen's Division	- 3 TA battalions
The King's Division	- 3 TA battalions
The Prince of Wales Division	- 3 TA battalions
The Light Division	- 2 TA battalions
The Parachute Regiment	- 1 TA battalions
The Royal Irish Regiment	- 1 TA battalion

In total the British Army has 40 regular battalions available for service and this total combined with the 15 TA battalions could give a mobilisation strength of 55 infantry battalions.

Outside the above listed Regiments are three companies of guardsmen each of 110 men, who are provided to supplement the Household Division Regiments while on public duties in London, to allow them to continue to carry out normal training on roulement from guard duties. Gibraltar also has its own single battalion of the Royal Gibraltar Regiment comprising one Regular and two volunteer companies.

During mid 2003 the infantry were grouped as follows:

United Kingdom	- 31 battalions (5 Resident in Northern Ireland)
Germany	- 6 battalions
Cyprus	- 2 battalions
Falkland Islands	- 1 company group on detachment
Bosnia	- 1 composite battalion on detachment
Kosovo	- 1 composite battalion on detachment
Brunei	- 1 battalion (Gurkha)
Iraq	- 4 battalions (on detachment from UK/Germany)

As explained previously, it would be most unusual for the Infantry to fight as battalion units especially in armoured or mechanised formations. The HQ of an infantry battalion will generally be the HQ of a battle group, and the force will be provided with armour, artillery, engineers and possibly aviation to enable it to become a balanced all arms grouping.

The Infantry accounts for about 25% of the Army

The Guards Division

1st Bn The Grenadier Guards	1 GREN GDS
1st Bn The Coldstream Guards	1 COLM GDS
1st Bn The Scots Guards	1 SG

| 1st Bn The Irish Guards | 1 IG |
| 1st Bn The Welsh Guards | 1 WG |

There are generally three battalions from the Guards Division on public duties in London at any one time. When a Regiment is stationed in London on public duties it is given an extra company to ensure the additional manpower required for ceremonial events is available.

The Scottish Division

1st Bn The Royal Scots	1 RS
1st Bn The Royal Highland Fusiliers	1 RHF
1st Bn The King's Own Scottish Borderers	1 KOSB
1st Bn The Black Watch	1 BW
1st Bn The Argyll & Sutherland Highlanders	1 A & SH
1st Bn The Highlanders	1 HLDRS

The Queen's Division

1st Bn The Princess of Wales's Royal Regiment (Queen's and Royal Hampshire)	1 PWRR
2nd Bn The Princess of Wales's Royal Regiment (Queen's and Royal Hampshire)	2 PWRR
1st Bn The Royal Regiment of Fusiliers	1 RRF
2nd Bn The Royal Regiment of Fusiliers	2 RRF
1st Bn The Royal Anglian Regiment	1 R ANGLIAN
2nd Bn The Royal Anglian Regiment	2 R ANGLIAN

The King's Division

1st Bn The King's Own Royal Border Regiment	1 KINGS OWN BORDER
1st Bn The King's Regiment	1 KINGS
1st Bn The Prince of Wales's Own Regiment of Yorkshire	1 PWO
1st Bn The Green Howards	1 GREEN HOWARDS
1st Bn The Queen's Lancashire Regiment	1 QLR
1st Bn The Duke of Wellington's Regiment	1 DWR

The Prince of Wales Division

1st Bn The Devonshire & Dorset Regiment	1 D and D
1st Bn The Cheshire Regiment	1 CHESHIRE
1st Bn The Royal Welch Fusiliers	1 RWF
1st Bn The Royal Regiment of Wales	1 RRW
1st Bn The Royal Gloucestershire, Berkshire and Wiltshire Regiment	1 RGBW
1st Bn The Worcestershire & Sherwood Foresters Regiment	1 WFR
1st Bn The Staffordshire Regiment	1 STAFFORDS

The Light Division
1st Bn The Light Infantry	1 LI
2nd Bn The Light Infantry	2 LI
1st Bn The Royal Green Jackets	1 RGJ
2nd Bn The Royal Green Jackets	2 RGJ

The Brigade of Gurkhas
1st Bn The Royal Gurkha Rifles	1 RGR
2nd Bn The Royal Gurkha Rifles	2 RGR

The Parachute Regiment
1st Bn The Parachute Regiment	1 PARA
2nd Bn The Parachute Regiment	2 PARA
3rd Bn THe Parachute Regiment	3 PARA

The Royal Irish Regiment
1st Bn The Royal Irish Regiment (Regular)	1 R IRISH
2nd Bn The Royal Irish Regiment (Home Service)	2 R IRISH
3rd Bn The Royal Irish Regiment (Home Service)	3 R IRISH
4th Bn The Royal Irish Regiment (Home Service)	4 R IRISH

From April 2002 there are four infantry training battalions at the Infantry Training Centre (ITC Catterick).

The Special Air Service Regiment
The 22nd Special Air Service Regiment	22 SAS

The SAS can be classed as an infantry unit but the members of the regiment are found from all arms and services of the Army after exhaustive selection tests.

Infantry Organisations

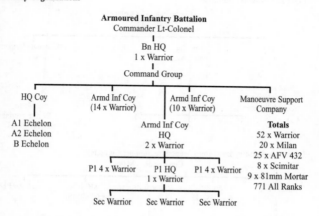

Armoured Infantry Battalion

Commander Lt-Colonel

Bn HQ
1 x Warrior

Command Group

| HQ Coy | Armd Inf Coy (14 x Warrior) | Armd Inf Coy (10 x Warrior) | Manoeuvre Support Company |

A1 Echelon
A2 Echelon
B Echelon

Armd Inf Coy
HQ
2 x Warrior

P1 4 x Warrior   P1 HQ 1 x Warrior   P1 4 x Warrior

Sec Warrior   Sec Warrior   Sec Warrior

Totals
52 x Warrior
20 x Milan
25 x AFV 432
8 x Scimitar
9 x 81mm Mortar
771 All Ranks

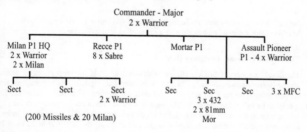

Armoured Infantry Battalion - Manoeuvre Support Company

Commander - Major
2 x Warrior

| Milan P1 HQ 2 x Warrior 2 x Milan | Recce P1 8 x Sabre | Mortar P1 | Assault Pioneer P1 - 4 x Warrior |

Sect   Sect   Sect 2 x Warrior

Sec   Sec 3 x 432 2 x 81mm Mor   Sec   3 x MFC

(200 Missiles & 20 Milan)

Note: (1) There are 9 x Armoured Infantry Battalions, 6 of which are in Germany with 1 (UK) Armoured Division and the remaining 3 in the UK with 3 (UK) Division. (2) There are longer term intentions to replace the AFV 432s on issue to armoured infantry battalions by other versions of Warrior or equivalent vehicles such as mortar carrier, ambulance, command vehicle etc.(3) Another 4 Milan firing posts are held by the section that is only activated on mobilisation.

87

Light Role Infantry Battalion

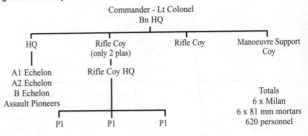

Light Role Infantry Battalion - Manoeuvre Support Company

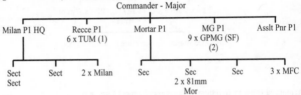

Notes: (1) TUM is the abbreviation for Truck-Utility-Medium; (2) General Purpose Machine Guns mounted on tripods with a range of up to 1,800 metres.

The Royal Regiment of Artillery (RA)

The Royal Regiment of Artillery (RA) provides the battlefield fire support and air defence for the British Army in the field. Its various regiments are equipped for conventional fire support using field guns, for area and point air defence using air defence missiles and for specialised artillery locating tasks. There are now three Regiments equipped with the Multiple Launch Rocket System (MLRS) which have now taken their place in the Order of Battle and these weapons were used with great effect during the 1991 war in the Gulf. In October 1993 1st Royal Horse Artillery became the first regiment to be equipped with the AS 90 self propelled howitzer. By 2000 the AS 90 self propelled howitzer was the primary 155 mm artillery weapon of the British Army and the towed 155 mm FH 70 has been retired from general service.

Following the Strategic Defence Review of 1990 the RA remains one of the larger organisations in the British Army with 17 Regiments included in its regular Order of Battle. It has the following structure in both the UK and Germany (ARRC).

	UK	Germany
Field Regiments (AS 90 SP Guns)	3	3
Field Regiments (Light Gun)	2(1)	-
Depth Fire Regiments (MLRS)	2(2)	-
Air Defence Regiments (Rapier)	2	-
Air Defence Regiment (HVM)	1	1
Surveillance and Target Acquisition Regiment	1	-
Training Regiment (School Assets Regt)	1	-
The Kings Troop (Ceremonial)	1	-

Note:

(1) Of these 2 Regiments one is a Commando Regiment (29 Cdo Regt) and the other is an Air Assault Regiment(7 PARA RHA*). This Regt has one battery in the Parachute role but the Regt is assigned to the 16th Air Assault Bde at Colchester. 7 RHA will, incidently, keep the designation "PARA" as well as the word "Horse" in their title. 7 RHA Battery titles are those of the famous horse drawn batteries at Waterloo,

(2)The third MLRS Regiment is now a TA Regt with 12 Launch vehicles in peace uprateable to 18 in war.

(3) Although the artillery is organised into Regiments, much of a "Gunner's" loyalty is directed towards the battery in which they serve. The guns represent the Regimental Colours of the Artillery and it is around the batteries where the guns are held that history has gathered. A Regiment will generally have three or four gun batterys under command.

The Royal Horse Artillery (RHA) is also part of the Royal Regiment of Artillery and its three regiments have been included in the totals above. There is considerable cross posting of officers and soldiers from the RA to the RHA, and some consider service with the RHA to be a career advancement.

Artillery training is carried out at the Royal School of Artillery at Larkhill in Wiltshire. After initial training officers and gunners will be posted to RA units worldwide, but soldiers will return to the RSA for frequent career and employment courses. Artillery recruits spend the first period of recruit training (Common Military Syllabus) at the Army Training Regiment - Lichfield.

Air Defence is a vital part of the role of the Royal Artillery and updates to the Rapier system are in the main complete, with batterys being upgraded to Field Standard B2 and Field Standard C. During 1994 a Starstreak HVM Regiment became operational in the UK. In addition, the air defences have been enhanced by the Air Defence Alerting Device.

The Royal Artillery provides the modern British armoured formation with a protective covering. The air defence covers the immediate airspace above and around the formation, with the field artillery reaching out to approximately 30 km in front and across the flanks of the formation. An armoured formation that moves out of this protective covering is open to immediate destruction by an intelligent enemy as the Egyptians discovered in 1973.

Divisional Artillery Group (DAG)

An armoured or mechanised division has it own artillery under command. This artillery usually consists of 3 Close Support Regiments, with a number of units detached from the

Corps Artillery and could include TA reinforcements. In war the composition of the DAG will vary according to the task.

The following is a diagram of the artillery support available to a UK division. Expect each brigade in the division to have one Close Support Regiment with AS90 under command.

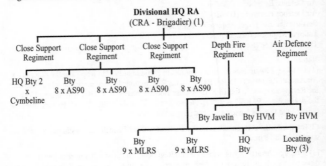

Divisional HQ RA
(CRA - Brigadier) (1)

Close Support Regiment — Close Support Regiment — Close Support Regiment — Depth Fire Regiment — Air Defence Regiment

HQ Bty 2 x Cymbeline | Bty 8 x AS90 | Bty 8 x AS90 | Bty 8 x AS90 | Bty 8 x AS90

Bty Javelin | Bty HVM | Bty HVM

Bty 9 x MLRS | Bty 9 x MLRS | HQ Bty | Locating Bty (3)

Notes:
(1) Air defended areas (ADAs) are provided by Rapier.
(2) The Staff of an armoured or mechanised division includes a Brigadier of Artillery known as the Commander Royal Artillery (CRA). The CRA acts as the artillery advisor to the Divisional Commander, and would probably assign one of his Close Support Regiments to support each of the Brigades in the division. These regiments would be situated in positions that would allow most of their batterys to fire across the complete divisional front. Therefore, in the very best case, a battlegroup under extreme threat could be supported by the fire of more than 96 guns.

The number of batterys and guns per battery in an AS 90 Close Support Regiment has changed post SDR 1999 to four batterys of six guns per battery in the UK Regiments, and three batteries each of six guns for the Regiments in Germany. In war all batteries will have eight guns each. These additional guns are currently in the training inventory at The Royal School of Artillery and at BATUS in Canada where regular field training takes place

Royal Artillery Regiments

1st Regiment RHA	1 RHA	(Field)
3rd Regiment RHA	3 RHA	(Field)
4th Regiment RA	4 REGT	(Field)
5th Regiment RA	5 REGT	(STA and Special Ops)
7th Regiment RHA	7 RHA	(Parachute & Air Assault)
12th Regiment RA	12 REGT	(Air Defence)
14th Regiment RA	14 REGT	(Training)
16th Regiment RA	16 REGT	(Air Defence)
19th Regiment RA	19 REGT	(Field)

22nd Regiment RA	22 REGT	(Air Defence)
26th Regiment RA	26 REGT	(Field)
29th Commando Regiment RA	29 REGT	(Field)
32nd Regiment RA	32 REGT	(MLRS)
39th Regiment RA	39 REGT	(MLRS)
40th Regiment RA	40 REGT	(Field)
47th Regiment RA	47 REGT	(Air Defence)

TA Artillery Regiments

The Honourable Artillery Coy	London	STA and Special Ops
100 Fd Regt RA (V)	Luton	Reinforcement Regt
101 Fd Regt RA (V)	Newcastle	MLRS (12 in peace)
103 Fd Regt RA (V)	Liverpool	Javelin
104 Fd Regt RA (V)	Newport	Javelin
105 Fd Regt RA (V)	Edinburgh	Javelin
106 Fd Regt RA (V)	London	Individual Reinforcements

Army Air Corps

The Army obtains its aviation support from the Army Air Corps (AAC), which is an Army organisation with 5 separate regiments and a number of independent squadrons. The AAC also provides support for Northern Ireland on a mixed resident and roulement basis and the two squadrons concerned are sometimes referred to as the sixth AAC Regiment, although the units would disperse on mobilisation and have no regimental title.

1 Regiment - Germany	(652 & 661 Sqns)
3 Regiment - Wattisham	(653,662 & 663 Sqns)
4 Regiment - Wattisham	(654,659 & 669 Sqns)
5 Regiment - Aldergrove	(655 & 665 Sqns)
7 Regiment - Netheravon	(658 & 666(V) Sqns)
9 Regiment - Dishforth	(656, 664 & 672 Sqns)
2 (Trg) Regiment - Depot	(651AH & 667D7T Sqns)

The HQ of 2 (Trg) Regiment is at Middle Wallop and there are 2 x TA Squadrons. One at Netheravon 658 Sqn(V) and 666 Sqn(V) with 3 Flight at RAF Leuchars and 6 Flight at RAF Shawbury. In addition to the Regiments in the UK and Germany there are small flights in Cyprus, Bruggen (Germany), Brunei, Suffield (Canada) and the Falkland Islands.

The AAC Centre at Middle Wallop in Hampshire acts as a focal point for all Army Aviation, and it is here that the majority of training for pilots and aircrew is carried out. From 1997, elementary flying training for all three services has been carried out at RAF Shawbury in Shropshire.

Although the AAC operates some fixed-wing aircraft for training, liaison flying and radar duties, the main effort goes into providing helicopter support for the ground forces. About 350 AAC helicopters are used for anti-tank operations, artillery fire control, reconnaissance, liaison flying and a limited troop lift.

Army Air Corps - Attack Regiment

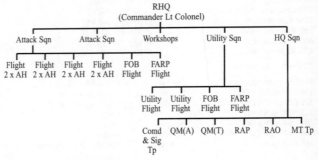

Totals: 8 x LUH (Light Utility Helicopters)
16 x AH (Attack Helicopters)

Notes: FOB - Forward Operating Base: FARP- Forward Area Rearm/Refuel Point.

By the end of 2003 we would expect 3 Regiment and 4 Regiment at Wattisham to be equipped with AH-64 Apache. Wattisham is also the home of 7 Bn REME - a unit configured as an aircraft workshops.

Army Air Corps - Regimental Designations	**AAC**
1st Regiment	1 REGT AAC
3rd Regiment	3 REGT AAC
4th Regiment	4 REGT AAC
5th Regiment	5 REGT AAC
7th Regiment	7 REGT AAC
9th Regiment	9 REGT AAC

Army Air Corps - Divisional Aviation Regiment

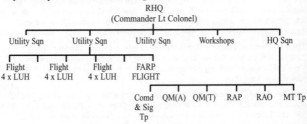

Total: 36 x LUH (Light Utility Helicopters), approx 450 personnel

Corps of Royal Engineers

The engineer support for the Army is provided by the Corps of Royal Engineers (RE). This large corps, currently composed of 16 regiments filled with highly skilled tradesmen is currently organised as follows:

	Germany	UKLF
Engineer Regiments	4	6
EOD Regiment	-	1
TA Engineer Regiments	-	5

There are also a number of independent engineer squadrons worldwide.

The Royal Engineers provide specialist support to the combat formations and engineer detachments can be found at all levels from the Combat Team/Company Group upwards. Combat Engineers tasks are amongst the following:

a. **Defence:** Construction of field defences; laying anti-tank mines; improvement and construction of obstacles.

b. **Attack:** Obstacle crossing; demolition of enemy defences (bunkers etc); mine clearance; bridge or ferry construction.

c. **Advance:** Building or strengthening roads and bridges; removal of booby traps; mine clearance; airfield construction; supply of water; survey.

d. **Withdrawal:** Demolition - of airfields, roads and bridges, fuel, ammunition and food dumps, railway tracks and rolling stock, industrial plant and facilities such as power stations; route clearance; laying anti-tank mines; booby trapping likely enemy future positions and items that might be attractive to the enemy. Often amongst the first soldiers into battle, and still involved in dangerous tasks such as mine clearance in the former Yugoslavia, the Sappers can turn their hands to almost any engineering task.

Recent UN tasks have highlighted the importance of combat engineers. Tasks for which engineer support was requested stretched the resources of the Corps to its limit and the first priority in almost any call from the UN for support is for engineers. Tracks have to be improved, roads must be built, wells dug and clean water provided together with camps for refugees. All of these are engineer tasks that soak up large amounts of manpower.

Engineer Organisations

The smallest engineer unit is the field troop which is usually commanded by a Lieutenant and consists of approximately 44 men. In an armoured division a field troop can be expected to have up to four sections and each section is mounted in an APC. Engineer Regiments in UKLF may have only three sections and may be mounted in wheeled vehicles such as Land Rovers and 4 Ton Trucks. An engineer troop will carry equipment, stores and explosives to enable it to carry out its immediate battlefield tasks.

Armoured Divisional Engineer Regiment (1)

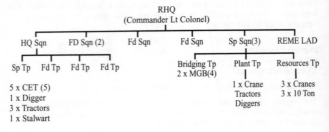

Strength: Approx 650 All Ranks

(1) This Regiment would send most of its soldiers to man the engineer detachments that provide support for a division's battlegroups; (2) Field Squadron (expect a field squadron to have approximately 68 vehicles and some 200 men; (3) Support Squadron; (4) Medium Girder Bridge; (5) Combat Engineer Tractor; (6) This whole organisation is highly mobile and built around the AFV 432 and Spartan series of vehicles; (7) In addition to the regimental REME LAD each squadron has its own REME section of approximately 12 - 15 men.

Engineer amphibious capability and specialist support is provided by elements of 28 Engineer Regiment in Germany and a TA Regiment in the UK.

The UK Engineer Field Regiment (Regular & TA) is generally a wheeled organisation that might be expected to have 2 Field Squadrons, a Support Squadron and possibly an Airfield Damage Repair (ADR) Squadron. Engineer regiments supporting 3(UK) Division could be structured along the lines of the Armoured Divisional Engineer Regiment.

Royal Engineers - Regimental Designations

1st RSME Regiment	1 RSME REGT RE
3rd RSME Regiment	3 RSME REGT RE
21st Engineer Regiment	21 ENGR REGT
22nd Engineer Regiment	22 ENGR REGT
23rd Engineer Regiment	23 ENFR REGT
25th Engineer Regiment	25 ENGR REGT
28th Engineer Regiment	28 ENGR REGT
32nd Engineer Regiment	32 ARMD ENGR REGT
33rd Engineer Regiment	33 ENGR REGT (EOD)
35th Engineer Regiment	35 ENGR REGT
36th Engineer Regiment	36 ENGR REGT
38th Engineer Regiment	38 ENGR REGT
39th Engineer Regiment	39 ENGR REGT

The Royal Corps of Signals

The Royal Corps of Signals (R Signals) provides the communications throughout the command system of the Army. Individual battlegroups are responsible for their own internal communications, but all communications from Brigade level and above are the responsibility of the Royal Signals.

Information is the lifeblood of any military formation in battle and it is the responsibility of the Royal Signals to ensure the speedy and accurate passage of information that enables commanders to make informed and timely decisions, and to ensure that those decisions are passed to the fighting troops in contact with the enemy. The rapid, accurate and secure employment of command, control and communications systems, maximises the effect of the military force available and consequently the Royal Signals act as an extremely significant 'Force Multiplier'.

The Royal Corps of Signals provides about 9% of the Army's manpower with 11 Regular (including 1 Training Regiment) and 11 Territorial Army Regiments, each generally consisting of between 3 and up to 6 Sqns with between 400 and 1,000 personnel. In addition, there are 20 Regular and 2 Territorial Army Independent Squadrons, each of which has about 200 men, and 4 Independent Signal Troops of between 10 and 80 men each. Royal Signals personnel are found wherever the Army is deployed including every UK and NATO headquarters in the world. The Headquarters of the Corps is at the Royal School of Signals (RSS) located at Blandford in Dorset.

Royal Signals units based in the United Kingdom provide command, control and communications for forces that have operational roles both in the UK itself, including Northern Ireland, and overseas including mainland Western Europe and further afield wherever the Army finds itself. There are a number of Royal Signals units permanently based in Germany, Holland and Belgium from where they provide the necessary command and control communications and Electronic Warfare (EW) support for both the British Army and other NATO forces based in Europe. Royal Signals units are also based in Cyprus, Hong Kong, the Falkland Islands, Belize and Gibraltar.

Armoured Divisional Signal Regiment Organisation

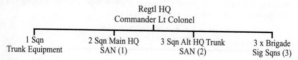

Notes: (1) SAN - Secondary Access Node (2) A Divisional HQ will have two HQs to allow for movement and possible destruction. The main HQ will be set up for approx 24 hrs with the alternative HQ (Alt HQ) set up 20-30 km away on the proposed line of march of the division. When the Main HQ closes to move to a new location, the Alt HQ becomes the Main HQ for another 24 hour period. (3) Expect a Brigade Sig Sqn to have a Radio Troop and a SAN Troop.

Regiments

1st (UK) Armd Div HQ and Signal Regiment	1 SIG REGT
2nd Signal Regiment	2 SIG REGT
3rd (UK) Div HQ & Signal Regiment	3 SIG REGT
7th (ARRC) Signal Regiment	7 SIG REGT
9th Signal Regiment (Radio)	9 SIG REGT
11th Signal Regiment (Trg Regt)	11 SIG REGT
14th Signal Regiment (Electronic Warfare)	14 SIG REGT
15th Signal Regiment	15 SIG REGT
16th Signal Regiment	16 SIG REGT
21st Signal Regiment (Air Support)	21 SIG REGT
30th Signal Regiment	30 SIG REGT

The Royal Logistic Corps (RLC)

The RLC is the youngest Corps in the Army and was formed in April 1993 as a result of the recommendations of the MoD's Logistic Support Review. The RLC results from the amalgamation of the Royal Corps of Transport (RCT), the Royal Army Ordnance Corps (RAOC), the Army Catering Corps (ACC), the Royal Pioneer Corps (RPC) and elements of the Royal Engineers (RE). The Corps makes up about 16% of the Army with 20,000 Regular soldiers and 10,000 Territorial Army soldiers wearing its cap badge.

The RLC has very broad responsibilities throughout the Army that include the movement of personnel throughout the world, the Army's air dispatch service, maritime and rail transport, operational re-supply, and explosive ordnance disposal which includes the hazardous bomb disposal duties in Northern Ireland and in mainland UK, the operation of numerous very large vehicle and stores depots both in the UK and overseas, the training and provision of cooks to virtually all units in the Army, the provision of pioneer labour and the Army's postal and courier service.

The principal field elements of the RLC are the Close Support and the General Support Regiments whose primary role is to supply the fighting units with ammunition, fuel and rations (Combat Supplies).

A division has an integral Close Support Regiment which is responsible for manning and operating the supply chain to Brigades and Divisional units.

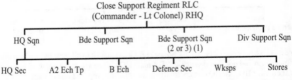

Close Support Regiment RLC
(Commander - Lt Colonel) RHQ

HQ Sqn — Bde Support Sqn — Bde Support Sqn (2 or 3) (1) — Div Support Sqn

HQ Sec — A2 Ech Tp — B Ech — Defence Sec — Wksps — Stores

Note:
(1) A regiment could have two or three brigade support sqns depending upon the size of the division being supported.
(2) Some of these regiments may have a Postal and Courier Squadron.
The General Support Regiment's role is primarily to supply ammunition to the Royal

Artillery using DROPS vehicles and to provide Tank Transporters that move armoured vehicles more rapidly and economically than moving them on their own tracks.

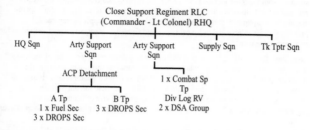

Both types of Regiment have large sections holding stores both on wheels and on the ground. A Division will typically require about 1,000 tons of Combat Supplies a day but demand can easily exceed that amount in high intensity operations.

Regiments

1 General Support Regiment	1 (GS) REGT
2 Close Support Regiment	2 (CS) REGT
3 Close Support Regiment	3 (CS) REGT
4 General Support Regiment	4 (GS) REGT
5 Territorial Army Training Regiment	5 (TRG) REGT
6 Support Regiment	6 (SP) REGT
7 Transport Regiment	7 (TPT) REGT
8 Artillery Support Regiment	8 (ARTY SP) REGT
9 Supply Regiment	9 (SUP) REGT
10 Transport Regiment	10 (TPT) REGT
11 Explosive Ordnance Disposal Regiment	11 (EOD) REGT
12 Supply Regiment	12 (SUP) REGT
13 Air Assault Support Regiment	13 (AIR ASSLT) REGT
14 Supply Regiment	14 (SUP) REGT
17 Port and Maritime Regiment	17 (PORT) REGT
21 Logistic Support Regiment	21 (LOG SP) REGT
23 Pioneer Regiment	23 (PNR) REGT
24 Regiment	24 REGT
27 Transport Regiment	27 (TPT) REGT
29 Regiment	29 REGT
89 Postal and Courier Regiment	89 (PC) REGT
Queen's Own Gurkha Logistic Regiment	QGLR

The Royal Electrical & Mechanical Engineers (REME)

The Logistic Support review of 1990 recommended that Equipment Support should remain separate from the other logistic pillar of Service Support and consequently the REME has retained not only its own identity but expanded its responsibilities. Equipment Support encompasses equipment management, engineering support, supply management, provisioning for vehicle and technical spares and financial management responsibilities for in-service equipment.

The aim of the REME is "To keep operationally fit equipment in the hands of the troops" and in the current financial environment it is important that this is carried out at the minimum possible cost. The equipment that REME is responsible for ranges from small arms and trucks to helicopters and Main Battle Tanks. All field force units have some integral REME support which will vary, depending on the size of the unit and the equipment held, from a few attached tradesmen up to a large Regimental Workshop of over 200 men.

In war, REME is responsible for the recovery and repair of battle damaged and unserviceable equipments.

The development of highly technical weapon systems and other equipment has meant that REME has had to balance engineering and tactical considerations. On the one hand the increased scope for forward repair of equipment reduces the time out of action but, on the other hand engineering stability is required for the repair of complex systems. In 1993, following the Options for Change and Logistic Support Reviews four extra REME battalions were formed, to provide second line support for the British contribution to the ACE Rapid Reaction Corps (ARRC).

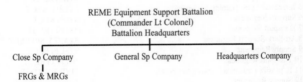

Note: Approx 450 personnel. In mid 2003 there are seven Regular REME Support battalions, three in Germany, three in the UK and one aviation support regiment in the UK. There are 4 battalions in the TA.

The Close Support Company will normally deploy a number of FRGs (Forward Repair Groups) and MRGs (Medium Repair Groups) in support of brigades. The company is mobile with armoured repair and recovery vehicles able to operate in the forward areas, carrying out forward repair of key nominated equipment often by the exchange of major assemblies. It is also capable of carrying out field repairs on priority equipment including telecommunications equipment and the repair of damage sustained by critical battle winning equipments.

The role of the General Support Company is to support the Close Support Companies and Divisional Troops. Tasks include the regeneration of fit power packs for use in forward repair and the repair of equipment backloaded from Close Support Companies. The General Support Company will normally be located to the rear of the divisional area in order to maximise productivity and minimise vulnerability.

Army Medical Services

Royal Army Medical Corps

In peace, the personnel of the RAMC are based at the various medical installations throughout the world or in field force units and they are responsible for the health of the Army.

The primary role of the Corps is the maintenance of health and the prevention of disease. On operations, the RAMC is responsible for the care of the sick and wounded, with the subsequent evacuation of the wounded to hospitals in the rear areas. Each Brigade has a medical squadron which is a regular unit that operates in direct support of the battlegroups. These units are either armoured, airmobile or parachute trained. In addition, each division has two TA field ambulance units that provide medical support for the divisional troops and can act as manoeuvre units for the forward brigades when required.

All medical squadrons have medical sections that consist of a medical officer and eight Combat Medical Technicians. These sub-units are located with the battlegroup or units being supported and they provide the necessary first line medical support. In addition, the field ambulance provides a dressing station where casualties are treated and may be resuscitated or stabilised before transfer to a field hospital. These units have the necessary integral ambulance support, both armoured and wheeled to transfer casualties from the first to second line medical units.

Field hospitals may be regular or TA and all are 200 bed facilities with a maximum of 8 surgical teams capable of carrying out life-saving operations on some of the most difficult surgical cases. Since 1990, most regular medical units have been deployed on operations either in the Persian Gulf or the former Yugoslavia.

Casualty Evacuation (CASEVAC) is by ambulance either armoured or wheeled and driven by RLC personnel or by helicopter when such aircraft are available. A Chinook helicopter is capable of carrying 44 stretcher cases and a Puma can carry 6 stretcher cases and 6 sitting cases.

The Queen Alexandra's Royal Army Nursing Corps (QARANC)

On 1 April 1992 the QARANC became an all-nursing and totally professionally qualified Corps. Its male and female officer and other rank personnel provide the necessary qualified nursing support at all levels covering a wide variety of nursing specialities. QARANC personnel can be found anywhere in the world where Army Medical services are required. During mid 2003 the QARANC strength was approximately 680 all ranks.

Royal Army Dental Corps (RADC)

The RADC is a professional corps that in late 2000 consisted of just over 290 officers and soldiers. The Corps fulfils the essential role of maintaining the dental health of the Army in peace and war, both at home and overseas. Qualified dentists and oral surgeons, hygienists, technicians and support ancillaries work in a wide variety of military units - from static and mobile dental clinics to field medical units, military hospitals and dental laboratories. During mid 2003 the RADC strength was approximately 367 all ranks (120 officers).

The Adjutant General's Corps (AGC)

The Adjutant General's Corps was formed on 1 April 1992 and its sole task is the management of the Army's most precious resource, its soldiers. The Corps absorbed the functions of six existing smaller corps; the Royal Military Police, the Royal Army Pay Corps, the Royal Army Educational Corps, the Royal Army Chaplain's Department, the Army Legal Corps and the Military Provost Staff Corps.

The Corps is organised into four branches, Staff and Personnel Support (SPS), Provost (PRP), Educational and Training Services (ETS) and Army Legal Services (ALS). In late 2000, the AGC consisted of over 7,000 officers and soldiers.

The Role of SPS Branch

The role of SPS Branch is to ensure the efficient and smooth delivery of Personnel Administration to the Army. This includes support to individual officers and soldiers in units by processing pay and Service documentation, first line provision of financial, welfare, education and resettlement guidance to individuals and the provision of clerical skills and information management to ensure the smooth day to day running of the unit or department.

AGC (SPS) officers are employed throughout the Army, in direct support of units as Regimental Administrative Officers or AGC Detachment Commanders. They hold Commander AGC(SPS) and SO2 AGC(SPS) posts in district/Divisional and Brigade HQs and fill posts at the Adjutant General's Information Centre (AGIC) and general staff appointments throughout the Army headquarters locations.

AGC(SPS) soldiers are employed as military clerks in direct support of units within the AGC Field Detachments, in fixed centre pay offices, in headquarters to provide staff support and in miscellaneous posts such as embassy clerks, as management accountants or in AGIC as programmer analysts.

Currently, about 62% of AGC(SPS) soldiers are based in UK, 27% in Germany and 11% elsewhere. The majority, currently 70% serving with field force units, with the remaining 30% in base and training units or HQs, such as MoD.

Members of AGC(SPS) are first trained as soldiers and then specialise as Military Clerks. AGC(SPS) officers complete the same military training as their counterparts in other Arms and Services, starting at the Royal Military Academy, Sandhurst. They are required to attend all promotion courses such as the Junior Command and Staff Course, and to pass the standard career exams prior to promotion to the rank of Major.

The Role of the Provost Branch

The Provost Branch was formed from the formerly independent Corps of Royal Military Police (RMP) and the Military Provost Staff Corps (MPSC). Although they are no longer independent they are still known as the AGC (PRO) and AGC (MPS) thus forming the two parts of the Provost Branch.

Royal Military Police

To provide the police support the Army requires the RMP has the following functions:

a. Providing operational support to units in the field.
b. Preventing crime.
c. Enforcement of the law within the community and assistance with the maintenance of discipline.
d. Providing a 24 hour response service of assistance, advice and information.

Operational support includes advising commanders and the staff who produce the operational movement plans. RMP traffic posts are deployed along the main operational movement routes and provide a constant flow of traffic information regarding the progress of front line troops and the logistical resupply. RMP units with a vehicle to man ratio of 1:3 are also a valuable force for the security of rear areas. In addition, there is a highly trained RMP close protection group that specialises in the protection of high risk VIPs.

The RMP provides the day to day police support for both the army in the UK and dependents and MoD civilians overseas. RMP units are trained and equipped to deal with the most serious crimes. The Special Investigation Branch (SIB) operates in a similar fashion to the civilian CID.

The Military Provost Staff

AGC(MPS) staff recruited from within the Army are carefully selected for the leadership, management and training skills necessary to motivate the predominantly young offenders with whom they work. The majority of AGC(MPS) personnel are located in the Military Corrective Training Centre (MCTC) at Colchester where offenders sentenced by military courts are confined.

The Role of the ETS Branch

The AGC(ETS) Branch has the responsibility for improving the efficiency, effectiveness and morale of the Army by providing support to operations and the developmental education, training, support and resettlement services that the Army requires to carry out its task. ETS personnel provide assistance at almost all levels of command but their most visible task is the manning of Army Education Centres wherever the Army is stationed. At these centres officers and soldiers receive the educational support necessary for them to achieve both civilian and military qualifications.

The Role of the ALS Branch

The AGC(ALS) Branch advises on all aspects of service and civilian law that may affect every level of the Army from General to Private soldiers. Members of the branch are usually qualified as solicitors or barristers. In addition to the AGC personnel attached to major units throughout the Army the Corps is directly responsible for the following:

Smaller Corps

THE INTELLIGENCE CORPS (Int Corps) - The Int Corps deals with operational intelligence, counter intelligence and security.

THE ROYAL ARMY VETERINARY CORPS (RAVC) - The RAVC looks after the many animals that the Army has on strength. Veterinary tasks in today's army are mainly directed towards guard or search dogs and horses for ceremonial duties.

THE ARMY PHYSICAL TRAINING CORPS (APTC) - Consists mainly of SNCOs who are responsible for unit fitness. The majority of major units have a representative from this corps on their strength.

THE GENERAL SERVICE CORPS (GSC) - A holding unit for specialists. Personnel from this corps are generally members of the reserve army.

SMALL ARMS SCHOOL CORPS (SASC) - A small corps with the responsibility of training instructors in all aspects of weapon handling.

The Royal Gibraltar Regiment
Consists of one infantry company and an artillery battery which assists in the defence of Gibraltar.

The Regular Army Reserve

The Regular Reserve

Individual Reservists (IR) are former members of the Regular Army who after completion of their full-time service may be recalled to the Colours, or who volunteer after their legal Reserve obligation has expired. They have varying degrees of liability for recall and training depending upon factors such as period of Regular Army service, age and sex. Categories of IR are described below:

a. The Regular Army Reserve of Officers (RARO). Retired Regular, Army Emergency Reserve or TA Officers. Those granted Commissions from 1 April 1983 have a compulsory training liability for six years after leaving the Active List. Others may volunteer to train;

b. The Regular Reserve. Ex-Regular soldiers (male and female) who have a compulsory training liability (normally for six years after leaving the Colours) or who have volunteered to join it from other categories;

c. The Long-Term Reserve. Men (but not women) who have completed their Regular Reserve liability and who serve in this category until aged 45. They have no training liability;

d. Army Pensioners. Ex-Regular soldiers (male and female) who are in receipt of a Service pension. They have a legal liability for recall to age 60 (but only to age 55 would be invoked). They have no training liability.

In October 2002 the Regular Army Reserve consisted of 33,100 personnel and IR's totalled 127,000.

The Territorial Army (TA)

Strength of the Territorial Army (1 January 2001)

Royal Armoured Corps	4 Regiments (Yeomanry)
Royal Artillery	7 Regiments (1)
Royal Engineers	5 Regiments
Infantry	15 Battalions

Special Air Service	2 Regiments
Signals	11 Regiments
Equipment Support	4 Battalions
Logistics	17 Regiments
Intelligence Corps	1 Battalion
Aviation	1 Regiment
Medical	15 Hospitals and Field Ambulances

Notes: (1) Including HAC.

TA ORDER OF BATTLE

Royal Armoured Corps

Royal Yeomanry
RHQ - London
Squadrons: Swindon; Leicester; Croydon; Nottingham; London.

Royal Wessex Yeomanry
RHQ - Bovington
Squadrons: Bovington; Salisbury; Cirencester; Barnstable.

Royal Mercian and Lancastrian Yeomanry
RHQ - Telford
Squadrons: Dudley; Telford; Chester; Wigan.

Queen's Own Yeomanry
RHQ - Newcastle
Squadrons: York; Ayr; Belfast; Cupar; Newcastle.

Royal Artillery

Honourable Artillery Company
RHQ - London
Squadrons: 5 all based in the City of London.

100 Regiment
RHQ - Luton
Batteries: Luton; Bristol; Nottingham.

101 Regiment
RHQ - Gateshead
Batteries: Blyth; Newcastle; South Shields.

103 Regiment
RHQ - St Helens
Batteries: Liverpool; Manchester; Bolton.

104 Regiment
RHQ - Newport
Batteries: Wolverhampton; Newport; Worcester.

105 Regiment
RHQ - Edinburgh
Batteries: Newtownards; Glasgow; Arbroath.

106 Regiment
RHQ - London
Batteries: Bury St Edmunds; London; Leeds: Southampton.

Central Volunteers HQ RA
London

Royal Engineers

Royal Monmouthshire RE (Militia)
RHQ - Monmouth
Squadrons: Cwmbran; Swansea; Warley.

71 Regiment
RHQ - Leuchars
Squadrons: Paisley; Newcastle.

73 Regiment
RHQ - Nottingham
Squadrons: Sheffield; Nottingham; Chesterfield; St Hellier(Jersey).

75 Regiment
RHQ - Failsworth
Squadrons: Birkenhead; Stoke on Trent; Walsall.

101 Regiment
RHQ - London
Squadrons: London; Rochester; Tunbridge Wells.

131 Independent Commando Squadron
London.

135 Topographical Squadron
Ewell.

412 Amphibious Engineer Troop
Hameln.

Central Volunteer HQ RE
Camberley.

Royal Signals

31 Signal Regiment
RHQ - London
Squadrons: Coulsdon; Eastbourne; London.

32 Signal Regiment
RHQ - Glasgow
Squadrons: Aberdeen; East Kilbride; Edinburgh.

33 Signal Regiment
RHQ - Huyton
Squadrons: Manchester; Liverpool; Runcorn.

34 Signal Regiment
RHQ - Middlesborough

Squadrons: Leeds; Darlington; Middlesborough.

35 Signal Regiment
RHQ - Coventry
Squadrons: Birmingham; Newcastle-Under-Lyme; Rugby; Shrewsbury.

36 Signal Regiment
RHQ - Ilford
Squadrons: Grays; Colchester; Cambridge.

37 Signal Regiment
RHQ - Redditch
Squadrons: Cardiff; Stratford-Upon-Avon; Manchester; Coventry.

38 Signal Regiment
RHQ - Sheffield
Squadrons: Derby; Sheffield; Nottingham.

39 Signal Regiment
RHQ - Bristol
Squadrons: Uxbridge; Banbury; Gloucester.

40 Signal Regiment
RHQ - Belfast
Squadrons: Belfast; Limavady; Bangor.

71 Signal Regiment
RHQ - London
Squadrons: Lincolns Inn; Bexleyheath; Chelmsford.

1 Signal Squadron
Bletchley.

2 Signal Squadron
Dundee.

5 Communications Company
Chicksands.

63 Signal Squadron (SAS)

97 (BRITFOR) Signals Squadron
For service in the Balkans

Infantry

The Tyne Tees Regiment
Bn HQ - Durham
Companies: Scarborough; Middlesborough; Bishop Auckland; Newcastle upon Tyne; Ashington.

The King's and Cheshire Regiment
Bn HQ - Warrington
Companies: Liverpool; Warrington; Manchester; Crewe.

51st Highland Regiment
Bn HQ - Perth
Companies: Dundee; Peterhead; Inverness; Dunbarton; Stirling.

52nd Lowland Regiment
Bn HQ - Glasgow
Companies: Edinburgh; Ayr; Glasgow; Galashiels.

The East and West Riding Regiment
Bn HQ - Pontefract
Companies: Huddersfield; Barnsley; Hull; York; Wakefield.

The East of England Regiment
Bn HQ - Bury St Edmunds
Companies: Norwich; Lincoln; Leicester; Mansfield; Chelmsford.

The London Regiment
Bn HQ - Battersea
Companies: Westminster; Edgeware; Balham; Camberwell; Mayfair; West Ham.

3rd (Volunteer) Battalion, The Princess of Wales's Royal Regiment (Queen's and Royal Hampshires)
Bn HQ - Canterbury
Companies: Farnham; Brighton; Canterbury.

The Royal Rifle Volunteers
Bn HQ - Reading
Companies: Oxford; Reading; Portsmouth; Milton Keynes.

The Rifle Volunteers
Bn HQ - Exeter
Companies: Gloucester; Taunton; Dorchester; Truro; Exeter.

The West Midlands Regiment
Bn HQ - Wolverhampton
Companies: Birmingham; Kidderminster; Burton upon Trent; Stoke-on-Trent; Shrewsbury.

The Royal Welsh Regiment
Bn HQ - Cardiff
Companies: Wrexham; Swansea; Cardiff; Colwyn Bay.

The Lancastrian and Cumbrian Volunteers
Bn HQ - Preston
Companies: Barrow in Furness; Blackburn; Workington; Preston.

The Royal Irish Rangers
Bn HQ - Portadown
Companies: Newtonards; Newtownabbey.

4th (Volunteer) Battalion, The Parachute Regiment
Bn HQ - Pudsey
Companies: London; Pudsey; Glasgow.

Army Medical Services

201 Field Hospital
RHQ - Newcastle upon Tyne
Squadrons: Newton Aycliffe; Stockton-on-Tees; Newcastle upon Tyne.

202 Field Hospital
RHQ - Birmingham

Squadrons: Birmingham; Stoke on Trent; Oxford; Shrewsbury.

203 Field Hospital
RHQ - Cardiff
Squadrons: Cardiff; Swansea; Abergavenny.

204 Field Hospital
RHQ - Belfast
Squadrons: Belfast; Ballymena; Newtownards; Armagh.

205 Field Hospital
RHQ - Glasgow
Squadrons: Glasgow; Aberdeen; Dundee; Edinburgh.

207 Field Hospital
RHQ - Manchester
Squadrons: Stockport; Blackburn; Bury.

208 Field Hospital
RHQ- Liverpool
Squadrons: Liverpool; Ellesmere; Lancaster.

212 Field Hospital
RHQ - Sheffield
Squadrons: Sheffield; Bradford; Nottingham; Leeds.

243 Field Hospital
RHQ - Keynsham
Squadrons: Keynsham; Exeter; Plymouth; Portsmouth.

256 Field Hospital
RHQ - Walworth, London
Squadrons: Walworth; Hammersmith; Kingston; Bow.

253 Field Ambulance
Belfast.

254 Field Ambulance
Cambridge.

152 Ambulance Regiment
RHQ - Belfast
Squadrons: Londonderry; Belfast; Bridgend.

C (144) Parachute Medical Squadron
London.

B (220) Medical Squadron
Maidstone.

B (250) Medical Squadron
Hull.

B (225) Medical Squadron
Dundee.

C (251) Medical Squadron
Sunderland.

C (222) Medical Squadron
Leicester.

HQ Army Medical Service TA
York.

Royal Logistic Corps

150 (Northumbria) Transport Regiment
RHQ - Hull
Squadrons: Hull; Tynemouth; Leeds; Doncaster.

151 (Greater London) Logistic Support Regiment
RHQ - Croydon
Squadrons: Romford; Sutton; Barnet; Southall.

156 (North West) Transport Regiment
RHQ - Liverpool
Squadrons: Liverpool; Birkenhead; Salford; Bootle.

157 (Wales and Midland) Logistic Support Regiment
RHQ - Cardiff
Squadrons: Cardiff; Telford; Swansea; Carmarthen; West Bromwich.

158 (Royal Anglain) Transport Regiment
RHQ - Peterborough
Squadrons: Peterborough; Kempston; Ipswich; Loughborough.

Scottish Transport Regiment
RHQ - Dunfermline
Squadrons: Dunfermline; Glasgow; Edinburgh; Glenrothes; Irvine.

168 Pioneer Regiment
RHQ - Grantham
Squadrons: Grantham; Cramlington; Coulby Newham.

CVHQ and HR RLC TA
Grantham.

Royal Electrical And Mechanical Engineers

101 Battalion REME
Bn HQ - Queensferry
Companies: Prestatyn; Coventry; Clifton; Grangemouth.

102 Battalion REME
Bn HQ - Newton Aycliffe
Companies: Newton Aycliffe; Rotherham; Scunthorpe; Newcastle upon Tyne.

103 Battalion REME
Bn HQ - Crawley
Companies: Portsmouth; Redhill; Ashford.

104 Battalion REME
Bn HQ - Bordon
Company: Northampton.

HQ REME TA
Bordon

Adjutant General's Corps

4 Regiment, Royal Military Police
RHQ - Aldershot
Companies: West Bromwich; Brixton.

5 Regiment, Royal Military Police
RHQ - Livingston
Companies: Livingston; Stockton-on-Tees.

CVHQ AGC:
Worthy Down.

Intelligence Corps

3 (Volunteer) Military Intelligence Battalion:
BHQ - London
Companies: London; Edinburgh; York; Keynsham; Birmingham.

Special Air Service

21 and 23 Regiments SAS

Army Air Corps

7 Regiment AAC
Netheravon.

Officer Training Corps
Aberdeen University Officer Training Corps
Birmingham University Officer Training Corps
Bristol University Officer Training Corps
Cambridge University Officer Training Corps
East Midlands University Officer Training Corps
City of Edinburgh University Officer Training Corps
Exeter University Officer Training Corps
Glasgow and Strathclyde Universities Officer Training Corps
Leeds University Officer Training Corps
Liverpool University Officer Training Corps
London University Officer Training Corps
Manchester and Salford University Officer Training Corps
Northumbrian University Officer Training Corps
Oxford University Officer Training Corps
Queens University Officer Training Corps
Sheffield University Officer Training Corps
Southampton University Officer Training Corps
Tayforth University Officer Training Corps
University of Wales Officer Training Corps

Currently the TA has 34,300 personnel. The TA acts as a General Reserve to the Army, with a secondary but vitally important function being the promotion of a nationwide link between the military and civilian community.

The MoD describes the role of the TA as follows:

a. To reinforce the Regular Army, as and when required, with individuals, sub-units and units, either in the UK or overseas;

b. To provide the framework for bringing units up to full War Establishment strength and the basis for forming new units in times of national emergency.

TA Infantry Units have a General Purpose structure which will give them flexibility of employment across the spectrum of military operations. All Infantry Battalions, including Parachute Battalions, have a common establishment of three Rifle Companies and a Headquarters Company. In addition there are four Fire Support Battalions, each with a Headquarters and two Heavy Weapons Companies. Each company will have Milan, Mortar and Machine Gun Platoons. These battalions will provide operational and training support to all TA Battalions.

The 1998 SDR produced a TA with an emphasis on reducing the old Home Defence Role and a new priority of providing highly trained and properly resourced units to support the Regular Army worldwide.

Major Army Equipment

Challenger 2

(386 Challenger 2 available for operational service) Crew 4; Length Gun Forward 11.55m; Hull Length 8.32m; Height to Turret Roof 2.49m; Width 3.52m; Ground Clearance 0.50m; Combat Weight 62,500 kg; Main Armament 1 x 120mm L30 CHARM Gun; Ammunition Carried 52 rounds - APFSDS, HESH, Smoke, DU; Secondary Armament Co-axial 7.62mm MG; 7.62mm GPMG Turret Mounted for Air Defence; Ammunition Carried 4,000 rounds 7.62mm; Engine CV12TCA 12 cylinder - Auxiliary Engine Perkins 4.108 4-stroke diesel; Gearbox TN54 epicyclic - 6 forward gears and 2 reverse; Road Speed 56 km/h; Cross Country Speed 40 km/h; Fuel Capacity 1,797 litres.

Although the hull and automotive parts of the Challenger 2 are based upon that of its predecessor Challenger 1, the new tank incorporates over 150 improvements aimed at increasing reliability and maintainability. The whole of the Challenger 2 turret is of a totally new design and the vehicle has a crew of four - commander, gunner, loader/signaller and driver. The 120mm rifled Royal Ordnance L30 gun fires all current tank ammunition plus the new depleted uranium (DU) round with a stick charge propellant system.

The design of the turret incorporates several of the significant features that Vickers had developed for its Mk 7 MBT (a Vickers turret on a Leopard 2 chassis). The central feature is an entirely new fire control system based on the Ballistic Control System developed by Computing Devices Company (Canada) for the US Army's M1A1 MBT. This second-generation computer incorporates dual 32-bit processors with a MIL STD 1553B databus and has sufficient growth potential to accept Battlefield Information Control System (BICS) functions and navigation aids (a GPS satnav system). The armour is an uprated version of Challenger 1's Chobham armour.

The first production models of the Challenger 2 were taken into service by the Royal Scots Dragoon Guards in mid 1994 and the regiment was the first to deploy to Germany with the new tank in mid 1995. Production of the UK's Challenger 2 contract was completed in 2001.

The only export order so far is an Omani order for 38 x Challenger which includes 2 x Driver Training Vehicles and 4 x Challenger Armoured Repair and Recovery Vehicles.

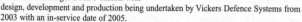

A contract has also been signed for 66 x Engineer Tank Systems (ETS) based on a modified Challenger 2 MBT chassis with design, development and production being undertaken by Vickers Defence Systems from 2003 with an in-service date of 2005.

There will be two versions of the ETS, the first is the Titan bridge-laying vehicle and the second the Trojan flexible obstacle/ mineclearing vehicle. Titan will be able to carry and lay the current in-service 26 m and 13.5 m long aluminium bridges with the crew under complete protection.

MCV - 80 Fv 510 (Warrior)

(575 in service) Weight loaded 24,500kg: length 6.34m: Height to turret top 2.78m: Width 3.0m: Ground Clearance 0.5m: Max Road Speed 75km/h: Road Range 500km: Engine Rolls Royce CV8 diesel: Horsepower 550hp: Crew 2 (carries 8 infantry soldiers): Armament L21 30mm Rarden Cannon: Coaxial EX-34 7.62mm Chain Gun: Smoke Dischargers Royal Ordnance Visual and Infra Red Screening Smoke (VIRSS).

Warrior is an armoured infantry fighting vehicle (AIFV) that replaced many of the AFV 432 in the armoured infantry battalions. Following drawdown, the original buy of 1,048 vehicles was reduced and in early 1993, it was announced that the total buy had been reduced to 789 units. The vehicle is in service with 2 armoured infantry battalions in the UK (with 3 (UK) Div) and 6 armoured infantry battalions in Germany (with 1 (UK) Armd Div). Warrior is armed with the 30mm Rarden cannon that gives the crew a good chance of destroying enemy APCs at ranges of up to 1,500m. The vehicle carries an infantry section of seven men.

The vehicle is NBC proof, and a full range of night vision equipment is included as standard. The basic Warrior is part of a family of vehicles which include a Milan ATGW carrier, a mechanised recovery vehicle, an engineer combat version and an artillery command vehicle to name but a few. Examination of the contract details reveal that each vehicle costs approximately £550,000 at 1990 prices.

The vehicle has seen successful operational service in the Gulf (1991), with the British contingent serving in the Balkans and more recently in Southern Iraq. The vehicle has proven protection against mines, and there is dramatic BBC TV footage of a Warrior running over a Serbian anti-tank mine in Bosnia with little or no serious damage to the vehicle.

A Warrior Mid-Life Improvement Programme is due to be implemented between 2007 and 2012. This will provide a new power pack, vehtronics enhancement, a digital fire control system (FCS)and a modern medium calibre cannon system. This extension of capability for Warrior will provide the necessary lead time for the introduction of future advanced capability systems vehicles to replace both Challenger 2 and Warrior.

The future digitisation programme in-service date (ISD) has slid to around 2017. Current thinking suggests that the British Army may replace existing rifle platoon Warrior with the improved Warrior 2000. This would release existing Warrior to be refitted to fulfil roles currently carried out by ageing and obsolescent FV 432s. This plan would create a new Battalion Assault Support Vehicle (BASV) which can carry Manoeuvre Support elements, principally 81 mm mortars, at the same pace as the Warrior fighting vehicles. This was a major failing of the FV 432 Mortar Vehicles in the 1990 Gulf War.

This solution would be cheaper than developing a new FIFV concept vehicle and then having to adapt it for digitisation and on board IT components. The scheme would also carry the Warrior through to its original replacement date of 2020 without the expense of planning and engineering a mid-life improvement which could have included the fitting of a new larger calibre cannon and turret.

The Kuwait MOD signed a contract for the purchase of warrior vehicles during the mid 1990s, some of which are Recce vehicles armed with a 90mm Cockerill gun. Industry sources confirm that the Kuwait contract was for 254 vehicles.

AT - 105 Saxon

(640 Saxon believed to be in operational service) Weight 10,670kg: Length 5.16m: Width 2.48m: Height 2.63m: Ground Clearance (axles) 0.33m: Max Road Speed 96km/h: Max Road Range 510km: Fuel Capacity 160 litres: Fording 1.12m: Gradient 60 degrees: Engine Bedford 600 6-cylinder diesel developing 164bhp at 2,800rpm: Armour proof against 7.62mm rounds fired at point blank range: Crew 2 + 10 max.

The Saxon was manufactured by GKN Defence and the first units for the British Army were delivered in late 1983. The vehicle, which can be best described as a battlefield taxi is designed around truck parts and does not require the enormous maintenance of track and running gear normally associated with APC/AIFVs.

As a vehicle capable of protecting infantry from shell splinters and machine gun fire in Europe during the Cold War years Saxon was a useful addition to the formerly larger Army. It does not, however, have the speed and agility which the lessons of recent mobile combat suggest will be necessary for infantry to survive in the assault in the future. The vehicle is fitted with a 7.62 mm Machine Gun for LLAD.

Each vehicle cost over £100,000 at 1984 prices and they are on issue to four mechanised infantry battalions assigned to 3 (UK) Division infantry battalions.

Essentially a mine-proof lorry rather than an armoured personnel carrier, the vehicle has been used very successfully by British mechanised battalions serving with the UN in Bosnia.

The Army holds a number of Saxon IS (Patrol) vehicle for service in Northern Ireland. In the recent more peaceful period in the province this vehicle seldom leaves its storage areas. The IS equipped vehicle has a Cummins BT 5.1 engine instead of the Bedford 6-cylinder installed on the APC version and other enhancements for internal security operations such as roof-mounted searchlights, improved armour, a barricade removal device and an anti-wire device.

Saxon Patrol comes in two versions, troop carrier and ambulance. The troop carrier carries 10 men and the ambulance two stretcher cases. Industry sources suggest that this latest contract was for 137 vehicles at a cost of some £20 million resulting in a unit cost per vehicle of approximately £145,000.

Saxon is in service with the following overseas customers:
Bahrain - 10: Brunei - 24: Hong Kong - 6: Malaysia - 40:
Oman - 15.

Milan 2 ATGW

Missile - Max Range 2,000m; Mix Range 25m; Length 918mm; Weight 6.73kg; Diameter 125mm; Wing Span 267mm; Rate of Fire 3-4rpm; Warhead - Weight 2.70kg; Diameter 115mm; Explosive Content 1.79kg; Firing Post- Weight 16.4kg; Length 900mm; Height 650mm; Width 420mm; Armour Penetration 352mm; Time of Flight to Max Range 12.5 secs; Missile Speed 720km/h; Guidance Semi-Automatic command to line of sight by means of wires:

Milan is a second generation, anti-tank guided weapon (ATGW), the result of a joint development project between France and West Germany, with British Milan launchers and missiles built under licence in the UK by British Aerospace Dynamics. We believe that the cost of a Milan missile is currently in the region of £15,000 and that to date, the UK MoD has purchased over 50,000 missiles. The Milan comes in two main components, which are the launcher and the missile. It is then a simple matter to clip both items together and prepare the system for use. On firing, the operator has only to keep his aiming mark on the target and the SACLOS guidance system will do the rest.

Milan was the first of a series of infantry anti-tank weapons that seriously started to challenge the supremacy of the main battle tank on the battlefield. During fighting in Chad in 1987, it appears that 12 Chadian Milan post mounted on Toyota Light Trucks were able to account for over 60 Libyan T-55s and T-62s. Reports from other conflicts suggest similar results.

Milan is on issue throughout the British Army and an armoured infantry battalion could be expected to be equipped with 24 firing posts and 200 missiles. Milan is in service with 36 nations worldwide and it is believed there are over 1,000 firing posts in service with the British Army.

Javelin ATGW

During early 2003 the MoD selected the Raytheon/Lockheed Martin Javelin as its new Light Forces ATGW.

Believed to be worth £300 million Javelin is scheduled to enter service in the UK during 2005 and should replace Milan 2 in rapid reaction formations such as 3 Command Brigade and 16 Air Assault Brigade.
It is expected that the initial requirement will be for at least 100 firing posts and 2,000 missiles. In addition to being capable of defeating main battle tanks (MBTs) from all aspects Javelin has a secondary capability against other battlefield targets such as fixed defences.

5.56mm Individual Weapon (IW) (SA 80A2)

Effective Range 400m: Muzzle Velocity 940m/s: Rate of Fire from 610-775rpm: Weight 4.98kg (with 30 round magazine): Length Overall 785mm: Barrel Length 518mm: Trigger Pull 3.12-4.5kg:

Following some severe criticism of the original SA80's mechanical reliability the improved SA 80A2 was introduced into service during late 2001. Some thirteen changes have been made to the weapon's breech block, gas regulation, firing-pin, cartridge extractor, recoil springs, cylinder and gas plug, hammer, magazine and barrel. Since modification the weapon has been extensively trialled.

Mean time before failure (MTBF) figures from the firing trials for stoppages, following rounds fired are as follow:

	SA 80A2	LSW
UK (temperate)	31,500	16,000
Brunei (hot/wet)	31,500	9,600
Kuwait (hot/dry)	7,875	8,728
Alaska (cold/dry)	31,500	43,200

The first SA 80A2 were in operational service during early 2002 and these weapons were in service with the majority of the UK infantry units during the 2003 operations in Iraq. First reports from Southern Iraq suggest that there were no major problems with the weapon.

The cost of the programme was £92 million and some 200,000 weapons have been modified.

In late 2001 the British Army Combat Shooting Team took part in the Australian Army's skill at arms meeting in Brisbane using the SA 80A2. Teams from eight nations took part in the competition and the British Army team won. The team's SA 80s fired 21,000 rounds in nine days without a stoppage.

AS 90

(179 in service) Crew 5: Length 9.07m: Width 3.3m: Height 3.0m overall: Ground Clearance 0.41m: Turret Ring Diameter 2.7m: Armour 17mm: Calibre 155mm: Range (39 cal) 24.7km (52 cal) 30km: Recoil Length 780mm: Rate of Fire 3 rounds in 10 secs (burst) 6 rounds per minute (intense) 2 rounds per minute (sustained): Secondary Armament 7.62mm MG: Traverse 6,400 mills: Elevation -89/+1.244 mills: Ammunition Carried 48 x 155mm projectiles and charges (31 turret & 17 hull): Engine Cummins VTA903T turbo-charged V8 diesel 660hp: Max Speed 53 km/h: Gradient 60 degrees: Vertical Obstacle 0.75m: Trench Crossing 2.8m: Fording Depth 1.5m: Road Range 420km.

AS 90 was manufactured by Vickers Shipbuilding and Engineering (VSEL) at Barrow in Furness. 179 Guns have been delivered under a fixed price contract for £300 million. These 179 guns have completely equipped 6 field regiments replacing the older 120 mm Abbot and 155 mm M109 in British service. Three of these Regiments are under the command of 1(UK) Armoured Division in Germany and three under the command of 3 (UK) Div in the United Kingdom.

AS 90 is currently equipped with a 39 calibre gun which fires the NATO L15 unassisted projectile out to a range of 24.7kms (Base Bleed ERA range is 30kms). Funding is available for the re-barreling of 96 x AS 90 with a 52 calibre gun with ranges of 30kms (unassisted) and 60 to 80 kms with improved accuracy and long range ERA ammunition. The current in service date for the 52 calibre gun is 2002/3 based on a firm programme which will fit 50% of the guns by November 2002 and up to 90% of them by April 2003.

AS 90 has been fitted with an autonomous navigation and gun laying system (AGLS), enabling it to work independently of external sighting references. Central to the system is an inertial dynamic reference unit (DRU) taken from the US Army's MAPS (Modular Azimuth Positioning System). The bulk of the turret electronics are housed in the Turret Control Computer (TCC) which controls the main turret functions, including gunlaying, magazine control, loading systems control, power distribution and testing.

227 mm MLRS

(62 launchers in service - 54 operational in 3 Regiments): Crew 3: Weight loaded 24,756kg: Weight Unloaded 19,573kg: Length 7.167m: Width 2.97m: Height (stowed) 2.57m: Height (max elevation) 5.92m: Ground Clearance 0.43m: Max Road Speed 64km/h: Road Range 480km: Fuel Capacity 617 litres: Fording 1.02m: Vertical Obstacle 0.76m: Engine Cummings VTA-903 turbo-charged 8 cylinder diesel developing 500 bhp at 2,300 rpm: Rocket Diameter 227mm: Rocket Length 3.93m: M77 Bomblet Rocket Weight 302.5kg: AT2 SCATMIN Rocket Weight 254.46kg: M77 Bomblet Range 11.5 -32km: AT2 SCATMIN Rocket Range 39km: One round "Fire for Effect" equals one launcher firing 12 rockets: Ammunition Carried 12 rounds (ready to fire).

The MLRS is based on the US M2 Bradley chassis and the system is self loaded with 2 x rocket pod containers, each containing 6 x rockets. The whole loading sequence is power assisted and loading takes between 20 and 40 minutes. There is no manual procedure.

A single round 'Fire for Effect' (12 rockets) delivers 644 bomblets or 336 scatterable mines and the coverage achieved is considered sufficient to neutralise a 500 m x 500 m target or produce a minefield of a similar size. Currently the weapon system accuracy is range dependent and therefore more rounds will be required to guarantee the effect as the range to the target increases. Future smart warhead sub munitions currently under development will enable pinpoint accuracy to considerably extended ranges. Ammunition for the MLRS is carried on the DROPS vehicle which is a Medium Mobility Load Carrier. Each DROPS vehicle with a trailer can carry 8 x Rocket Pod Containers and there are 15 x DROPS vehicles supporting the 9 x M270 Launcher vehicles within each MLRS battery.

The handling of MLRS is almost a military 'art form' and is an excellent example of the dependence of modern artillery on high technology. Getting the best out of the system is more than just parking the tubes and firing in the direction of the enemy. MLRS is the final link in a chain that includes almost everything available on the modern battlefield, from high speed communications, collation of intelligence, logistics and a multitude of high technology artillery skills and drills. Unmanned aerial vehicles (UAVs)can be used to acquire targets, real time TV and data links are used to move information from target areas to formation commanders and onward to the firing positions. Helicopters can be used to dump ammunition and in some cases to move firing platforms. The refining of this capability is an interesting and dynamic future development area in which available technologies are currently being harnessed and applied.

There are currently two Regular and one TA MLRS Regiments. The Regular Regiment operates 18 launcher vehicles and the TA Regiment 12 in peace and 18 in war.

The US Army is currently operating 857 MLRS, the French have 58, the West Germans 154 and the Italians 21.

Starstreak HVM
(135 Fire Units on Stormer and 145 on Light Mobile Launcher) Missile Length 1.39m: Missile Diameter 0.27m: Missile Speed Mach 3+: Maximum Range 5.5 kms:

Short Missile Systems of Belfast were the prime contractors for the HVM (High Velocity Missile) which continues along the development path of both Blowpipe and Javelin. The system can be shoulder launched or can be mounted on the LML (lightweight multiple launcher) or vehicle borne on the Alvis Stormer APC. The Stormer APC has an eight round launcher and 12 reload missiles can be carried inside the vehicle.

HVM has been optimised to counter threats from fast pop-up type strikes by attack helicopters and low flying aircraft. The missile employs a system of three dart type projectiles which can make multiple hits on the target. Each of these darts has an explosive warhead. It is believed that the HVM has an SSK (single shot to kill) probability of over 95%.

12 Regiment RA stationed at Sennelager in German is equipped with HVM and supports 1 (UK) Division. The UK HVM Regiment is 47 Regiment RA stationed at Thorney Island. 12 Regiment is believed to have 108 launchers divided amongst the three missile batteries. An HVM detachment of 4 is carried in a Stormer armoured vehicle and in each vehicle there are 4 personnel. Inside the vehicle there are twelve ready to use missiles with a further 8 stored inside as reloads.

In mid 2001 Thales Air Defence was awarded a £66 million order for an Identification Friend-or-Foe (IFF) system for the Starstreak HVM.

Rapier
(70 fire units in service) Guidance Semi Automatic to Line of Sight (SACLOS): Missile Diameter 13.3 cm: Missile Length 2.35 m: Rocket Solid Fuelled: Warhead High Explosive: Launch Weight 42 kg: Speed Mach 2+: Ceiling 3,000 m: Maximum Range 6,800 m: Fire Unit Height 2.13 m: Fire Unit Weight 1,227 kg: Radar Height (in action) 3.37 m: Radar Weight 1,186 kg: Optical Tracker Height 1.54 m: Optical Tracker Weight 119 kg: Generator Weight 243 kg: Generator Height 0.91 m.

The Rapier system provides area 24 hour through cloud, Low Level Air Defence (LLAD) over the battlefield. The two forms of Rapier in service are as follows:-

The latest version of the system Rapier Field standard C (FSC) incorporates a range of technological improvements including an advanced 3 dimensional radar tracker acquisition system designed by Plessey. The towed system launcher will mount eight missiles (able to fire two simultaneously) which are manufactured in two warhead versions. One of these is a proximity explosive round and the other a kinetic energy round. The total cost of the Rapier

FS'C' programme is £1,886 million.

The into-action time of the system is thought to be less than 15 minutes and the surveillance radar is believed to scan out to around 15 km. Each fire unit can therefore cover an Air Defence Area (ADA) in excess of 100 square kms.

Current plans are for the Royal Artillery to continue to field 2 x Towed Rapier Regiments. One Regiment will field FSC version (three batteries each of two troops with four fire units per troop) and the other the FSB2 version (three batteries each of two troops with four fire units per troop and a commander's troop with two fire units). Under the command of 22 Regiment RA (one of the two Rapier Regiments)is 20 Commando Battery RA the unit that provides air defence for 3 Commando Brigade Royal Marines. The other Rapier Regiment is 16 Regiment RA.

Rapier has now been sold to the armed forces of at least 14 nations. We believe that sales have amounted to over 25,000 missiles, 600 launchers and 350 Blindfire radars.

In the Falklands Campaign, Rapier was credited with 14 kills and 6 probables from a total of 24 missiles fired.

Lynx AH - Mark 7/9

(108 in service). Length Fuselage 12.06 m: Height 3.4 m: Rotor Diameter 12.8 m: Max Speed 330 kph: Cruising Speed 232 kph: Range 885 km: Engines 2 Rolls-Royce Gem 41: Power 2 x 850 bhp: Fuel Capacity 918 litres(internal): Weight (max take off) 4,763 kg: Crew one pilot, one air-gunner/observer: Armament 8 x TOW Anti-Tank Missiles: 2-4 7.62 mm machine guns: Passengers-able to carry 10 PAX: Combat radius approximately 100kms with 2 hour loiter.

Armed with 8 x TOW missiles, for many years the Lynx was the mainstay of the British armed helicopter fleet. However, in addition to its role as an anti-tank helicopter, Lynx can be used for fire support using machine guns, troop lifts, casualty evacuation and many more vital battlefield tasks.

During hostilities we would expect Lynx to operate on a section basis, with 2 or 3 Lynx aircraft armed with TOW directed by a Section Commander possibly flying in a Gazelle. The Section Commander would control what is in reality an airborne tank ambush and following an attack on enemy armour decide when to break contact. Having broken contact, the aircraft would return to a forward base to refuel and rearm. Working from forward bases, some of which are within 10kms of the FEBA, it is suggested that a Lynx section could be "turned around" in less than 15 minutes. Lynx with TOW replaced SCOUT with SS11 as the British Army's anti-tank helicopter.

We believe the majority of Lynx in British service to be Lynx Mark 7 and that there are currently 24 Lynx Mark 9 (the latest version) in the inventory.

The MoD is currently awaiting the results of a study into the future of Lynx. There is a possibility that 80 Lynx will be upgraded to a new configuration to meet the requirements for the proposed Future Lynx Battlefield Light Utility Helicopter (BLUH).

The BLUH proposal envisages a helicopter capable of transporting up to eight combat-equipped personnel and other materiel. In addition the BLUH could also undertake command and control and communications relay duties, the reconnaissance of potential forward operating bases and the immediate extraction of downed aircrew.

Lynx is known to be in service with France, Brazil, Argentina, The Netherlands, Qatar, Denmark, Norway, West Germany and Nigeria. The naval version carries anti-ship missiles.

Longbow Apache (AH Mk 1)

(67 On Order) Gross Mission Weight 7,746 kgs (17,077 lb; Cruise Speed at 500 meters 272 kph; Maximum Range (Internal Fuel with 20 minute reserve) 462 kms; General Service Ceiling 3,505 meters (11,500 ft); Crew 2; Carries - 16 x Hellfire II missiles (range 6,000 meters approx); 76 x 2.75" rockets; 1,200 30mm cannon rounds; 4 x Air to Air Missiles; Engines 2 x Rolls Royce RTM-332.

The UK MoD ordered 67 Longbow Apache from Westland during mid 1995 with the first aircraft being delivered to the Army Air Corps during 2000. From this figure of 67 aircraft we believe that there will be 48 aircraft in two regiments (each of 24 aircraft). The remaining 19 aircraft will be used for trials, training and a war maintenance reserve (WMR).

In September 1999 the first production Apache made its maiden flight and was handed over to GKN Westland (the UK contractor) at the Boeing aircraft plant in Arizona. Boeing has built the first aircraft and will partially assemble the other 59. GKN Westland will undertake final assembly, flight testing and programme support at its Yeovil factory.

The aircraft were purchased for a unit cost of £27.5 million, the AH Mk 1 was declared in-service in January 2001 and the last aircraft is due for completion during mid 2004. The first 37 aircraft should be brought up to the final production standard by the middle of 2005. By mid 2003 we believe that 36 aircraft have been delivered. Under current assumption it should be possible for the Army Air Corps to field a brigade level attack helicopter regiment by early 2007.

The Hellfire anti-tank guided missile (ATGW) has a range approaching 6 kms and is capable of defeating all types of armour. The missile has a length of 1.78 metres and weighs 43.1 kg. The guidance system is semi-active laser homing.

It is believed that an air-to-air weapon capability will continue to be investigated and trials of the Shorts Starstreak missile onboard an AH-64 will continue in the US. Any longer term decision to proceed will be based on the results of these US Army trials.

The procurement of an attack helicopter of this type gives the British Army the "punch" necessary for operations during the next decade. These aircraft had a significant effect upon operations during the 1991 Gulf War where the US Army deployed 288 x AH-64 Apache in 15 Army Aviation battalions. The US Army claims that these aircraft destroyed 120 x APCs, 500 x MBT, 120 x artillery guns, 10 radar installations, 10 x helicopters, 30 x air defence units, about 300 soft skinned vehicles and 10 x fixed-wing aircraft on the ground. A single US Army Aviation battalion is believed to have destroyed 40 x APCs and over 100 x MBT in an engagement that lasted over 3 hours, firing 107 Hellfire missiles and over 300 x 70 mm rockets.

Once in service with the Joint Helicopter Command the AH Mk 1 is expected to remain in service until at least 2030.

BR90 Family of Bridges
In early 1994 the UK MoD announced that the production order had been placed for the BR90 family of bridges that should have entered service between January 1996 and June 1997 as follows:

January 1996   - General Support Bridge
November 1996   - Close Support Bridge
May 1997   - Two Span Bridge
June 1997   - Long Span Bridge

BR90 will be deployed with Royal Engineer units in both Germany and the UK. The production order, valued at approximately £140 million, was issued and accepted in October 1993.

The components of the system are:

Close Support Bridge - This consists of three tank-launched bridges capable of being carried on the in-service Chieftain bridgelayer and a TBT (Tank Bridge Transporter) truck.

	Weight	**Length**	**Gap**
No 10 Bridge	13 tons	26 m	24.5 m
No 11 Bridge	7.4 tons	16 m	14.5 m
No 12 Bridge	5.3 tons	13.5 m	12 m

The existing No 8 and No 9 bridges previously carried in the Chieftain AVLB will be retained in service.

The Unipower TBT 8 x 8 truck can carry 1 x No 10 Bridge, 1 x No 11 Bridge or 2 x No 12 Bridges. The TBT has an unladen weight of 21 tons and is also used to transport the General Support Bridge.

General Support Bridge - This system utilises the Automated Bridge Launching Equipment (ABLE) that is capable of launching bridges up to 44 metres in length. The ABLE vehicle is positioned with its rear pointing to the gap to be crossed and a lightweight launch rail extended across the gap. The bridge is then assembled and winched across the gap supported by the rail, with sections added until the gap is crossed. Once the bridge has crossed the gap the ABLE launch rail is recovered. A standard ABLE system set consists of an ABLE vehicle and a TBT carrying a 32 metre bridge set. A 32m bridge can be built by 10 men in about 25 minutes.

Spanning Systems - There are two basic spanning systems. The long span systems allows for lengthening a 32 metre span to 44 metres using ABLE and the two span system allows 2 x 32 metre bridge sets to be constructed by ABLE and secured in the middle by piers or floating pontoons, crossing a gap of up to 60 metres.

Chapter 4 – THE ROYAL AIR FORCE

General - Royal Air Force Squadrons (as at 1 April 2003)

	2003	1980
Strike/Attack Squadrons	5	14
Offensive Support Squadrons	5	5
Air Defence Squadrons	4	16
Maritime Patrol Squadrons	3	4
Reconnaissance Squadrons	5	5
Airborne Early Warning Squadrons	2	1
Transport/Tanker Squadrons	9	9
Helicopter Squadrons (2 SAR)	10	4
Surface to Air Missile Squadrons	4	8
Ground Defence Squadrons	7	5
	54	**71**

Note: 1980 figures are for comparison purposes.

As of 1 April 2003, total RAF personnel numbered 52,804, of which 1,145 were aircrew and a further 170 were aircrew under training. The most recent RAF personnel figures are shown in the table.

RAF Personnel (1 April 2003)	Trained	Under Training	Total
General Duties	3,555	753	4,308
Ground Branch Officers	6,027	531	6,558
Airmen Aircrew	1,145	170	1,315
Ground Trades	37,908	2,715	40,623
Grand Total	48,635	4,169	52,804

Royal Air Force Squadron Listing (as at 1 April 2003)

We estimate that there were some 420 combat aircraft (plus 142 held in reserve) capable of delivering missiles or ordnance in front-line service on 1 April 2003.

1 Sqn	13 x Harrier GR7 1 x Harrier T10	RAF Cottesmore (JFH)
2 Sqn	12 x Tornado GR4A	RAF Marham
3 Sqn	13 x Harrier GR7 1 x Harrier T10	RAF Cottesmore (JFH)
4 Sqn	13 x Harrier GR7 1 x Harrier T10	RAF Cottesmore (JFH)
5 Sqn	5 x Sentinel (ASTOR)	RAF Waddington (from 1 April 2004)
6 Sqn	11 x Jaguar GR3/3A (1) 1 x Jaguar T4	RAF Coltishall
7 Sqn	5 x Chinook HC2	RAF Odiham (JHC)

	1 x Gazelle	
8 Sqn	3 x Sentry AEW1	RAF Waddington
9 Sqn	12 x Tornado GR4	RAF Marham
10 Sqn	10 x VC10 C1K	RAF Brize Norton
11 Sqn	16 x Tornado F3	RAF Leeming
12 Sqn	12 x Tornado GR4	RAF Lossiemouth
13 Sqn	12 x Tornado GR4A	RAF Marham
14 Sqn	12 x Tornado GR4	RAF Lossiemouth
18 Sqn	18 x Chinook HC2	RAF Odiham (JHC)
22 Sqn	8 x Sea King HAR3/3A	RAF St Mawgan (Sqn HQ)*
23 Sqn	3 x Sentry AEW	RAF Waddington
24 Sqn	11 x Hercules C1/C3, C4/C5	RAF Lyneham
25 Sqn	16 x Tornado F3	RAF Leeming
27 Sqn	10 x Chinook HC2	RAF Odiham (JHC)
28 Sqn	22 x Merlin HC3	RAF Benson
30 Sqn	11 x Hercules C1/C3, C4/C5	RAF Lyneham
31 Sqn	12 x Tornado GR4	RAF Marham
32 (The Royal) Sqn	5 x BAe 125 CC3	RAF Northolt
	2 x BAe 146 CC2	
	3 x Twin Squirrel HCC1	
33 Sqn	15 x Puma HC1	RAF Benson (JHC)
39 Sqn (1 PRU)	4 x Canberra PR9	RAF Marham
	1 x Canberra T4	
41 Sqn	12 x Jaguar GR3/3A	RAF Coltishall
	1 x Jaguar T4	
43 Sqn	16 x Tornado F3	RAF Leuchars
47 Sqn	11 x Hercules C1/C3, C4/C5	RAF Lyneham
51 Sqn	3 x Nimrod R1	RAF Waddington
54 Sqn	11 x Jaguar GR3/3A	RAF Coltishall
	1 x Jaguar T4	
70 Sqn	11 x Hercules C1/C3,C4/C5	RAF Lyneham
72 Sqn	8 x Wessex HC2	RAF Aldergrove (JHC) (disbanded 2002)
	5 x Puma HC1	
78 Sqn	1 x Chinook HC2	RAF Mount Pleasant (JHC) (Falklands)
	2 x Sea King HAR3	
84 Sqn	4 x Griffin HAR2	RAF Akrotiri
99 Sqn	4 x C-17	RAF Brize Norton (from May 2001)
100 Sqn	16 x Hawk T1/T1A	RAF Leeming
101 Sqn	7 x VC10 K3/K4	RAF Brize Norton
111 Sqn	16 x Tornado F3	RAF Leuchars
120 Sqn	6 x Nimrod MR2	RAF Kinloss
201 Sqn	6 x Nimrod MR2	RAF Kinloss

202 Sqn	8 x Sea King HAR3/3A	RAF Boulmer (Sqn HQ)*
206 Sqn	5 x Nimrod MR2	RAF Kinloss
216 Sqn	8 x Tristar K1/KC1/C2	RAF Brize Norton
230 Sqn	18 x Puma HC1	RAF Aldergrove (JHC)
617 Sqn	12 x Tornado GR4	RAF Lossiemouth
1312 Flight	1 x Hercules C1	RAF Mount Pleasant
	1 x VC10 K3/4	
1435 Flight	4 x Tornado F3	RAF Mount Pleasant, Falklands

Notes:

(1) * Headquartered at RAF St Mawgan, 22 Sqn maintains three detachments at Chivenor ('A' Flight), Wattisham ('B' Flight) and Valley ('C' Flight). 202 Sqn has detachments at Boulmer ('A' Flight and Headquarters), Lossiemouth ('D' Flight) and Leconfield ('E' Flight).

(2) JFH means that a squadron is assigned to the Joint Force Harrier and JHC means that a squadron is assigned to the Joint Helicopter Command.

(3) There are RAF flying units deployed in Cyprus, Falklands and periodically Gibraltar on national missions.

(4) RAF flying units are supporting UN/NATO operations in the area of the former Yugoslavia (Op Oculus), Afghanistan (Op Oracle), and Cyprus.

(5) As of early 2003, RAF flying units were deployed in the Bahrain, Kuwait and periodically Saudi Arabia in the Persian Gulf area (Op Resinate South), in Turkey (Op Resinate North), and in Italy (Op Deliberate Forge) in support of United Nations Operations Southern and Northern Watch to enforce the Iraq no-fly zones.

The 2003 Iraq War (Operation Telic)

For the 2003 war with Iraq, the RAF deployment under the US-led coalition was the largest since the 1990/91 Gulf War. The air component deployed on Operation Telic from January to April 2003 numbered about 100 fixed-wing aircraft and 27 support helicopters, supported by some 7,000 RAF personnel. Aircraft types involved included: Sentry AEW1, Tornado GR4, Jaguar GR3, Harrier GR7, Tornado F-3, VC-10 tanker aircraft, Tristar tanker aircraft, Hercules transport aircraft, Nimrod MR2, Chinook HC2 and Puma helicopters. RAF Regiment units provided ground defence for the force.

US, UK and other coalition aircraft flew more than 41,000 sorties and dropped nearly 30,000 bombs and 31 million leaflets on Iraq during the conflict, according to the first detailed report. Coalition air strength numbered some 1,800 military aircraft flown by all four US military services as well as armed forces of the United Kingdom, Australia and Canada. Their missions consumed 417 million pounds of jet fuel from flying tankers. Between 21 March and mid-April 2003, coalition aircraft dropped some 19,948 satellite or laser guided bombs, more than twice as many as the 9,251 unguided bombs. The RAF accounted for about 10% of the average 1,200 coalition sorties a day.

The Afghanistan campaign from 2001 through 2003 (Operations Veritas, Oracle and Fingal)

RAF Forces participated in the military operation (Operation Veritas) against the Al Qaeda terrorist organisation and the Taliban regime harbouring them in Afghanistan from October 2001 to July 2002. RAF Tristar and VC-10 tanker aircraft were deployed, and a capability has been retained in theatre to support the continuing operations in the area. Their refuelling system is compatible with US Navy and US Marine Corps aircraft, allowing them to offer particular support to US carrier-borne assets. Other RAF aircraft supporting the operation have included: Sentry AEW1, Nimrod R1, Nimrod MR2, and Canberra PR9. Under Operation Oracle, RAF Sentry AEW1, Nimrod MR2, and Hercules transport aircraft were deployed in support of International Security Assistance Force (ISAF) in Afghanistan. Since June 2002, Operation Fingal has provided troops to the ISAF to assist the new Afghan Interim Authority with the provision of security and stability in Kabul. RAF air transport aircraft are providing air transport support for the deployment of ISAF personnel.

Training Units

Unit	Aircraft	Base
15 (R) Sqn	26 x Tornado GR4	RAF Lossiemouth
16 (R) Sqn	8 x Jaguar GR3/T4	RAF Lossiemouth
19 (R) Sqn	35 x Hawk T1	RAF Valley*
20 (R) Sqn	9 x Harrier GR7	RAF Wittering
	6 x Harrier T10	
42 (R) Sqn	3 x Nimrod MR2	RAF Kinloss
45 (R) Sqn	11 x Jetstream T1	RAF Cranwell
55 (R) Sqn	9 x Dominie T1	RAF Cranwell
56 (R) Sqn	20 x Tornado F3	RAF Leuchars
57 (R) Sqn	5 x Hercules C3/C4/C5	RAF Lyneham
60 (R) Sqn	7 x Griffin HT1	RAF Shawbury
	28 x Squirrel HT1	
72 (R) Sqn	34 x Tucano T1	RAF Linton-on-Ouse (from July 2002)
203 (R) Sqn	3 x Sea King HAR3	RAF St Mawgan
207 (R) Sqn	33 x Tucano T1	RAF Linton-on-Ouse (from July 2002)
208 (R) Sqn	34 x Hawk T1/T1A	RAF Valley

Note: The (R) in a squadron designation represents a training unit/reserve squadron. In the majority of cases this reserve squadron is the Operational Conversion Unit (OCU) for the particular aircraft type and the reserve squadron has a mobilisation role.
- There are 69 x Hawk at RAF Valley.
- CFS stands for Central Flying School.

Elementary Flying Training

Unit	Base	Aircraft
JEFTS*	RAF Barkston Heath	18 x Firefly M260
	RAF Cranwell	6 x Firefly M260
	RAF Church Fenton	14 x Firefly M260
University Air Squadrons	Throughout UK	91 x Tutor T1

Basic Flying Training

Unit	Base	Aircraft
1 Flying Training School	RAF Linton-on-Ouse	67 x Tucano
3 Flying Training School	RAF Cranwell	11 x Jetstream T1
		9 x Dominie
		8 x Tutor T1

Advanced Flying Training

4 Flying Training School	RAF Valley	69 x Hawk T1/1A
DHFS*	RAF Shawbury	28 x Squirrel HT1
		7 x Griffin HT1
Search & Rescue Training Unit	RAF Valley	4 x Griffin HT1
Sea King Training Unit	RAF St Mawgan	Sea King
JFACTSU*	RAF Leeming	2 x Hawk T1/T1A

Note: * JEFTS - Joint Elementary Flying Training School; DHFS - Defence Helicopter Flying School; JFACTSU - Joint Forward Air Control Training and Standards Unit.

Miscellaneous Units

SAOEU	Boscombe Down	2 x Tornado GR4
(Strike Attack Operational Evaluation Unit)		1 x Jaguar GR3/GR3A
		3 x Harrier GR7
Tornado F3 OEU	RAF Coningsby	3 x Tornado F-3
(Operational Evaluation Unit)		
RAF Aerobatic Team	RAF Scampton	10 x Hawk T1A
(The Red Arrows)		
Station Flight	RAF Northolt	1 x Islander CC2
RAF Centre of Aviation Medicine	RAF Henlow	2 x Hawk T1

Royal Air Force Regiment

1 Sqn RAF Regt	RAF St Mawgan	Ground Defence
2 Sqn RAF Regt	RAF Honington	Ground Defence with airborne capability
3 Sqn RAF Regt	RAF Aldergrove	Ground Defence
15 Sqn RAF Regt	RAF Honington	6 x Rapier
16 Sqn RAF Regt	RAF Honington	6 x Rapier
26 Sqn RAF Regt	RAF Waddington	6 x Rapier
34 Sqn RAF Regt	RAF Leeming	Ground Defence
(Reaction Force Air)		
37 Sqn RAF Regt	RAF Wittering	6 x Rapier
(RAF Bruggen closed in 2002)		
51 Sqn RAF Regt	RAF Lossiemouth	Ground Defence
63 (QCS) Sqn	RAF Uxbridge	Ground Defence & Ceremonial
RAF Regt Depot	RAF Honington	Training & Administration
Rapier FSC OCU	RAF Honington	2 x Rapier (Joint Training and Conversion Unit)
RAF STO Centre	RAF Honington	(Tactical Survive to Operate Centre)
No 1 RAF STO HQ	RAF Wittering	(Tactical Survive to Operate HQ)
No 2 RAF STO HQ	RAF Leeming	(Tactical Survive to Operate HQ)

| No 3 RAF STO HQ | RAF Marham | (Tactical Survive to Operate HQ) |
| No 4 RAF STO HQ | RAF Honington | (Tactical Survive to Operate HQ) |

Royal Auxiliary Air Force

No 1 Maritime HQ	RAF Northolt	Maritime HQ Unit
No 2 Maritime HQ	Edinburgh	Maritime HQ Unit
No 3 Maritime HQ	RAF St Mawgan	Maritime HQ Unit
3 Sqn	RAF Henlow	Tactical Provost Wing
501 Sqn	RAF Brize Norton	Operations Support Sqn
504 Sqn	RAF Cottesmore	Harrier Support Sqn
600 Sqn	RAF Northolt	Headquarters Augmentation Unit
603 Sqn	Edinburgh	Operations Support Sqn
606 Sqn	RAF Benson	Helicopter Support Sqn
609 Sqn	RAF Leeming	Air Defence Support Unit
612 Sqn	RAF Leuchars	Air Transportable Surgical Squadron
2503 Sqn Regt	RAF Waddington	RAuxAF Regiment Field Squadron
2620 Sqn Regt	RAF Marham	RAuxAF Operations Support Squadron
2622 Sqn Regt	RAF Lossiemouth	RAuxAF Regiment Field Squadron
2623 Sqn Regt	RAF Honington	RAuxAF Regiment Rapier Squadron
2624 Sqn Regt	RAF Brize Norton	RAuxAF Operations Support Squadron
2625 Sqn Regt	RAF St Mawgan	RAuxAF Regiment Field Squadron
4624 Sqn Regt	RAF Brize Norton	RAuxAF Movements Squadron
4626 Sqn	RAF Lyneham	RAuxAF Aeromedical Evacuation Unit
7006 Flight	RAF High Wycombe	Intelligence squadron
7010 Flight	RAF High Wycombe	Photographic Interpretation squadron
7630 Flight	DISC Chicksands	Intelligence squadron
7644 Flight	RAF High Wycombe	Corporate Communication squadron
Mobile Met Unit	RAF Benson	RAFVR Meteorological Services
1359 Flight	RAF Lyneham	Hercules Reserve Aircrew
Marham Support Flight	RAF Marham	Ground Crew
TSS	RAF Shawbury	Training & Standardisation Sqn

British Airline Fleets

In an emergency, the Government has the power to enlist the assistance of the United Kingdom's civil airline and aircraft charter fleets. In total, there are over 50 registered airlines and aircraft charter companies operating over 900 fixed-wing passenger and transport aircraft and over 200 helicopters. The largest of the British-registered airlines is

British Airways with some 61,500 employees, operating about 350 aircraft, carrying on average about 34 million passengers per year. Other major British airlines include Virgin Atlantic with 21 aircraft, British Midland Airways with 41 aircraft, the discount airline Easyjet with 67 aircraft, and the charter airline Air 2000 with 30 aircraft. Bristow Helicopters - UK subsidiary of Offshore Logistics - is the largest helicopter charter operator with a fleet of some 120 helicopters. British companies employ some 10,000 trained pilots active in commercial operations in the UK.

Air Force Board

The routine management of the Royal Air Force is the responsibility of the Air Force Board, the composition of which is shown in the next diagram:

Air Force Board
The Secretary of State for Defence

Minister of State (Armed Forces)	Chief of the Air Staff
Minister of State (Defence Procurement)	Air Member for Personnel
Under-Secretary of State (Armed Forces)	Controller of Aircraft
Under-Secretary of State (Defence Procurement)	Air Member for Logistics
2nd Permanent Under Secretary of State	AOC Strike Command
	Assistant Chief of Air Staff

Decisions made by the Defence Council or the Air Force Board are implemented by the air staff at various headquarters worldwide. The Chief of the Air Staff is the officer ultimately responsible for the Royal Air Force's contribution to the national defence effort. He maintains control through the AOC (Air Officer Commanding), and the staff branches of each of these headquarters.

Chief of The Air Staff (As at 1 August 2003)

Air Chief Marshal Sir Jock Stirrup KCB AFC ADC FRAeS FCMI RAF

Air Chief Marshal Stirrup was educated at Merchant Taylors' School, Northwood and the Royal Air Force College Cranwell, and was commissioned in 1970. After a tour as a Qualified Flying Instructor he served on loan with the Sultan of Oman's Air Force, operating Strikemasters in the Dhofar War. Returning to the United Kingdom in 1975 he was posted to No 41(F) Squadron, flying Jaguars in the Fighter Reconnaissance role, before taking up an exchange appointment on RF-4C Phantoms in the United States.

He then spent two years at Lossiemouth as a flight commander on the Jaguar Operational Conversion Unit, and subsequently attended the Joint Service Defence College in 1984. He commanded No II(AC) Squadron, flying Fighter Reconnaissance Jaguars from Royal Air Force Laarbruch, until 1987 when he took up the post of Personal Staff Officer to the Chief of the Air Staff. He assumed command of Royal Air Force Marham in 1990, just in time for Operation GRANBY, and then attended the 1993 Course at the Royal College of Defence Studies. He completed No 7 Higher Command and Staff Course at Camberley prior to becoming the Director of Air Force Plans and Programmes in 1994. He became Air Officer

Commanding No 1 Group in April 1997 and was appointed Assistant Chief of the Air Staff in August 1998.

During 2000 he was appointed as Deputy Commander-in-Chief Strike Command. At the same time he assumed the additional roles of Commander of NATO's Combined Air Operations Centre 9 and Director of the European Air Group. He spent the last few months of his tour, from September 2001 to January 2002, as UK National Contingent Commander and Senior British Military Advisor to CINCUSCENTCOM for Operation VERITAS, the UK's contribution to the United States led Operation ENDURING FREEDOM in Afghanistan. Air Chief Marshal Stirrup was appointed KCB in the New Year Honours List 2002 and became Deputy Chief of the Defence Staff (Equipment Capability) in March 2002. He was appointed Chief of the Air Staff, on promotion, on 1 August 2003.

Air Chief Marshal Stirrup is married with one son and enjoys golf, music, theatre and history.

ACM Stirrup

Chain of Command

On the 1 April 2000, the Royal Air Force was reorganised. The command structure of the RAF was rationalised into the two Commands, Strike Command and Personnel and Training Command. Logistics support for all three Services was to be the responsibility of the new Defence Logistics Organisation under independent command. The resultant RAF "Chain of Command" is as follows:

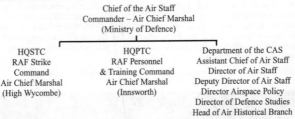

Chief of the Air Staff
Commander – Air Chief Marshal
(Ministry of Defence)

HQSTC	HQPTC	Department of the CAS
RAF Strike	RAF Personnel	Assistant Chief of Air Staff
Command	& Training Command	Director of Air Staff
Air Chief Marshal	Air Chief Marshal	Deputy Director of Air Staff
(High Wycombe)	(Innsworth)	Director Airspace Policy
		Director of Defence Studies
		Head of Air Historical Branch

Strike Command

From its headquarters at RAF High Wycombe, Strike Command (STC) now controls all of the United Kingdom's front-line aircraft world wide. Its assets include fighters, strike/attack, transport and maritime aircraft and helicopters. As the commander of Strike Command, the AOCinC is responsible for the day to day national peacetime operations of the Command. In war, Strike Command is an essential part of the NATO organisation and as such is a component of SACEUR European Theatre air assets.

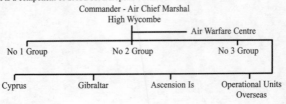

Commander - Air Chief Marshal
High Wycombe

Air Warfare Centre

No 1 Group   No 2 Group   No 3 Group

Cyprus   Gibraltar   Ascension Is   Operational Units Overseas

HQ Strike Command

Notes:
(1) The Air Warfare Centre (formerly CTTO) is responsible for the Tornado F3 OEU and the SAOEU.
(3) Groups are normally commanded by Air Vice Marshals.

Reorganised in 2000 and again in 2003, Strike Command is based on three Groups. In 2000, these groups were re-organised around operational capability and collocated at High Wycombe to streamline command and control as well as generate better links between force elements with a similar role. A further reorganisation of the three groups is scheduled for implementation between April 2003-April 2004. As of April 2002, Strike Command controlled about 5,600 civilians and 29,600 servicemen and women – well over half of the present strength of the Royal Air Force. The personnel and aircraft are spread through some 200 units of various sizes, the majority of which are in the United Kingdom.

Air Warfare Centre (AWC)

The Air Warfare Centre is responsible for formulating tactical doctrine and conducting operational trials. Formed from the old CTTO, DAW, EWOSE, ORB and OEUs, the AWC also maintains liaison with MoD research establishments and industry, and close contact with RAF operational commands as well as with the Royal Navy, Army and Allied air forces. The AWC HQ is collocated with the Defence Electronic Warfare Centre at RAF Waddington. The AWC is administered by HQ Strike Command, but is responsible jointly to the Assistant Chief of Air Staff, and to the Commander-in-Chief for the conduct of trials, and development of tactics for all Royal Air Force operational aircraft. Branches and locations of the AWC are as follows:

HQ	Waddington
Operational Doctrine (OD&T)	Cranwell & High Wycombe
Tactics (TD&T)	Waddington
Electronic Warfare (EWOS)	Waddington
Operational Analysis (OA)	High Wycombe, Waddington & Cranwell
Operational Testing & Evaluation (OT&E)	Boscombe Down, Coningsby, Odiham & Ash

No 1 Group

Until April 2003, No 1 Group was responsible for all strike attack and offensive support aircraft. With the exception of the Harrier, the reformed No 1 Group operated all the frontline RAF aircraft including, in the future, Eurofighter. Between April 2003 and April 2004, No 1 Group is to become an Air Combat Group containing all fast jet assets including the Joint Force Harrier (JFH), formerly part of No 3 Group, and the Joint Force Air Component (JFAC) HQ, which is currently a centrally provided asset. The JFAC HQ provides the deployable Air Command and Control required to support expeditionary warfare and links in to the other Joint Force Component HQs under PJHQ direction.

Strike Attack	Aircraft	Location
9 Squadron	12 x Tornado GR4	Marham
12 Squadron	12 x Tornado GR4	Lossiemouth
14 Squadron	12 x Tornado GR4	Lossiemouth
31 Squadron	12 x Tornado GR4	Marham
617 Squadron	12 x Tornado GR4	Lossiemouth
15 (Reserve) Squadron	26 x Tornado GR4	Lossiemouth

Air Defence	Aircraft	Location
11 Squadron	16 x Tornado F3	Leeming
25 Squadron	16 x Tornado F3	Leeming
43 Squadron	16 x Tornado F3	Leuchars
111 Squadron	16 x Tornado F3	Leuchars
1435 Flight	4 x Tornado F3	Mount Pleasant
56 (Reserve) Squadron	20 x Tornado F3	Leuchars

Strike Command OEU	3 x Tornado F-3	Coningsby
Offensive Support	**Aircraft**	**Location**
6 Squadron	11 x Jaguar GR3/3A	Coltishall
	1 x Jaguar T4	
54 Squadron	11 x Jaguar GR3/3A	Coltishall
	1 x JaguarT4	
16 (Reserve) Squadron	4 x Jaguar GR3/3A	Lossiemouth
	4 x Jaguar T4	
Joint Force Harrier	**Aircraft**	**Location**
1 Squadron	13 x Harrier GR7	Cottesmore
	1 x Harrier T10	
3 Squadron	13 x Harrier GR7	Cottesmore
	1 x Harrier T-10	
4 Squadron	13 x Harrier GR7	Cottesmore
	1 x Harrier T10	
20 (Reserve) Squadron	9 x Harrier GR7	Wittering
	6 x Harrier T10	
800 Sqn (Fleet Air Arm)	8 x Sea Harrier F/A2	Cottesmore
801 Sqn (Fleet Air Arm)	8x Sea Harrier F/A2	Cottesmore
899 Sqn (Fleet Air Arm)	10 x Sea Harrier F/A2	Wittering
	4 x Harrier T4/T8	
Miscellaneous	**Aircraft**	**Location**
100 Squadron	16 x Hawk T1/1A	Leeming (target towing)

The Harriers and Sea Harriers are based at RAF Cottesmore and RAF Wittering as a joint force capable of operating either from land or the Royal Navy's carriers. Plans announced in 2002 will see the withdrawal of the Sea Harrier by 2006 with the Harrier GR7/GR9s being operated by RAF and Royal Navy squadrons. By 1 April 2007, JFH will be an all Harrier GR9 Force. The force will achieve 50/50 RAF/RN manning shortly after this date. There is to be 4 front line squadrons, with 2 squadrons manned predominantly by the RN, and 2 manned predominantly by the RAF. The Harrier GR9 will be maintained in service until the Future Joint Combat Aircraft is in service.

No 2 Group

Until April 2003, No 2 Group operated all the aircraft and force elements that supported frontline operations. These included the air transport and air-to-air refuelling aircraft, and the Nimrod R and Sentry aircraft as well as the RAF Regiment and Ground Based Air Defence systems. The Group was also to be responsible, in the future, for ASTOR but that role is now to go to No 3 Group. Between April 2003-April 2004, No 2 Group will be reorganised to become the Air Combat Support Group containing all Air Transport/Air-to-Air Refuelling assets, the Force Protection assets, and the Air Combat Service Support Units (ACSSU) which include deployable supporting elements covering, engineering, armament, communications, supply, movements, medical, administrative and catering. Currently, the ACSSUs are commanded centrally within HQSTC.

Air Transport	Aircraft	Location
24 Squadron	11 x Hercules C1/C3/C4/C5	Lyneham
30 Squadron	11 x Hercules C1/C3/C4/C5	Lyneham
47 Squadron	11 x Hercules C1/C3/C4/C5	Lyneham
70 Squadron	11 x Hercules C1/C3/C4/C5	Lyneham
32 Squadron (The Royal)	5 x Bae 125	Northolt
	3 x Bae 146	
	3 x Twin Squirrel	
57 (Reserve Sqn)	5 x Hercules C3/C4/C5	Lyneham

Air Movements/Tankers	Aircraft	Location
99 Squadron	4 x C-17A	Brize Norton
10 Squadron	10 x VC10 C1K	Brize Norton
101 Squadron	3 x VC10 K2	Brize Norton
	4 x VC10 K3	
	5 x VC10 K4	
216 Squadron	8 x Tristar K1/KC1/C2/A	Brize Norton
1312 Flight	1 x VC10 K2	Mount Pleasant
	1 x Hercules C1	(Air transport only)

10 Sqn has been involved in almost all of the UK's major operations and recently became a dual tanker/transport squadron when its aircraft were fitted with air-to-air refuelling pods.

No 3 Group

From 2000, No 3 Group was the first home of the new Joint Force Harrier (JFH). The Group also included Nimrod maritime patrol aircraft, Search and Rescue helicopters and the RAF's Mountain Rescue Teams. From April 2003, JFH is under No 1 Group control, and no longer part of No 3 Group. Between April 2003-April 2004, No 3 Group is to become a Battle Management Group containing all Information, Surveillance, Target Acquisition and Reconnaissance (ISTAR), Air Surveillance and Control System (ASACS), Maritime and SAR assets. In addition, AOC No 3 Group will assume responsibility for the RAF element of Joint Helicopter Command (JHC). ASTOR will be operated by No 3 Group when it enters service around 2005.

Airborne Early Warning	Aircraft	Location
8 Squadron	3 x Sentry AEW1	Waddington
23 Squadron	3 x Sentry AEW1	Waddington

Electronic Warfare	Aircraft	Location
51 Squadron	3 x Nimrod R1	Waddington

Maritime Patrol	Aircraft	Location
120 Squadron	6 x Nimrod MR2	Kinloss
201 Squadron	6 x Nimrod MR2	Kinloss
206 Squadron	5 x Nimrod MR2	Kinloss
42 (Reserve) Squadron	3 x Nimrod MR2	Kinloss

Reconnaissance	Aircraft	Location
2 Squadron	12 x Tornado GR4A	Marham
13 Squadron	12 x Tornado GR4A	Marham
41 Squadron	12 x Jaguar GR3/3A	Coltishall
	1 x Jaguar T4	
39 (1 PRU) Sqn	4 x Canberra P9	Marham
	1 x Canberra T4	

Search & Rescue	Aircraft	Location
22 Squadron	Headquarters	St Mawgan
A Flight	3 x Sea King HAR3	Chivenor
B Flight	3 x Sea King HAR3	Wattisham
C Flight	2 x Sea King HAR3	Valley
202 Squadron	Headquarters	Boulmer
A Flight	3 x Sea King HAR3	Boulmer
D Flight	3 x Sea King HAR 3	Lossiemouth
E Flight	2 x Sea King HAR 3	Leconfield
203 (Reserve) Squadron	3 x Sea King HAR3	St Mawgan
78 Squadron	2 x Sea King HAR3	Mount Pleasant
78 Squadron total includes	1 x Chinook HC2	

Note: MoD figures show both 22 and 202 Squadrons as having 8 aircraft on strength.

Joint Helicopter Command

The UK armed forces' Joint Helicopter Command (JHC) became operational on 1 April 2000. Its first commander was Air Vice Marshal David Niven, who had under his command about 12,000 service personnel. By 1 April 2003, total helicopter assets of the JHC numbered some 454, including 67 WAH-64D Apache Longbow attack helicopters on order and whose delivery is to be completed by April 2004. In total, as of 2003, the JHC incorporates 44 Royal Navy helicopters (29 x Sea King Mk4, 6 x Lynx AH7, 9 x Gazelle), 306 British Army helicopters (117 x Gazelle, 117 x Lynx utility/TOW, 67 x Apache (final deliveries in 2004), and 103 RAF helicopters (33 x Puma, 48 x Chinook HC2/2A/3, and 22 x Merlin Mk3). The British Army helicopters include those operated by the British Army's 16 Air Assault Brigade (using Lynx light utility and anti-tank helicopters, and by 2005 to include 48 of the 67 WAH-64D Apache Longbow attack helicopters). The Chinook HC3 is to enter RAF service in 2003. The following RAF aircraft are assigned to the JHC.

Support Helicopters	Aircraft	Location
7 Squadron	5 x Chinook HC2	Odiham
	1 x Gazelle	
18 Squadron	18 x Chinook HC2	Odiham
27 Squadron	10 x Chinook HC2	Odiham
33 Squadron	15 x Puma HC1	Benson
78 Squadron	1 x Chinook HC2	Mount Pleasant
	2 x Sea King HAR3	(SAR capable)
84 Squadron	3 x Griffin HAR2	Akrotiri (SAR capable)
230 Squadron	13 x Puma HC1	Aldergrove

UK Air Surveillance and Control System (ASACS)

One of Strike Command's main responsibilities is the UK Air Surveillance and Control System (ASACS). AOC Strike Command is tasked with providing early warning of air attack against the UK air defence region; to provide fighter and missile defences and the associated ground control system; fighter co-ordination with Royal Naval ships operating in adjacent waters and to maintain the integrity of UK air space in war. ASACS comprises of a number of individual static and mobile units that provide the minute-to-minute information on air activity required to defend the UK and NATO partners. Manned by officers of Fighter Control under the Operations Support Branch with the support of airmen Aerospace Systems Operators, ASACS is a computer-based system which gathers and disseminates information on all aircraft flying in and around the UK Air Defence Region. The information within is used by the Air Defence Commander when deciding whether to investigate or perhaps even destroy an aircraft flying in an area without permission. Information comes from the RAF's ground-based radars and from the air defence systems of neighbouring NATO partners. ASACS can also receive information via digital data-links from other ground, air or sea-based units including No 1 Air Control Centre, which is part of the UK's Rapid Reaction Force.

ASACS has 2 operational Control and Reporting Centres (CRCs) based at RAF Buchan north of Aberdeen, and at RAF Neatishead which is north-east of Norwich. An additional stand-by CRC is found at RAF Boulmer in Northumberland. Each CRC has geographical areas of responsibility, roughly split north and south of Newcastle. Within their own areas, the CRCs receive and process information provided round-the- clock by military and civilian radars. In addition to this radar data, the CRCs also exchange information using digital data-links with neighbouring NATO partners, AEW aircraft and ships. The second ASACS function is the control of air defence aircraft. Fighter Controllers at Buchan and Neatishead provide the tactical control required for Air Defence aircraft to police the UK's airspace in peace and war, and they are also involved in the peacetime training of the RAF Air Defence assets. Fighter Controllers also provide support to Ground Attack forces when undertaking training with their Air Defence counterparts.

The CRCs are supported by a number of Reporting Posts (RPs) across the UK. In addition to those found at the CRCs, the locations of the RPs reflect the locations of the main RAF Air Defence radars that feed information into the UK ASACS. In addition to the radars, units have varying capabilities for the exchange of data-link information. The RPs are found at: RAF Saxa Vord in the Shetlands; RAF Benbecula in the Hebrides; RAF Staxton Wold near Scarborough; RP Portreath which is a satellite of RAF St Mawgan on the north coast of Cornwall.

Mobile Elements of the ASACS

No 1 Air Control Centre (1 ACC) provides the RAF with a mobile command and control capability able to deploy within the UK or anywhere in the world at short notice. Although operating as an interim ACC at present, the Unit will soon be transformed into a fully capable Tactical Air Command and Control System (TACCS) following delivery of state-of-the-art communications and data-link equipment to supplement the 2 new mobile radars recently delivered into its inventory. No 1 ACC is based at RAF Boulmer when in garrison.

Sentry AEW

The Sentry AEW1 makes a large contribution to ASACS using digital datalinks. The Sentry can deploy rapidly in response to crisis or conflict to provide the Air Defence Commander with information on potential aggressors. The roles within the Mission Crew of the Sentry mirror those within the UK ASACS CRCs, the posts being filled again with Fighter Controllers and Aerospace Systems Operators.

United Kingdom Combined Air Operations Centre

The nerve centre of ASACS is the United Kingdom Combined Air Operations Centre (UKCAOC) at Headquarters Strike Command at RAF High Wycombe. The UKCAOC is responsible for the overall coordination of the Air Defence, Ground Attack and Maritime Air elements of the RAF together with the air forces and navies of our NATO partners. ASACS information is monitored and controlled 24 hours a day. Within the UKCAOC, control and reporting centres are linked with other elements of the NATO Air Defence Ground Environment (NADGE) and with the Ballistic Missile Early Warning Systems (BMEWS) station at RAF Fylingdales in North Yorkshire. The latter is networked with the US operated BMEWS at Thule (Greenland) and Clear (Alaska). By extending high-level radar cover some 3,000 miles across eastern Europe, Fylingdales would give advance warning of intermediate range ballistic missiles launched against the UK and Western

Europe, and of inter-continental ballistic missiles against the North American continent. Fylingdales also tracks satellites and space debris.

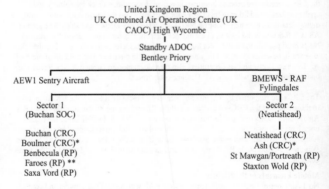

```
                    United Kingdom Region
            UK Combined Air Operations Centre (UK
                   CAOC) High Wycombe
                            |
                      Standby ADOC
                      Bentley Priory
                            |
 AEW1 Sentry Aircraft                    BMEWS - RAF
                                          Fylingdales

      Sector 1                             Sector 2
    (Buchan SOC)                         (Neatishead)

   Buchan (CRC)                         Neatishead (CRC)
   Boulmer (CRC)*                       Ash (CRC)*
   Benbecula (RP)              St Mawgan/Portreath (RP)
   Faroes (RP) **                      Staxton Wold (RP)
   Saxa Vord (RP)
```

* Denotes Reserve SOC
** Operated by the Royal Danish Air Force
In Reserve - STC Mobile Radar Reserve (144 Signals Unit)
Key: SOC - Sector Operations Centre
          CRC - Control and Reporting Centre
          RP - Reporting Post

In the Falkland Islands there are Reporting Posts at Mount Kent, Mount Alice and Byron Heights.

Until April 2003, the majority of UK ASACS units are under the command of 2 Group. Between April 2003-April 2004, the ASACS role is to transfer to No 3 Group.

I-UKADGE (Improved-UK Air Defence Ground Environment) is the communications system upon which the air defences depend for their operational effectiveness. The system is fully automated and integrated with the NATO Air Defence Ground Environment (NADGE), which includes sites stretching from Northern Norway to Eastern Turkey, and the Portuguese Air Command and Control System (POACCS). These systems integrate the various sites which are equipped with modern radars, data processing and display systems and are linked by modern digital communications. Computerised data exchange and information from a number of sources such as radars, ships and aircraft is moved around the system on a number of routes to minimise the disruptive effects of enemy action. ICCS (Integrated Command and Control System) provides to the commanders and air defence staff the information gathered in the system and UNITER brings together all the nodes on a digital network.

JTIDS (Joint Tactical Information Distribution/Display System) is a secure tactical datalink network to enable the UK armed forces to participate in Allied operations. JTIDS is now in service throughout the UK armed Forces. The RAF is believed to operate some 60 terminals and the majority of these equip 2 Tornado F3 squadrons and the AEW1 Sentry aircraft.

BACCS

The Backbone Air Command & Control System (BACCS) will replace ASACS as a component of the North Atlantic Treaty Organisation (NATO) Integrated Air Defence System (NATINADS) around 2009. The programme will be based on NATO ACCS requirements with additional UK requirements being nationally funded. BACCS will provide computer-based static capability covering early warning, air policing and operational training using the existing ASACS radar sensors and communications infrastructure.

RAF Personnel & Training Command (RAF PTC)

HQ PTC controls all personnel aspects ranging from conditions of service, recruiting, training, education, manning, career management, resettlement and pensions. The headquarters also deals with all policy matters relating to medical, dental, legal and chaplaincy. The Command employs 17,000 people, including 4,000 civilians, at more than 30 locations. It is responsible for over 500 training aircraft of which 150 are gliders. Headquarters staff number some 1500, of whom a half are civilian.

```
                         AOC in C & AM Personnel
                         Commander - Air Marshal
                             (HQ Innsworth)
            COS ————————————————|———————————————— Command Secretary

Chaplain in   Air Secretary   Director    Director    Cmdt      AOC
  Chief                        Legal       Medical    Cranwell  Training
                               Services    Services   AOC Air   Group
                                                      Cadets    Defence
                                                                Agency
```

Chief of Staff's Branch (COS)

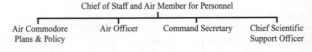

Chief of Staff and Air Member for Personnel

| Air Commodore | Air Officer | Command Secretary | Chief Scientific |
| Plans & Policy | | | Support Officer |

Air Secretary

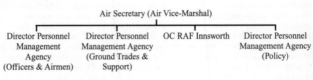

Air Secretary (Air Vice-Marshal)

Director Personnel	Director Personnel	OC RAF Innsworth	Director Personnel
Management	Management Agency		Management Agency
Agency	(Ground Trades &		(Policy)
(Officers & Airmen)	Support)		

Director Medical Services

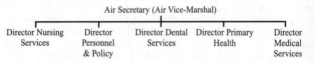

Air Secretary (Air Vice-Marshal)

Director Nursing	Director	Director Dental	Director Primary	Director
Services	Personnel	Services	Health	Medical
	& Policy			Services

Air Officer Commanding Training and Chief Executive Training Group Defence Agency

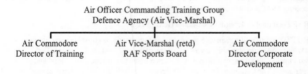

Air Officer Commanding Training Group
Defence Agency (Air Vice-Marshal)

Air Commodore	Air Vice-Marshal (retd)	Air Commodore
Director of Training	RAF Sports Board	Director Corporate
		Development

The RAF Training Group Defence Agency forms an integral part of the Command administered from Innsworth. The Agency comprises nine RAF stations UK-wide with additional minor units elsewhere. It also has responsibility for administering the RAF Aerobatic Team, the Red Arrows.

136

PTC Flying Training Units

Elementary Flying Training	Aircraft	Location
Joint Elementary Flying Training School (JEFTS)	18 x Mk 1 Firefly	Barkstone Heath
University Air Squadrons (UAS)	91 x Tutor	Various locations
Volunteer Gliding Schools (VGS)	135 Gliders including Viking & Vigilant	Various locations

Basic Flying Training	Aircraft	Location
No 1 Flying Training School (1 FTS)	67 x Tucano T1	Linton (includes Central Flying School at Topcliffe)
No 3 Flying Training School (3 FTS)	11 x Jetstream T1 9 x Dominie T1 8 x Tutor	Cranwell

Advanced Flying Training	Aircraft	Location
No 4 Flying Training School (4 FTS)	69 x Hawk T1/1A	Valley
SAR Training Unit	4 x Griffin HT1	Valley
Defence Helicopter Flying School (DHFS)	28 x Squirrel HT1 7 x Griffin HT1	Shawbury

Operational Conversion Unit (OCU)

The RAF has a number of OCU's designed to train pilots for front-line squadron service as follows:

Tornado OCU	26 x Tornado GR4	RAF Lossiemouth	(15 Reserve Sqn)
Tornado F3 OCU	20 x Tornado F3	RAF Leuchars	(56 Reserve Sqn)
Jaguar OCU	8 x Jaguar GR3/T4	RAF Lossiemouth	(16 Reserve Sqn)
Harrier OCU	9 x Harrier GR7 6 x Harrier T10	RAF Wittering	(20 Reserve Sqn)
Nimrod OCU	3 x Nimrod MR2	RAF Kinloss	(42 Reserve Sqn)
Hercules OCU	5 x Hercules	RAF Lyneham	(57 Reserve Sqn)
Sea King OCU	3 x Sea King HAR3	RAF St Mawgan	(203 Reserve Sqn)

The organisation of an OCU is obviously tailored to fit the size of the aircraft fleet being supported. As an example No 56 Reserve Sqn (Tornado F3 OCU) is organised along the following lines:

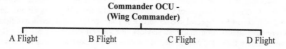

A and B Flights provide flying training with about 19 x staff crews and 12 x student crews. C Flight is a standards flight - training instructors, and D Flight provides simulators and a dome air combat trainer.

137

RAF Armament Support Unit

The RAF Armament Support Unit (RAFASU) is headquartered at RAF Marham. RAF Wittering houses the RAF Explosive Ordnance Disposal (EOD) Squadron (5131 BD), which is the part of RAFASU responsible for all aspects of RAF EOD training and trials, as well as actual clearance operations. RAFASU also trains aircrew and ground crew in all aspects of special weapons functions and moves weapons as required.

RAF Signals

As of April 2003, RAF Signals units are as shown below:

Unit	Location
9 SU	RAF Boddingtons
11 SU	RAF Rheindahlen, Germany
81 SU	RAF Bampton Castle
303 SU	Falkland Islands
591 SU	RAF Digby
1001 SU	RAF Oakhanger
Tactical Communications Wing	RAF Brize Norton

RAF signals communications fall into three categories. First, there is a large complex of HF transmitter and receiver facilities in the UK, including communications centres with automatic message routing equipment. Operations include those on behalf of Strike Command, the Military Air Traffic Organisation, NATO, and the Meteorological Office. Second, the RAF Signals Staff operate message relay centres, both automatic and manual and also manage the RAF's General Purpose Telephone network. RAF command operating procedures are monitored on all networks to ensure high standards are achieved and maintained. To reduce risk of compromise, all RAF communications facilities designed to carry classified information are checked for communications electrical security by Command staff. For the use of all armed forces, the MoD has procured a fixed telecommunications network called Boxer under a Private Finance Initiative (PFI) contract, which will save the increasing expense of renting lines from the private sector. Third, the main operation of the Skynet Satellite Communications System, which offers overseas formations telegraphed, data and speech communications, is controlled by RAF Command. RAF Oakhanger is the focal point of military satellite communications in the UK. Two satellite communications (Satcom) units are based at Oakhanger, No 1001 Signals Unit and a NATO Satellite Ground Terminal. From 1998, 3 x Skynet 4 Stage 2 replaced the existing Skynet satellites when they reached the end of their operational life, and entered service late in 1998. In addition, a management service for the NATO 4 series of satellites is provided. From 2008, Skynet 5 is expected to enter service and provide the next generation of flexible and survivable satellite communications services for military use and will replace the Skynet 4 constellation at the end of its predicted life. Robust military satellite communications services are essential to support inter and intra-theatre information exchange requirements and ensure that deployed and mobile forces are not constrained by the need to remain within the range of terrestrial communications. RAF command operating procedures are monitored on all networks to ensure high standards are achieved and maintained. To reduce risk of compromise, all RAF communications facilities designed to carry classified information are checked for communications electrical security by Command staff.

AOC Signals has a large engineering design staff of engineers, technicians and draughtsmen. Manufacturing resources include a general mechanical engineering and calibration capacity at RAF Henlow, plus a facility for the systems design, development and installation of certain airborne signals role equipment.

RAF Procurement

Like logistics, UK procurement is managed on a tri-service basis by the Defence Procurement Agency (DPA). The DPA was launched on 1 April 1999 as an Executive Agency of the Ministry of Defence (MoD), replacing the MoD Procurement Executive. The core role of the DPA is the procurement of military equipment to meet the operational requirements of the armed forces. RAF operational requirements are formulated and managed by Integrated Project Teams (IPT). RAF personnel are seconded to the DPA for the duration of their appointments - usually two to three years.

RAF Logistics

Since the MoD-wide reorganisation of 2000, logistics support for all three Services is the responsibility of Defence Logistics Organisation. Three DLO business units do most of the RAF support - the Equipment Support (Air) (ES Air), the Defence Supply Chain (DSC) and the Defence Communication Service Agency (DSCA). Most DLO units supporting the RAF are based at RAF Brampton, Wyton and Henlow. The three sites retain their own identities, but are run under single command, with many of the support functions centralised. RAF personnel are seconded to the DLO for the duration of their appointments - usually two to three years.

RAF Wyton is the largest of the three sites and provides the principal home for Equipment Support (Air) (ESAir). In addition, it houses Corporate Technical Services, another DLO element. RAF Brampton provides support to a number of other lodger units including elements of the DLO. It is also the base for the Defence Security Standards Organisation and RAF Infrastructure Organisation East Region. Henlow has been a ground-training base specialising in electronics since the end of the Second World War and was for many years the base for the RAF Signals Engineering Establishment (RAFSEE). The Station is now home to the Directorate of Engineering Interoperability (DEI), which is part of the Defence Communications Services Agency (DCSA) within the DLO.

Equipment Support (Air) - Defence Logistics Organisation

The majority of RAF Logistic support is incorporated within the Defence Logistics Organisation under the Equipment Support (Air) business unit. ES(Air) provides in-service logistic support for all Ministry of Defence aircraft and helicopters. It is responsible for the maintenance and support of everything from Chinook helicopters to fast jets such as Tornado, from avionics to ground support equipment. ES(Air) manages an extensive inventory of different products and supports over 1,000 aircraft in over 30 fleets. It also contracts out design specifications for new aircraft parts; oversees aircraft modification programmes; provides logistics support for air launched munitions; avionics and radar systems and works with industry to improve aircraft capabilities. The organisation controls a budget of around £4.3 billion, the majority of which goes to industry for the purchase of spares, repairs and post-design services. ES(Air) manages over 7,000 contracts with some 200 firms - the vast majority of which are British based companies.

ES(Air) is organised into Integrated Project Teams (IPT), which focus on the whole life support of equipment and inventory items used by the Armed Forces, and Directorates, which provide common support services to the IPTs (for example financial services and business improvements). As of 2003, ES (Air) is led by DG (Director General) Air Vice-Marshal Peter Liddell. He reports to the Chief of Defence Logistics who sits on the top MoD executive committee - the Defence Management Board as the executive arm of the Defence Council.

ES(Air) workforce of around 4,000 is made up of Army, Royal Navy, Royal Air Force and civil servants. The Headquarters of ES(Air) is located at RAF Wyton and, whilst members of ES(Air) work in over 50 locations, the majority work in nine main sites - Abbey Wood, Brampton, Gosport, Middle Wallop, St Athan, Sherborne, Waddington, Wyton and Yeovilton.

Material Supply

Under the MoD-wide reorganisation of 2000, the DLO became responsible for the centralised storage and supply of RAF material through its Defence Supply Chain (DSC) arm. The DSC comprises four agencies whose duties divide into storage and distribution, medical supplies, defence transport and movement and British Forces post. In addition to these four agencies it also contains six business units, ranging from the Defence Supply Chain Operations to the Defence Catering Corp. One of these units, Defence Munitions was recently charged with the task of retrieving ammunition from HMS Nottingham.

Operationally, the DLO through ES (Air) also supports major force deployments through PJHQ via a rapid deployment unit based at RAF Stafford. This organisation is equipped to move at very short notice to provide a range of support facilities, including fuel and spares, anywhere in the world.

Equipment Repair and Maintenance - Defence Communication Services Agency

Since the establishment of the DLO, support for the ground-based signals infrastructure is the responsibility of the Air Defence Ground Based Systems Integrated Project Team, dual accountable to the Defence Logistics Organisation and the Defence Procurement Agency, This IPT forms part of the Defence Communication Services Agency (DCSA) located at RAF Brampton. The deep maintenance and repair of ground radio and radar equipments is carried out by the Ground Radio Servicing Centre (GRSC) based at RAF Sealand. This includes radars, radio navigation aids and point-to-point and ground-to-air communications. The DCSA provides support to technician training facilities located at RAF Cosford and the Ground Radio Servicing Centre based at RAF Sealand.
The DLO ES (Air) provides an antenna systems maintenance service on a worldwide basis, embracing the fields of communications, radar and navigation aids. The men required for this highly specialised work are trained at the Aerial Erector School at RAF Digby.

Equipment Repair and Maintenance - Defence Aviation Repair Agency

Launched on 1 April 1999, the Defence Aviation Repair Agency (DARA) brought together the RAF Maintenance Group Defence Agency (MGDA) and the Naval Aircraft Repair Organisation (NARO). DARA has trading fund status within the MoD, and is not part of the DLO. It will probably be privatised at some stage. Repair and maintenance activities at DARA are divided into five main groups - fixed-wing aircraft, helicopters, engines, electronics and components. Scheduled major maintenance, repair, rectifications, reconditioning and modification for a wide variety of aircraft are undertaken for tasks beyond the normal capability of operational stations.

Work on aircraft is carried out at RAF St Athan. The DARA engineering unit at St Athan is manned jointly by service personnel and civilians, with an Aircraft Servicing Wing and a General Engineering Wing. In February 2003, DARA announced the construction of a new state-of-the-art £77m facility at the Agency's headquarters base in St Athan. The new repair and maintenance facility will be constructed within a 100-acre site on the existing RAF St Athan base. It consolidates DARA interests and replaces the present facilities, currently spread around the 1000-acre site. The new facility will have the capacity to house 48 jet aircraft, and will be capable of adapting capacity to suit the needs of customers.

The DARA facility at RAF Sealand near Chester is the main engineering unit for airborne electronic and instrument equipment. Large workshops and test facilities are laid out on production lines to enable the unit to service more than 100,000 items of airborne radio, radar, electrical, instrument and missile engineering equipment per year. The unit also provides a test equipment calibration service and manufactures test equipment, aircraft cables and looms.

Overseas Bases

Strike Command has responsibility for all RAF bases overseas.

RAF Akrotiri, Cyprus

The RAF use the airfield at Akrotiri as a staging post for transport aircraft, and as a temporary operating base for aircraft carrying out Armament Practice Camps. Akrotiri is the permanent base of 84 Squadron who perform Search and Rescue duties as well as a support role for the UN peacekeeping forces on the island. In addition, a detachment of the RAF Regiment is stationed at Akrotiri to assist with airfield defence.

RAF Gibraltar

Although aircraft are no longer stationed at RAF Gibraltar, Hercules and Nimrod and Tornado aircraft make regular visits.

RAF Ascension Island

Situated in the middle of the Atlantic Ocean, and over 700 miles from its nearest neighbour, Ascension Island was used extensively as a staging base during the Falklands War. This is still the major role for the Station, which it performs for both the RAF and the USAF.

RAFU Goose Bay, Canada

A team of RAF personnel is stationed at Goose Bay in Labrador to support RAF fast jet aircraft carrying out low level flying training over Labrador. The fast jets are usually accompanied by VC-10s, Tristars or Hercules aircraft, providing AAR or transport support.

Mount Pleasant, Falkland Islands

Mount Pleasant was opened in 1984 to establish a fighter and transport presence in the Islands following the Falklands War. Currently based at Mount Pleasant are No 1435 Flight with 4 Tornado F3s, No 1312 Flight, with a single VC10 tanker and one Hercules C1, as well as No 78 Squadron with Chinook and Sea King helicopters. Ground units include No 7, 303 and 751 Signals Units and a Rapier detachment from the RAF Regiment.

RAF Nordhorn, Germany

Nordhorn is one of the largest bombing and gunnery range complexes in NATO, and is used by the RAF and other NATO air forces for weapons training and exercises.

Mobile Air Movement Squadron (MAMS)

During operations and exercises, aircraft often visit overseas airfields where no regular RAF ground handling organisation exists. For this purpose, Strike Command has a Mobile Air Movement Squadron (MAMS) at RAF Lyneham, which provides teams who are expert in all aspects of loading and unloading aircraft.

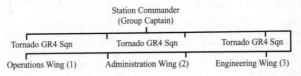

RAF Station Organisation

An indication of the manner in which an RAF Station might be organised is as follows. This example is an RAF Station with 3 x Tornado GR1 flying squadrons - each with 12 x aircraft. The 36 aircraft will have cost at least £780 million in total purchase costs, and the combined running costs for the operation of these three squadrons will be in the region of some £90 million pounds per annum.

Notes: (1) Ops Wing; (2) Admin Wing; (3) Eng Wing; (4) Expect the commanders of the Tornado Sqns to be Wing Commanders aged between 34-40; Ops, Admin and Eng Wings will almost certainly be commanded by Wing Commanders from their respective branch specialities - these Wing Commanders will probably be a little older than the commanders of the flying squadrons.

Flying Squadron Organisation

Note: Generally 1 x Tornado GR4 will be held in reserve (IUR)
Note: (1) These departmental leaders have responsibility for weapons, airframes, propulsion, electronics, flight guidance and control systems, communications, automatic navigation and attack controls and report to the squadron commander.

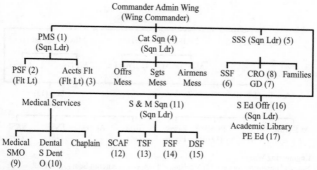

Administration Wing Organisation

Notes: (1) Personnel Management Squadron; (2) Personal Services Flight; (3) Accounts Flight; (4) Catering Sqn; (5) Station Services Sqn; (6) Station Services Flight; (7) General Duties Flight; (8) Community Relations Officer (9) Senior Medical Officer; (10) Senior Dental Officer; (11) Supply & Movements Sqn; (12) Supply Control & Accounts Flight; (13) Technical Supply Flight; (14) Forward Supply Flight; (15) Domestic Supply Flight; (16) Senior Education Officer; (17) Physicial Education.

Operations Wing Organisation

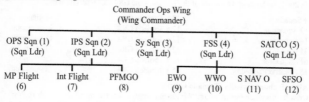

Notes: (1) Operations Sqn; (2) Intelligence & Planning Sqn; (3) Security Sqn - includes RAF Police & Station Defence Personnel; (4) Flying Support Sqn; (5) Senior Air Traffic Control Officer; (6) Mission Plans Flight; (7) Intelligence Flight; (8) Pre-flight Message Generation Officer; (9) Electronic Warfare Officer; (10) Wing Weapon Officer; (11) Senior Navigation Officer; (12) Station Safety Officer.

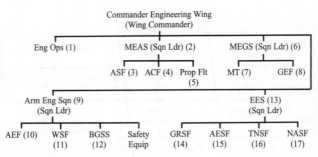

Engineering Wing

Notes: (1) Engineering Ops; (2) Mechanical Engineering Aircraft Sqn; (3) Aircraft Servicing Flight; (4) Aircraft Components Flight; (5) Propulsion Flight; (6) Mechanical Engineering Ground Squadron; (7) Mechanical Transport; (8) General Engineering Flight; (9) Armament Engineering Sqn; (10) Armament Engineering Flight; (11) Weapon Storage Flight; (12) Bomb Group Supply Section; (13) Electrical Engineering Squadron; (14) Ground Radio Servicing Flight; (15) Avionics Electrical Systems Flight; (16) Tornado Navigation Systems Flight; (17) Navigation and Attack Systems Flight.

RAF Aircraft

Tornado GR-4

In 2003, the latest strike variant of the Tornado - the GR4 - is in service with:

9 Squadron	12 x Tornado GR4	Marham
12 Squadron	12 x Tornado GR4	Lossiemouth
14 Squadron	12 x Tornado GR4	Lossiemouth
31 Squadron	12 x Tornado GR4	Marham
617 Squadron	12 x Tornado GR4	Lossiemouth
15 (Reserve) Squadron	26 x Tornado GR4	Lossiemouth

Aircraft characteristics (Tornado GR4)

Crew 2; Wingspan (open) 13.9m; Wingspan (swept) 8.6m; Height 5.9m; Length 16.7m; Max Weapon Load 18,000lb/8,180kg; Max Take Off Weight 27,900kg; Max Speed Mach 2.2 (1,452 mph/2,333kph); Max Ferry Range approx 3,900km; Required Runway Length approx 900m. Engines 2 x Turbo-Union RB 199-34R Mk103 Turbofans; Armament 1 x 27mm Mauser Cannon, 3 x weapon points under fuselage, 4 x weapon points under wings; AIM-9L Sidewinder AAM; ALARM; JP233; BL755 CBU; Paveway II, III, EPR (IV); Brimstone; Storm Shadow CASOM.

The Tornado Multi-Role Combat aircraft (MRCA) has been the RAF's principal strike weapon system over the past two decades. Designed in the Cold War to penetrate Soviet air

defence at low level, the Tornado is nuclear-capable. Since the withdrawal from service of the WE177 nuclear bomb in 1998, the Tornado strike capability has been restricted to conventional weapons. The Tornado MRCA was jointly developed by the UK, West Germany and Italy under a collaborative agreement and manufactured by a consortium of companies formed under the name of Panavia. The Tornado GR-1 was the most numerous and important aircraft in the RAF inventory, and the GR-1 operated in the strike/attack and reconnaissance roles. The first prototype flew in 1974 and the first RAF Squadron equipped with the GR-1 became operational in 1982.

During the Gulf War, Tornado GR1s were amongst the first aircraft in action from 17 January 1991. During the war, the Tornado GR1 force flew 1,500 operational sorties divided almost equally between offensive counter air targets such as airfields and air defence sites, and interdiction targets such as bridges. Between them, Tornado GR1 and Jaguar GR1As dropped some 100 x JP233 airfield denial weapons, 5,000 x 1,000 pound bombs, 1,000 x LGBs, 100 x ALARM missiles and 700 x Air to Ground Rockets onto Iraqi positions. The RAF deployed 48 x GR1 in the area during hostilities.

A total of six GR1s was lost in action, five of which were involved in low-or medium- level attacks with 1,000 pound bombs and one that was flying a low-level JP233 mission. The final three weeks of the air war saw the Tornado GR1 force concentrating almost exclusively on day and night precision attacks dropping LGBs from medium altitude.

There are plans to maintain the Tornado GR4 in service until 2018. 142 x Tornado GR-1s have been upgraded to GR4 standard under the Tornado Mid-Life Update (MLU) programme costing some £943m. Deliveries began in 1998 and were scheduled for completion by the end of 2002. Compared to the GR1, the GR4 has a Forward-Looking Infra-Red (FLIR), a wide angle Head-Up Display (HUD), improved cockpit displays, Night-Vision Goggle (NVG) compatibility, new avionics and weapons systems, updated computer software, and Global Positioning System (GPS). The upgrade also re-arms the Tornado with the Storm Shadow stand-off missile, Brimstone advanced anti-armour weapon, and the Paveway EPW LGB. New sensors include the RAPTOR and Vicon reconnaissance pods and an improved Thermal Imaging Airborne Laser Designator (TIALD) targeting pod. A separate programme covered an integrated Defensive Aids Suite consisting of the radar warning receiver, Sky Shadow radar jamming pod and BOZ-107 chaff and flare dispenser. The standard Tornado GR4 can also fulfil tactical reconnaissance tasks when equipped with an external camera pod.

During the Iraq War of 2003 (Op Telic), GR4s from all five active Tornado squadrons were deployed. One Tornado was lost to friendly fire. The Storm Shadow air-launched cruise missile was fired operationally for the first time during the Iraq conflict - from a Tornado GR4.

Expect a Tornado GR4 squadron to have 15 established crews.

Tornado GR4A

In service with:

2 Squadron	12 x Tornado GR4A	Marham
13 Squadron	12 x Tornado GR4A	Marham

The Tornado GR4A is used as a combat reconnaissance aircraft - also upgraded under the GR1 series MLU - and has no cannons mounted in the forward fuselage. Replacing these are an internally-mounted Sideways Looking Infra-Red system and a Linescan infrared surveillance system.

Tornado F3

In service with:

11 Squadron	16 x Tornado F3	Leeming
25 Squadron	16 x Tornado F3	Leeming
43 Squadron	16 x Tornado F3	Leuchars
111 Squadron	16 x Tornado F3	Leuchars
1435 Flight	4 x Tornado F3	Mount Pleasant
56 (Reserve) Squadron	20 x Tornado F3	Leuchars

Crew 2; Wingspan (open) 13.9m; Wingspan (swept) 8.6m; Height 5.9m; Length 18.7m; Max Weapon Load 8,500kg; Max Take Off Weight 27,900kg; Max Speed Mach 2.2 (1,452 mph/2,333kph); ; Engines 2 x Turbo-Union RB 199-34R-Mk104 Turbofans; Intercept Radius 1,850 km (subsonic) or 550 km (supersonic).Armament 1 x 27mm Mauser Cannon;

AAM 4 x Sky Flash, AMRAAM; 4 x AIM-9L Sidewinder, ASRAAM; ALARM.

The Air Defence Variant (ADV) of the Tornado from which the F3 was developed flew for the first time in October 1979. The aircraft has a long-range, autonomous capability that enables operations to be conducted some 350 nm away from bases in bad weather, in an ECM environment and operating against multiple targets at high or low level, which can be engaged at distances in excess of 20 nm. With tanker support, the Tornado F3 Combat Air Patrol (CAP) time is increased from 2 hrs and 30mins to a loiter time of several hours. The Tornado F3 was originally armed with 4 x semi-recessed Sky Flash, 4 x Sidewinder AIM-9L missiles, and a single Mauser 27 mm cannon and has about 80% commonality with the Tornado GR1. The main difference is the extended fuselage, longer range air intercept Foxhunter Radar (replacing the terrain-following/ground mapping radar of the Tornado GR1) and the armament. Extension of the fuselage provides additional space for avionics and an extra 900 litres of fuel. RAF Tornado F3s are equipped with the Joint Tactical Information Distribution System (JTIDS). Operating in conjunction with Sentry AEW1 airborne early warning aircraft and other allied fighters, the system gives a real-time picture of the air battle, including information obtained by other sensors in other fighters or airborne early warning (AEW) aircraft.

RAF Tornado F3s were sent to the Gulf in August 1990 and by the end of hostilities on the 28 February 1991, 18 x F3 aircraft had flown some 2,500 sorties during their deployment including 700 sorties during the period of hostilities. Tornado F-3s from all four active UK squadrons were deployed during the 2003 Iraq War (Op Telic).

Under the recent £140 million Tornado F3 Capability Sustainment Programme (CSP), 100 F-3s were upgraded to incorporate the Raytheon AIM-120 Advanced Medium-Range Air-to-Air Missile (AMRAAM), and the Matra BAe Dynamics Advanced Short- Range Air-to-Air Missile (ASRAAM). For the Iraq War, F-3s were also modified to carry the ALARM anti-radiation missile. The F3 will almost certainly stay in service until 2007-2010. Its replacement is the Eurofighter Typhoon. Expect a Tornado F3 Squadron to have between 16 and 20 established crews.

Tornado in World Service
(Original Procurement Figures)

	GR1/IDS	F2/F3/ADV	ECR/GR1A/Recce
UK	199	170	26
Germany	302	-	36
Italy	70	24 (leased from UK)	-
Saudi Arabia	96	24	-

Jaguar GR3/3A and T4
In service with:

6 Squadron	11 x Jaguar GR3	Coltishall
	1 x Jaguar T4	
54 Squadron	11 x Jaguar GR3	Coltishall
41 Squadron	12 x Jaguar GR3	Coltishall
	1 x Jaguar T4	
16 (Reserve Squadron)	8 x Jaguar GR1A/T4	Lossiemouth

Crew (GR3/3A) 1 (T4) 2; Length (GR 3/3A) 16.83m; Wingspan 8.69m; Height 4.89m; All Up Operational Weight approx 11,000kg; Max Weapons Load 10,000lb/4,500kg; Max Speed 1,056mph/1,690k/ph; Engines 2 x Rolls-Royce Turbomeca Adour Mk 106s; Armament 2 x 30mm Aden Cannon, (T4)1 x 30mm Aden Cannon; 2 x Sidewinder AAM;

JP233; CBU-87; Paveway II, III; BL 755; CRV-7 rockets.

Produced to meet a joint Anglo-French requirement in 1965 for a dual-role advanced/operational trainer and tactical support aircraft, the Jaguar has been transformed into a potent fighter-bomber. The RAF originally intended to use the aircraft purely as an advanced trainer, but this was later changed to the offensive support role on cost grounds.

The first RAF aircraft took to the air in October 1969, and each air force placed orders for 200 aircraft - the RAF opting for 165 single-seat and 35 two-seat aircraft. Deliveries to No 226 Operational Conversion Unit at Lossiemouth began in 1973, and at its peak the Jaguar equipped 8 front-line squadrons in the UK and Germany. The Jaguar has a nuclear capability.

During the 1990-91 Gulf War, the RAF deployed a Squadron of 12 x Jaguar GR1A to the region. This squadron was employed on a variety of battlefield interdiction (BAI) and close air support (CAS) missions. Although only operating during daylight, the Jaguars displayed great versatility and flew over 600 operational sorties without loss. In addition to their operations over land, the Jaguars were also successful in destroying Iraqi patrol boats and landing craft in the Gulf. Jaguars also flew tactical reconnaissance sorties. Tornado GR1 and Jaguar GR1As dropped some 100 x JP233 airfield denial weapons, 5,000 x 1,000 pound bombs, 1,000 x LGBs, 100 x ALARM missiles and 700 x Air-to-Ground Rockets onto Iraqi positions. For the 2003 Iraq War (Op Telic), Jaguars from all three Coltishall squadrons were deployed.

61 of the RAF's Jaguar fleet of some 66 aircraft have recently undergone a major upgrade programme and been designated as the Jaguar GR3 (T4 for the 2-seat variant). The Adour 104 engine has been changed for the more powerful Adour 106 under a £61m contract. The upgrade also included improved avionics: Global Positioning System (GPS) and Terrain Referenced Navigation (TRN) integrated into the Inertial Navigator (IN) internal and external Night Vision Goggles (NVG) compatible lighting, helmet mounted sight and ASRAAM capability, and new Head Up Display (HUD) and Head Down Displays (HDD). Also incorporated are a Thermal Imaging and Laser Designator series 400 capability integrated with Map and Symbol Generator graphics, a new Jaguar Mission Planner system, provision for the Vicon 18-601 Electro-Optic reconnaissance pod, provision for a Jaguar Replacement Reconnaissance Pod, and a Paveway III and EPR Laser Guided Munitions capability.

The Jaguar is expected to be operational until at least 2008. Expect a Jaguar GR1A Squadron to have 16 established crews.

Harrier

The RAF's Harriers are in service with:

1 Squadron	13 x Harrier GR7	Cottesmore
	1 x Harrier T10	
3 Squadron	13 x Harrier GR7	Cottesmore
	1 x Harrier T-10	
4 Squadron	13 x Harrier GR7	Cottesmore
	1 x Harrier T10	
20 (Reserve Squadron)	9 x Harrier GR7	Wittering
	6 x Harrier T10	

Note: All of these aircraft are now part of the Joint Force Harrier (JFH) organisation.

Crew (GR7, GR7A, GR9, GR9A) 1; (T Mark 10, T12) 2; Length (GR7, GR7A,GR9) 14.1m; Length (T10, T12) 17m; Wingspan (normal) 9.2m; Height (GR7) 3.45m; Height (T10) 4.17m; Max Speed 1,065 k/ph (661mph) at sea level; All Up Operational Weight approx 13,494 kg; Engine (GR7, GR9, T10, T12) 1 x Rolls-Royce Pegasus Mk 105 (GR7A, GR9A) 1 x Rolls-Royce Pegasus Mk 107; Ferry Range 5,382 km (3,310 miles) with 4 x drop tanks. Armament on seven available wing stations: 2 x 30mm Aden guns, 4 x wing weapon pylons and 1 x under-fuselage weapon pylon, conventional or cluster bombs; 2 x Sidewinder AIM-9L AAM, ASRAAM; up to 16 x Mk 82 or six Mk 83 bombs; 4 x Maverick air-to-ground anti-armour missiles, Paveway II and III laser-guided bombs;

Brimstone anti-armour missiles, CRV-7 rocket pods; 2 x Storm Shadow CASOM.

The Harrier GR7 (two seat variant T-10) is the latest of Harrier 'Jump Jets' originating from the 1960s. Capable of taking off and landing vertically, the Harrier is not tied to airfields with long concrete runways but can be dispersed to sites in the field close to the forward edge of the battle area. The normal method of operation calls for a short take-off and vertical landing (STOVL), as a short ground roll on take-off enables a greater weapon load to be carried. The second-generation GR5 and GR7 versions replaced the original Harrier GR3s in the late 1980s/early 1990s in the offensive support role. First flight of the Harrier GR7 was in 1989, and deliveries to RAF squadrons began in 1990. A total of 96 aircraft were ordered, including 62 interim GR5s which were later modified to GR7 standard.

The Harrier is to receive a number of upgrades in the near future. These are expected to cost some £500m. New Pegasus 107 engines giving more thrust at higher temperatures as well as reduced maintenance costs will be fitted to 30 aircraft, these becoming Harrier GR7As. Also, a major upgrade to the aircraft's avionics and weapons systems will enable the Harrier to carry a variety of current and future weapons. These include Maverick air-to-surface missiles, Brimstone anti-armour missiles and AIM-9L Sidewinder air-to-air missiles for self-defence. A new, stronger composite rear fuselage will also be fitted. These aircraft will become Harrier GR9s, whilst those with the uprated engines and weapons systems will be Harrier GR9As. The programme also includes an upgrade of the two-seater T10 aircraft to the equivalent GR9 standard known as the Harrier T12.

All three Harrier squadrons from Cottesmore were deployed for the 2003 Iraq War in Operation Telic. Expect a Harrier GR7 Squadron to have 17 established crews.

Eurofighter Typhoon

The first production aircraft flew in 2003, and delivery should start later in 2003. Typhoon is scheduled to enter RAF service in the very near future, and reach its full operational capability some three years later. The Typhoon is to replace the Tornado F3 and then the Jaguar. It is planned that the Typhoon frontline will comprise 7 squadrons, of which 4 will be primarily Air Defence, 2 Swing-role, and one Offensive Support covering a full range of Combat Air Operations. Initial deliveries will be to the Eurofighter Operational Conversion Unit at RAF Coningsby. Subsequent aircraft will go to Tornado F3 squadrons at Leeming and Leuchars before Jaguar squadrons are re-equipped.

Crew 1; Length 15.96m; Height 5.23m; Wingspan 10.95m; Max Speed 1,321mph/2,125 kph; Empty Weight 22,000lb/9,999kg; Max Take-Off Weight 46,305lb/21,000kg; Engine 2 x Eurojet EJ200 turbofans; Ferry Range 5,382 km (3,310 miles) with 4 x drop tanks. Armament 1 x 27mm (first RAF batch only); Air Interdiction: 2 x Storm Shadow, 2 x ALARM, 4 x AMRAAM, 2 x ASRAAM, 2 x1,500 litre fuel tank, 1 x 1,000 litre fuel tank; Close Air Support: 18 x Brimstone, 4 x AMRAAM, 2 x ASRAAM, 1 x 1,000 litre fuel tank: SEAD: 6 x ALARM, 4 x AMRAAM, 2 x ASRAAM, 1 x 1,000 litre fuel tank: Maritime Attack: 4 x Penguin, 4 x AMRAAM, 2 x ASRAAM, 2 x 1,500 litre fuel tank, 1 x 1,000 litre fuel tank: also Sidewinder AAM; Meteor BVRAAM; Paveway II,III, EPR (IV) LGB; JDAM or other PGB.

The Eurofighter Typhoon (formerly EFA) is a single seat, STOL capable aircraft optimised for air superiority/air defence and ground attack roles. Germany, Italy and Spain are UK partners in the most costly European collaboration programme to date. As of 2002, the estimated procurement cost of the RAF Typhoons was some £18.6bn, including research and development costs - making it the most expensive weapon system yet produced for the UK armed forces. The air forces of the four countries have ordered a total of 620 Eurofighters (UK 232, Germany 180, Italy 121, and Spain 87).

Eurofighter is a fifth-generation combat aircraft with fully digital, integrated aircraft, avionics and weapon systems. Eurofighter is designed to perform at least five air missions: air superiority, air interdiction, Suppression of Enemy Air Defence (SEAD), Close Air Support (CAS) and Maritime Attack. It may in time be modified to fulfil naval aircraft carrier roles. The aircraft is designed to carry 6 x medium-range and 2 x short-range air-to-air missiles. The aircraft has 13 x store stations and an internal gun fitted on the starboard side. A range of air-to-ground weapons can be carried, including the new Storm Shadow CASOM, Brimstone anti-armour weapon, and the future Precision Guided Bomb (PGB). No modifications will be necessary to carry "smart" weapons and 3 stations can carry external fuel pods. The Captor radar is a collaboration European design. Other sensors include the Infra-Red Search and Track (IRST) system. The Defensive Aids Sub-System (DASS) equipment is carried in 2 x wing pods that are an integral part of the wing. The datalink is provided by the Multiple Image Data System (MIDS). The aircraft will be able to operate from a 500 metre strip.

Future Joint Combat Aircraft
The Future Joint Combat Aircraft will replace the Harrier in RAF and RN service, and be based on the US Joint Strike Fighter (JSF). The estimated in-service date is 2012 to coincide with the first of the new aircraft carriers (CVF) entering service. The US DoD placed a contract for the Lockheed Martin F-35 in October 2001. The JSF/FJCA programme is driven by the US requirement for up to 3,000 aircraft. BAe Systems and Rolls-Royce form the principal partners of Lockheed Martin, along with the US company Northrop Grumman and General Electric. Other international parties to the programme include Italy, Netherlands, Turkey, Canada, Denmark and Norway. The UK is to select either the Short Take Off Vertical Landing (STOVL) or Carrier Variant (CV) version of JSF, or possibly both. The likely date for a production contract is 2005/06. The joint RAF/RN requirement for the FJCA is 150. The projected UK procurement cost is some £4.3bn including £2bn for R&D and £2.3bn for production. Possible total production of the JSF is

estimated to be some 5,000 aircraft, including export models.

The F-35B for the UK Royal Air Force, Royal Navy, and US Marine Corps employs a short takeoff/vertical-landing (STOVL) capability. This takeoff and landing operation succeeds through a very innovative technology known as the shaft-driven lift fan propulsion system. Besides the propulsion system, the STOVL variant differs only slightly from the USAir Force F-35A variant to meet the F-16 replacement requirement. It carries a refuelling probe fitted into the right side of the forward fuselage, rather than the US Air Force standard refuelling receptacle normally located on the top surface of the aircraft. The STOVL variant carries no internal gun, though an external gun is an option. It shares all the electronic equipment of the US Air Force variant, and virtually an identical cockpit layout except for a lever to switch between wingborne and jetborne modes. Performance and stealth characteristics are also very similar. The STOVL variant, designed to replace the AV-8B Harrier, has more than twice the range on internal fuel, operates at supersonic conditions, and houses internal weapons. The third JSF variant is the F-35C. US Navy carrier operations account for most of the differences between the F-35C and the other JSF variants. The aircraft has larger wing and tail control surfaces to better manage low-speed carrier approaches. The F-35C, along with the F-35B, is a candidate for the new RN future aircraft carrier (CVF).

Future Offensive Air System (FOAS)

The Future Offensive Air System (FOAS) is planned to fill the Deep Strike capability gap when the Tornado GR4 reaches the end of its service life around 2018. Studies to define the kind of weapon system FOAS will be - derivative aircraft, new-design stealth bomber, cruise missile or unmanned combat air vehicle - are still underway. This programme was launched in December 1996 when £35 million was assigned for allocation to feasibility studies of the broadest possible range of options. The FOAS programme currently consists of 'System of Systems' concept studies and technology demonstration projects. Candidate system components could include manned aircraft; uninhabited air vehicles; cruise missiles; and a command, control, communications, computers, and intelligence (C4I) system. The programme is expected to move from the Concept phase into the Assessment phase in 2003.

A complete range of technologies including fly-by-light, stealth, virtual reality cockpits and integrated modular avionics is being considered. Over 100 companies are working on FOAS feasibility. A firm requirement for the aircraft will be issued in 2008. The current in service date is 2018, although this is expected to slip until 2020. If a crewed aircraft is selected, the RAF requirement would be for approximately 200.

Sentry AEW1

In service with:

8 Squadron	3 x Sentry AEW1	Waddington
23 Squadron	3 x Sentry AEW1	Waddington

Crew; 5 x Flight Crew and 12/13 x Mission Crew; Length 46.61m; Wingspan 44.42m; Height 12.73m; All Up Operational Weight 147,400kg; Max Speed 853 k/ph (530 mph); Patrol Endurance 6 hrs (can be enhanced by AAR); (Ferry Range 3,200 km; Engines 4 x CFM-56-2A-3; Armament provision for self-defence air-to-air missiles.

Deliveries of the Sentry AEW1, commenced in March 1991 and delivery of all seven airframes was complete in early 1992. These seven aircraft are of the same type as the 18 delivered to the multi national NATO early warning force between 1982/1985. Powered by four CFM 56-2A-3 engines, the Sentry is designed to cruise at 29,000 feet whilst detecting

air and surface contacts with its AN/APY-2 surveillance radar. Information is then transmitted back to interceptor aircraft and, ground air-and-ship-based units using a wide variety of digital datalinks. All are equipped with the Joint Tactical Information Distribution System (JTIDS) and a 665,360 word memory secure communication system. Between1998-2000, RAF Sentry aircraft were upgraded under the Radar System Improvement Programme (RSIP) costing some £120 million. New Global Positioning System navigation equipment was also installed. Most recently, Sentry AEW1 aircraft were deployed in support of Operation Telic during the 2003 Iraq War, and for Operation Oracle in support of ISAF in Afghanistan from 2002.

Nimrod
In service with:

120 Squadron	6 x Nimrod MR2	Kinloss
201 Squadron	6 x Nimrod MR2	Kinloss
206 Squadron	5 x Nimrod MR2	Kinloss
42 (Reserve) Squadron	3 x Nimrod MR2	Kinloss

Note: This group of units is known as the Kinloss Air Wing. We are reasonably certain that there are approximately 21 aircraft in this group at any one time. Aircraft are shown as being allocated to squadrons for ease of accounting - real numbers may change almost daily.

51 Squadron	3 x Nimrod R1	Waddington

Nimrod MR2: Crew 13; Length 38.63m; Span 35m; Height 9.08m; Max Speed 575mph/926km; Max All Up Weight 87,090 kg; Endurance 10-12 hrs; Operating range 3,800 miles, 6,080 km; Ferry Range 9,265 km; ; Engines 4 x Rolls Royce Spey RB 168-20 Mark 250 Turbofans; Armament: Sidewinder AIM-9, Harpoon, 9 x Mark 46 or Stingray Torpedoes, bombs.

Nimrod is a development of the basic Comet No 4C airframe that dates from the late 1940's. Both the current variants are descended from the original Nimrod MR Mark 1 version (first flight May 1967) upgraded during the 1980s. The first is the MR Mark 2P, which has been developed for long-range maritime patrol. The Nimrod MR2 carries out 3 main roles; Anti-Submarine Warfare (ASW), Anti-Surface Unit Warfare (ASUW) and

Search and Rescue (SAR). Its long ferry range enables the crew to monitor maritime areas far to the north of Iceland and up to 4,000 km out into the Western Atlantic. With AAR (Air-to-Air Refuelling), its range and endurance is greatly extended. The MR Mark 2 is a very lethal submarine killer carrying the most up to date sensors and data processing equipment linked to the weapon systems. In addition to weapons and sonar-buoys, a searchlight mounted in the starboard wing pod can be used for search and rescue (SAR) operations. Crew members comprise 2 Pilots and a flight engineer operate the flight deck, 2 Navigators, an Air Electronics Officer (AEO), the sonobuoy sensor team of 3 Air Electronic Operators and 4 Air Electronic Operators to manage a wide range of avionics and weapon systems.

The second version is the R Mark 1, an aircraft specially fitted out for the gathering of electronic intelligence and only three are known to be in service. This is a highly secret aircraft that has been in RAF service since 1971 and about which little is known except that it has been spotted on patrol over the Baltic Sea. The Nimrod R1s are externally distinguishable from the maritime reconnaissance version by the absence of the magnetic anomaly detection tail booms and a distinctive pod on the leading edge of the port wing. In-flight refuelling probes were added in 1982.

Under a £2.2 billion contract in July 1996, the Nimrod upgrade programme involved 21 Nimrod MR2 aircraft to Maritime Reconnaissance Attack 4 (MRA4) standard, together with training and integrated logistics support packages. The programme would involve the total replacement of the aircraft's systems and over 80 % of its airframe, resulting in the RAF receiving back practically a new aircraft. There has been a substantial programme cost escalation (estimated programme cost £2.8bn by 2002) and a two-year slippage. Numbers of MR4 to be procured have reduced from 21 to 18 as a result of cost escalation. The consequence of the Nimrod MRA4 in service date slip is that the Nimrod MR2 will remain in service until mid-2008. The operational impact of the slippage will be partly mitigated by existing measures to introduce upgrades to some Nimrod MR2 systems, notably Replacement Acoustic Processors (RAP), navigation systems, datalinks and other communications to address inter-operability issues. In-service date of the Nimrod MRA4 is planned for 2005.

Nimrod MRA4 will have a reach extending to some 6,000 miles, compared to the current MR2 capability of some 3800 miles. Rolls BR710 engines replace RR Spey engines. Other capability improvements over MR2 include increased time on station, a major improvement in overall sensor performance and weapon carrying capability. The new digital, integrated mission system features the Searchwater 2000 radar, UYS503/AQS970 sonar, DASS 2000 ECM, and EL/L8300UK ESM. The crew complement has reduced by 25%.

ASTOR

The Airborne Stand-off Radar (ASTOR) is a new British capability for operations over and around the battlefield. It is to form the UK equivalent to the US E-8 Joint Surveillance Target Attack Radar System (JSTARS). ASTOR is to provide a long range all weather theatre surveillance and target acquisition system capable of detecting moving, fixed and static targets. It is designed to meet a joint Army and RAF requirement. The production contract was signed in December 1999 for the supply of 5 air-platforms, 8 ground stations, and contractor logistic support. The principal elements of ASTOR are the Bombardier Global Express aircraft and the Raytheon ASARS-2 side looking airborne radar used on the U-2. The radar operates at high altitude and in all weathers to provide high resolution. ASARS-2 has been reported to provide images of the battlefield at ranges of 160 km, at altitudes up to 47,000 feet. High speed data links transfer the data from aircraft to ground stations in near real time. The system has directional and broadcast data links which are interoperable with existing US U-2Rs, JSTARS and command and control networks. ASTOR has a target in-service date of September 2005. Full operational capability should be achieved by 2008. The main ASTOR operating centre will be based at RAF Waddington in the UK. The projected procurement cost is just over £1bn.

Crew 2 aircrew, 3 mission systems operators; Length 30.3m; Height 7.57m; Wingspan 28.6m; Empty Weight 22,817kg; Max Take-Off Weight 43,094kg; Range 6,500nm/12,000km; Endurance 14 plus hours; Operating altitude 15,000m; Engines 2 x RR BR710; Systems ASARS-2 radar derivative; narrowband datalink subsystem (NDLS), wideband data link based on Common Data Link (CDL); Defensive Aids Subsystem (DASS) developed for the Nimrod MRA4, including missile warning system, radar warning receiver, towed radar decoy and chaff and flare dispensers.

Hawk

In service with:

100 Squadron	16 x Hawk T1/1A	Leeming (target towing)
No 4 Flying Training School (4 FTS)	69 x Hawk T1/1A	Valley
Red Arrows	10 x Hawk T1A	Scampton

Crew 2; Span 9.39m; Length 11.96m; Height 3.99m; Weight Empty 3,647kg; Max Take Off Weight 8,569kg; Max Speed 622 mph/1,000 kph at sea level; Combat Radius 556 km (345 miles); Engine 1 x Rolls Royce/Turbomeca Adour Mk 151 turbofan; Armament: (Hawk T1) 1 x 30mm Aden cannon pack and up to 5,600lb (2,540kg) of under-wing stores for rockets, bombs and missiles, (Hawk T1A) - in addition has inboard pylons for Sidewinder AIM-9 AAM.

The Hawk first flew in 1974, and entered RAF service two years later both as an advanced flying trainer and a weapons training aircraft. It has an economical Adour engine - an un-reheated version of the same turbofan powering the Jaguar. Hawks are used to teach

operational tactics such as air-to-air and air-to-ground firing, air combat and low-level operating procedures to pilots destined for the "fast-jet" squadrons. As a weapons trainer, the Hawk is armed with an Aden cannon carried beneath the fuselage, and rocket pods or practice bombs can be fitted to under-wing pylons. To fulfil its mobilisation role as a fighter aircraft, the Hawk carries a 30 mm Aden cannon and two Sidewinder air-to-air missiles, and is designated T1A (89 delivered to the RAF). The Hawk is a strong and rugged aircraft designed to cut training and maintenance costs. The aircraft has a long fatigue life to ensure a service career throughout the 1990s and beyond.

During January 1998, the MoD announced plans to extend the fatigue life of the Hawk T1/1A in RAF service. Up to 80 Hawks will be involved in a 'return-to-works' (RTW) programme that will see their centre and rear fuselage sections being replaced with new production units from the Hawk Series 60 production line. RAF Hawks have already received re-lifed wings and tail planes. The programme began in September 1999 and 2 aircraft per month were to be completed until the end of 2003. The first refurbished aircraft was delivered back to the RAF in May 2000. By June 2002, the UK's Defence Aviation Repair Agency (DARA) at St Athan in South Wales had delivered 55 of the 80 aircraft involved in the Royal Air Force (RAF) Hawk T.1/1A fuselage replacement programme (FRP). This programme will extend the Hawk's service life to 2010.

The Hawk has been widely exported as a trainer and single-pilot fighter ground attack aircraft - in numerical terms, by far the most successful British export programme since the Hawker Hunter. By 2003, over 780 Hawks had been exported or ordered, including 189 for the US Navy under licence arrangements, in addition to the 176 delivered to the RAF. For the future, RAF may buy a quantity of new-build Hawk trainers with modern "glass cockpits" and more powerful engines, and upgrade a quantity of existing Hawks to the same standard.

Tucano

In service with:
No 1 Flying Training School (1 FTS)
67 x Tucano T1
Linton (includes Central Flying School at Topcliffe)

Crew 2; Length 9.86m; Height 3.40m; Span 11.28m; Max Speed 507 kph/315mph; Service Ceiling 8,750m; Range 1,916kms; Engine 1,100shp Garrett TPE-331 turboprop.
Originally designed by the Brazilian aerospace company Embraer, the Tucano was selected

in 1985 to replace the Jet Provost as the RAF basic trainer. The development and production contract was awarded to Shorts of Belfast under licence. The first squadron aircraft was delivered in June 1988. Student training on the aircraft started at RAF Church Fenton in December 1989. The RAF version of the Tucano, designated the Tucano T1, has been modified in many ways from the basic Embraer 312. A Garrett TPE 331 engine is fitted in place of the original PT6 and represents a 50% power increase. Fatigue life has been extended from 8,000 to 12,000 hours by fitting strengthened wings and landing gear, a ventral air brake has been added, plus a new canopy which is bird strike resistant up to 270 knots. The original RAF purchase was for 126 x Tucano.

C-130 Hercules

In service with:

24 Squadron	11 x Hercules C1/C3/C4/C5	Lyneham
30 Squadron	11 x Hercules C1/C3/C4/C5	Lyneham
47 Squadron	11 x Hercules C1/C3/C4/C5	Lyneham
70 Squadron	11 x Hercules C1/C3/C4/C5	Lyneham
57 (Reserve Sqn)	5 x Hercules C3/C4/C5	Lyneham

The LTW (Lyneham Transport Wing) appears to have a total of 49 aircraft (including 5 in reserve). The squadron totals are given as a guide to what we believe are the average aircraft figures per squadron and the OCU at any one time.

Hercules C1/C3

Crew 5/6; Capacity 92 troops or 64 paratroops or 74 medical litters; Max freight capacity 43,399lb/19,685kg; Length C1 29.79m C3 34.69m; Span 40.41m; Height 11.66m; Weight Empty 34,287kg; Max All-up Weight 45,093kg; Max speed 374mph/602 kph; Service Ceiling 13,075m; Engines 4 x Allison T-56A-15 turboprops.

The C-130 Hercules C1 is the workhorse of the RAF transport fleet. Over the years it has proved to be a versatile and rugged aircraft, primarily intended for tactical operations including troop carrying, paratrooping, supply dropping and aeromedical duties. The Hercules can operate from short unprepared airstrips, but also possesses the endurance to mount-long range strategic lifts if required. The aircraft is a derivative of the C-130E used by the United States Air Force, but is fitted with British Avionic equipment, a roller-conveyor system for heavy air-drops and with more powerful engines. The crew of five includes, pilot, co-pilot, navigator, air engineer and air loadmaster.

As a troop carrier, the Hercules can carry 92 fully armed men, while for airborne operations 64 paratroops can be dispatched in two simultaneous "sticks" through the fuselage side doors. Alternatively, 40 paratroops can jump from the rear loading ramp. As an air ambulance the aircraft can accommodate 74 stretchers. Freight loads that can be parachuted from the aircraft include: 16 x 1 ton containers or 4 x 8,000 pound platforms or 2 x 16,000 pound platforms or 1 x platform of 30,000 pounds plus. Amongst the many combinations of military loads that can be carried in an air-landed operation are: 3 x Ferret scout cars plus 30 passengers or 2 x Land Rovers and 30 passengers or 2 x Gazelle helicopters.

Of the original 66 C1 aircraft, some 31 have been given a fuselage stretch producing the Mark C3. The C3 "stretched version" provides an additional 37% more cargo space. Refuelling probes have been fitted above the cockpit of both variants and some have received radar warning pods under the wing tips. One aircraft, designated Mark W2, is a special weather version and is located at the DRA Farnborough.

Hercules C-130J C4/C5

The RAF has replaced some of its Hercules C1/C3 aircraft with second-generation C-130Js on a one-for-one basis. Twenty-five Hercules C4 and C5 aircraft were ordered in December 94, and the first entered service in 2000 – two years behind schedule. Deliveries were completed by 2003 at a total cost of just over £1bn. The C4 is the same size as the older Hercules C3 which features a fuselage lengthened by 4.57 m (15ft 0 in) than the original C1. The Hercules C5 is the new equivalent of the shorter model. With a flight deck crew of two plus one loadmaster, the C-130J can carry up to 128 infantry, 92 paratroops, 8 pallets or 24 CDS bundles. The Hercules C4/C5s have new Allison turboprop engines, R391 6-bladed composite propellers and a Full Authority Digital Engine Control (FADEC). This propulsion system increases take-off thrust by 29% and is 15% more efficient. Consequently, there is no longer a requirement for the external tanks to be fitted. An entirely revised 'glass' flight deck with head-up displays (HUD) and 4 multi-function displays (MFD) replacing many of the dials of the original aircraft. These displays are compatible with night-vision goggles (NVG).

C-17 Globemaster

In service with:

99 Squadron	4 x C-17A	Brize Norton

Crew of 2 pilots and 1 loadmaster. Capacity Maximum of 154 troops. Normal load of 102 fully-equipped troops, up to 172,200lb (78,108 kg) on up to 18 standard freight pallets or 48 litters in the medevac role; Wingspan 50.29m; Length overall 53.04m; Height overall 16.8 m; Loadable width 5.5m; Cruising speed 648 kph (403 mph); Range (max payload) 4,444 km (2,400 miles); Engines 4 x Pratt and Whitney F117 turbofans.

The C-17 meets an RAF requirement for an interim strategic airlift capability pending the introduction of Future Transport Aircraft (A400). The decision to lease four C-17 aircraft for some £771m from Boeing was taken in 2000, and the aircraft entered service in 2001. The lease is for seven years, with the option of extending for up to a further two years. The C-17 fleet is capable of the deployment of 1,400 tonnes of freight over 3,200 miles in a 7 day period. The aircraft is able to carry one Challenger 2 MBT, or a range of smaller armoured vehicles, or up to three WAH-64 Apache aircraft at one time. Over 150 troops can be carried. Inflight refuelling increases the aircraft range.

No 99 Sqn has some 158 flight crew and ground staff.

A400

The MoD committed to 25 x Airbus A400M in 2000 to meet the Future Transport Aircraft (FTA) requirement for an air lift capability to replace the remaining Hercules C-130K C1/C3 fleet. The A400 is a collaborative programme involving eight European nations (Germany, France, Turkey, Spain, Portugal, Belgium, Luxembourg and United Kingdom), procuring a total of 196 aircraft. The expected UK cost is some £2.4 billion for 25 aircraft. The projected in-service date has slipped from 2007 to 2010.

The FTA requirement is to provide tactical and strategic mobility to all three Services. The capabilities required of FTA include: the ability to operate from well established airfields and semi-prepared rough landing areas in extreme climates and all weather by day and night; to carry a variety of vehicles and other equipment, freight, and troops over extended ranges; to be capable of air dropping paratroops and equipment; and to be capable of being unloaded with the minimum of ground handling equipment. The FTA should also meet a requirement for an airlift capability to move large single items such as attack helicopters and some Royal Engineers' equipment. In May 2003, the European consortium engine TP400-D6 was selected for the A400M military transport aircraft over the rival Pratt & Whitney proposal. The Europrop International Consortium comprises Rolls-Royce (UK), SNECMA (France), MTU (Germany), and ITP Spain.

The most commonly quoted argument in favour of the A400M over the C-130J is that this aircraft could carry a 25 ton payload over a distance of 4,000 km. Thus, it is argued that a fleet of 40 x FLA could carry a UK Brigade to the Gulf within 11.5 days, as opposed to the 28.5 days required to make a similar deployment with 40 x C-130s. In any event, the RAF seems likely to retain its C-17s, and to operate a mixed transport fleet comprising the C-130J, A-400 and C-17.

Air-to-Air Refuelling Aircraft
The RAF Air-to-Air Refuelling fleet mainly comprises 7 x the single-role VC10 K3 and K4 aircraft flown by No 101 Squadron based at RAF Brize Norton. These are supported by 10 x VC10 C1K (10 Sqn, Brize Norton) and 8 x Tristar K1/KC1/C2/C2A (216 Sqn, Brize Norton) aircraft used for both transport and AAR. The RAF AAR capability is the most specialised in NATO, and has been extensively deployed in recent allied coalition wars in Kosovo, Afghanistan, and Iraq.

Future Strategic Tanker Aircraft
The Future Strategic Tanker Aircraft (FSTA) is planned to replace the air-to-air refuelling (AAR) and some elements of air transport (AT) capability currently provided by the RAF's fleet of VC10 and TriStar aircraft. AAR is a key military capability that provides force multiplication and operational range enhancement for front line aircraft across a range of defence roles and military tasks. The projected in-service date is 2008-2010. The projected life cycle cost of the programme under Public Finance Initiative (PFI) arrangements is some £13.1bn.

Chinook
In service with:

7 Squadron	5 x Chinook HC2	Odiham
18 Squadron	18 x Chinook HC2	Odiham
27 Squadron	10 x Chinook HC2	Odiham
78 Squadron	1 x Chinook HC2	Mount Pleasant

All the above aircraft are under the control of the Joint Helicopter Command (JHC).

Crew 3/4; Fuselage Length 15.54m; Width 3.78m; Height 5.68m; Weight (empty) 10,814kg; Internal Payload 8,164kg; Rotor Diameter 18.29m; Cruising Speed 158mph/270 kph; Service Ceiling 4,270m; Mission Radius (with internal and external load of 20,000kgs including fuel and crew) 55kms; Rear Loading Ramp Height 1.98m; Rear Loading Ramp Width 2.31m; Engines 2 x Avco Lycoming T55-712 turboshafts.

The Chinook is a tandem-rotored, twin-engined medium-lift helicopter. The first Chinooks entered service with the RAF in 1982. It has a crew of four (pilot, navigator and two crewmen) and is capable of carrying 54 fully equipped troops or a variety of heavy loads up to approximately 10 tons. The triple hook system allows greater flexibility in load carrying and enables some loads to be carried faster and with greater stability. In the ferry configuration with internally mounted fuel tanks, the Chinook's range is over 1,600 km (1,000 miles). In the medical evacuation role the aircraft can carry 24 stretchers. RAF Chinook aircraft were upgraded to the HC2 standard between 1993-1996 for some £145m. The HC2 upgrade modified the RAF Chinooks to the US CH-47D standard. New equipment included infrared jammers, missile approach warning indicators, chaff and flare dispensers, a long-range fuel system, and machine gun mountings. In 1995, the UK MoD purchased a further 14 x Chinooks (6 x HC2 and 8 x HC3) for £240 million. In June 2000, the UK MoD formally refused to accept delivery of the first of eight Chinook Mk3 helicopters configured for special operations. Current indications are that the first HC3 aircraft may enter service in 2003.

Puma

In service with:

33 Squadron	15 x Puma HC1	Benson
72 Squadron	5 x Puma HC1	Aldergrove
230 Squadron	13 x Puma HC1	Aldergrove

All the above aircraft are under the control of the Joint Helicopter Command (JHC).

Crew 2 or 3; Capacity up to 20 troops or 7,055lb underslung; Fuselage Length 14.06m Rotors Turning 18.15m; Width 3.50m; Height 4.38m; Weight (empty) 3,615kg; Maximum Take Off Weight 7,400kg; Max Speed 163mph/261 kph; Service Ceiling 4,800m; Range 550kms; 2 x Turbomeca Turmo 111C4 turbines.

Following the retirement of the last Wessex in 2003, the Puma is the oldest helicopter in RAF service. The "package deal" between the UK and France on helicopter collaboration dates back to February 1967. The programme covered the development of three helicopter types - the Puma, Gazelle and Lynx. Production of the aircraft was shared between the two countries, the UK making about 20% by value of the airframe, slightly less for the engine, as well as assembling the aircraft procured for the RAF. Deliveries of the RAF Pumas started in 1971. Capable of many operational roles, Puma can carry 16 fully equipped troops, or 20 at light scales. In the casualty evacuation role (CASEVAC), 6 stretchers and 6 sitting cases can be carried. Underslung loads of up to 3,200 kg can be transported over short distances and an infantry battalion can be moved using 34 Puma lifts. 41 x RAF Puma helicopters received an avionics upgrade between 1994-1998.

Sea King HAR3

In service with:

22 Squadron	Headquarters	RMB Chivenor
A Flight	3 x Sea King HAR3	RMB Chivenor
B Flight	3 x Sea King HAR3	Wattisham
C Flight	2 x Sea King HAR3	Valley
202 Squadron	Headquarters	Boulmer
A Flight	3 x Sea King HAR3	Boulmer
D Flight	3 x Sea King HAR 3	Lossiemouth
E Flight	2 x Sea King HAR 3	Leconfield
203 (Reserve) Squadron	3 x Sea King HAR3	St Mawgan
78 Squadron	2 x Sea King HAR3	Mount Pleasant

Note: Both 22 and 202 Squadrons have 8 x Sea King HAR3. Numbers of aircraft have been allocated to flights for rounding purposes.

Crew 4; Length 17.01m; Height 4.72m; Rotor Diameter 18.9m; Weight (empty) 6,201kg; Cruising Speed 129mph/208 kph; Range 1,230kms; Engine 2 x Rolls Royce Gnome H1400-1 turboshafts.

The Westland Sea King HAR3 Search and Rescue helicopter entered RAF service in 1978. The aircraft is fitted with advanced all-weather search and navigation equipment, as well as autopilot and onboard computer to assist positioning and hovering at night or in bad weather. In addition to four crew members, the HAR3 can carry up to six stretchers, or 18 survivors. Under normal conditions, expect the HAR3 to have an operational radius of approximately 448 km (280 miles). The Sea King HAR3 replaced the Wessex HC2 in the SAR role in 1996. An early 1990s MoD report concluded that a total of 25 Sea Kings was required to ensure that SAR duties were carried out effectively and an announcement was made in 1992 of an order for 6 more HAR3, to bring the total up to the required 25. Of these 25 aircraft, 16 are allocated for SAR duties in the UK, 2 in the Falkland Islands, 3 for conversion training and the remaining 3 form an engineering and operational pool.

EH101 Merlin Mk3

In service with:

28 Squadron	22 x Merlin Mk 3	Benson (from 2001)

All the above aircraft are under the control of the Joint Helicopter Command (JHC).

Crew 4; Capacity up to 24 combat-equipped troops, or 16 stretchers and a medical team, or 4 tonnes of cargo (2.5 tonnes as an underslung load). Length 22.81m; Rotor Diameter 18.59m; Max Speed 309k/ph (192mph); Engine 3 x Rolls Royce/Turbomeca RTM 322 turboshafts.

The EH101 Merlin Mk 3 is the newest RAF helicopter. The RAF ordered 22 EH101 (Merlin) support helicopters for £755m in March 1995. Merlin is a direct replacement for the Westland Wessex, and it operates alongside the Puma and Chinook in the medium-lift role. Its ability to carry troops, artillery pieces, light vehicles and bulk loads, means that the aircraft is ideal for use with the UK Army's 16 Air Assault Brigade. Deliveries took place between 2000-2002.

The aircraft can carry a maximum load of 24-30 troops with support weapons. The maximum payload is 4,000 kg and Merlin has a maximum range of 1,000 km, which can be extended by external tanks or by air-to-air refuelling. The Merlin Mk 3 has sophisticated defensive aids, and the aircraft is designed to operate in extreme conditions and is corrosion-proofed for maritime operations. All weather, day/night precision delivery is possible because of GPS navigation, a forward-looking infrared sensor and night vision goggle compatibility. In the longer term, the aircraft could be fitted with a nose turret mounting a .50 calibre machine gun.

RAF Weapons
Air to Air Missiles

Sidewinder AIM-9L

Diameter 0.13m; Span 0.63m; Length 2.85m; Total Weight 85.3 kg; Warhead Weight 9.5 kg; Propulsion Solid fuel rocket; Speed Mach 2.5; Range 10-18km; Guidance Solid-state, infrared homing system.

The *Sidewinder* missile, which is carried by all the RAF combat aircraft as well as the Hawk and Nimrod MR2, is an infrared weapon which homes onto the heat emitted by a hostile aircraft's engines. *Sidewinder* can operate independently of the aircraft's radar, and provides the air defence aircraft with an alternative method of attacking targets at shorter ranges. Sidewinder has an excellent dogfight capability.

Sky Flash

Length 3.66 m; Diameter 0.203 m; Span 1.02 m; Weight 192 kg; Warhead Weight 30 kg; Range 50kms; Marconi monopulse semi-active radar homing system.

Sky Flash is an advanced radar-guided air-to-air missile based on the US-designed AIM-7 *Sparrow* which was taken into service in 1977, but with improved guidance and fusing systems. Designed to operate in severe electronic counter-measure conditions, it has an all-weather high/low altitude attack capability. *Sky Flash* is in service on F3 air defence variant of the Tornado. It was the RAF's major air defence weapon before the acquisition of AMRAAM.

AMRAAM

Length 3.66 metres; Diameter 0.18m; Span 0.48m; Weight 161.4kg/336 lbs; Cruising speed Mach 4; Range approx 30 miles; Guidance System Active radar terminal/inertial midcourse

AMRAAM (Advanced medium-range air-to-air missile) is a US air fighting weapon that matches the fire-and-forget capability of the ASRAAM, but with greater range. There is increased immunity over electronic countermeasures and a low-smoke, high-impulse rocket motor to reduce the probability of an enemy sighting the missile. This system is in use by Tornado F3, and will be used by the Eurofighter Typhoon. In addition, trials were underway during late 2000 with AMRAAM fitted to Jaguar GR1B. AMRAAM has been in service with the Fleet Air Arm since 1995, and the initial purchase was believed to be some 210 missiles worth some £50m. For Eurofighter, the current cost for AMRAAM procurement is £214m with deliveries planned to begin from mid 2005.

ASRAAM

Length 2.9 metres; Diameter 0.17m; Weight 88kg; Cruising speed Mach 3.5+; Range over 10 miles.

Guidance Imaging IR 128x128 element focal plane array.

ASRAAM is a fast, highly agile, fire and forget IR missile for short range air-to-air combat, able to counter intermittent target obscurity in cloud and severe infrared countermeasures. It is carried on Tornado F3, Harrier GR7/9, and Sea Harrier FA2, and the Eurofighter Typhoon. It will replace Sidewinder AIM-9L albeit that this will remain in service in parallel for a period. The programme cost some £857m. There were considerable technical problems and delays.

Meteor (BVRAAM)

The Beyond Visual Range Air-to-Air Missile (BVRAAM) (also known as *Meteor*) should provide Eurofighter with the capability to combat projected air-to-air threats and sustain air superiority throughout the life of the aircraft. The weapon is required to operate in all weather conditions and will complement the Eurofighter Advanced Short Range Air-to-Air Missile (ASRAAM). Until *Meteor* enters service, Eurofighter will be armed with the Advanced Medium Range Air-to-Air Missile (AMRAAM). *Meteor* is a collaborative programme with five partner nations; Germany, Spain and Italy (for Eurofighter), Sweden (for JAS 39 Gripen) and France (for Rafale). The full development and initial production contract worth £1.2bn was signed by the parties in December 2002. In-service date has slipped from 2005 to 2008, and may slip further. Projected RAF cost overall is some £1.4bn.

Air-launched Air-to-Ground Cruisemissile

Storm Shadow

Length 5.1m; Diameter 0.48m; Span 2.84m; Weight 1,300kg; Range Estimate 350km; Propulsion TRI 60-30 Turbofan; Guidance Navigation using TERrain PROfile Matching system as well as GPS, Terminal guidance using imaging infrared sensor, Autonomous target recognition algorithms, BROACH warhead.

Storm Shadow (also known as Conventionally-Armed Stand-Off Missile or CASOM) is a long-range, air-launched, stand-off attack missile that will allow the RAF to attack high-priority targets deep inside enemy territory without exposing the launch aircraft to high-intensity enemy air defences. The missile is the BAe version (with some UK enhancements) of the French Matra APACHE/SCALP missile and entered service in late 2002. It will be fitted to Tornado GR4, Harrier GR7 and the Eurofighter Typhoon. The RAF is believed to have purchased an initial batch of 500 missiles. The programme cost is some £980m. Storm Shadow was deployed operationally and fired during the 2003 Iraq War.

Air-to-Ground Anti-Radiation Missile

ALARM

Length 4.3m: Diameter 0.22m: Span 0.72m: Weight 265kg: Propellant 1 x Royal Ordnance Nuthatch solid fuel two-stage rocket: Guidance Passive Radar Homing/Strap-down INS; Range 93km.

ALARM stands for Air-Launched Anti-Radiation Missile and this type was introduced into

RAF Service in the early 1990s. The missile is launched at low level near the suspected site of an enemy radar and, after launch, rapidly climbs to about 12,000 m. At this height, a small parachute opens and the missile descends earthwards while the on-board radar searches the broadband for emissions from enemy radar. Once a target has been identified, the motor is re-ignited and the missile makes a supersonic dive onto the target. The total RAF buy in the first manufacturing run was believed to be some 750 missiles. Since its original entry into service, radars have become increasingly more sophisticated in their ability to avoid detection and attack by anti-radiation weapons such as ALARM. As a result, the missile has upgraded and the improved capability ALARM is now entering service with the Tornado GR4 and (for the 2003 Iraq War) F-3 squadrons.

Area Weapons

BL 755 Cluster Bomb
Length 2.45m: Diameter 0.41m: Weight 277kg: Warhead 147 bomblets.

The BL 755 is a system that was designed to cope with some of the very large area targets that might have been encountered on the Soviet Central Front, especially large armoured formations of Regimental strength (90+ tanks) or more. The weapon can be carried by Tornado GR1, Harrier, Jaguar, Buccaneer and Phantom and consists of a large container which is divided into seven compartments. Each of these compartments contains 21 bomblets making a total of 147 bomblets in all. After the bomb has been released from the aircraft, the 147 bomblets are ejected and fall to the ground covering a wide area. As each individual bomblet hits a target, a HEAT charge is detonated which can fire a large slug of molten metal through up to 250 mm of armour. In addition, the casing of the bomblet disintegrates and hundreds of fragments of shrapnel are dispersed over a wide area, with resultant damage to personnel and soft- skinned vehicles. The BL 755 can be released at very low altitude and this is essential if pilots are to survive in high-density SAM conditions. Aircraft will only have the chance to make one pass over the target before the defences are alerted, and for a pilot to make a second pass to ensure accuracy would be suicidal.

Brimstone
Length 1.81m; Diameter 0.18m; Weight 49 kg; Propulsion cast double-base propellant rocket motor; Guidance inertial guidance + seeker determination to target acquisition, then seeker control; Cruising speed boost to supersonic; Range 8 km.

The Advanced Air-launched Anti-Armour Weapon (AAAW), known as Brimstone, is an area weapon to attack enemy armoured forces as early and as far forward as possible. It replaces the BL 755 cluster bomb in the anti-armour role, and will be carried by Tornado GR4/4a, Harrier GR7/9 and Eurofighter Typhoon. These fixed-wing aircraft will compliment the capability provided by the Apache AH64-D, which is armed with the Hellfire anti-armour weapon. Brimstone operates automatically after launch, which helps reduce the hazard to the attacking aircraft from enemy fire. Development and procurement of Brimstone has cost the RAF some £822m since 1996, and the weapon was to enter service in late 2002.

Air-to-Ground Anti-Armour Missiles
Maverick

Length 2.6m; Diameter 0.31m: Span 0.71m; Weight 286kg; Range 27km; IR Guidance (Laser and EO also available).

The Maverick missile, which is used by the Harrier GR7 as an anti-armour weapon, entered RAF service in early 2001 and is one of the latest additions to the RAF inventory. The missile has a number of seeker heads available for use in a variety of operational scenarios. The RAF bought the Maverick with an Imaging Infrared (IIR) seeker head, which allows the missile to be employed both by day and by night and in poor atmospheric conditions. The Maverick missile will complement the Brimstone missile that is entering RAF service with a millimetric wave all-weather seeker head. The RAF version of the Maverick is a fire-and-forget weapon, which sends a picture from the IIR seeker head to the Multi-Purpose Colour Display (MPCD) in the cockpit. The pilot identifies the target, locks the missile onto it and fires the missile once the target is in range. The Maverick will then home onto the target while the delivery aircraft carries out escape manoeuvres, thus minimising its exposure to enemy air defence systems.

Precision Guided Munitions

Paveway II
Length 3.7m; Weight 520kg; Laser Guidance

Paveway II is the standard 1,000 lb (454 kg) general purpose bomb for use against moderately well-protected targets. Paveway II can be fitted with a laser guidance kit, and the bomb can be used in the freefall or retarded Mode. Used on the Tornado GR4, Harrier, Jaguar, and Eurofighter Typhoon.

Paveway III
Length 4.4m; Weight 1,130kg; Laser Guidance

Paveway III is a 2,000 lb (908 kg) laser guided bomb (LGB) for use against well-protected targets. The bomb is guided to its target by a TIALD (Thermal Imaging and Laser Designation) pod that is carried on the aircraft or by a ground based observer using a target designator. The weapon can be carried on the Tornado GR4, Jaguar, Harrier, and Eurofighter Typhoon. Unlike the Paveway II, this weapon uses proportional guidance - the control canards on the front of the bomb move only the exact amount necessary to guide the weapon. This conserves energy, improves accuracy capability and increases the range of the weapon, thus allowing delivery aircraft to engage their targets with greater stand-off. When the weapon is released, it flies a pre-programmed autopilot profile into the target area, using the energy given to it by the releasing aircraft. These autopilot profiles are designated to provide the best attack conditions for different types of target and also to use to maximum effectiveness the increased stand-off capability of the weapon.

Enhanced Paveway
Length (EPW2)3.7m; (EPW3) 4.4m);Weight (EPW2) 545kg (EPW3) 1,130 kg); GPS guidance.

Shortcomings in target acquisition during the 1999 Kosovo conflict resulted in a requirement for the RAF to obtain a weapon to satisfy all-weather 24-hour tasking. The

Enhanced Paveway (EPW) family of weapons meets this requirement, and the EPWII entered service in 2001 and the larger EPWIII entered service in late 2002. Both EPWII and EPWIII are based on their laser-guided bomb variants, the Paveway II and Paveway III respectively, and utilise the same warheads and fin sections. However, the EPW weapons have a modified guidance section and wiring to accommodate a Global Positioning System Aided Inertial Navigation System (GAINS). EPW (also known as Paveway IV) is carried by the Tornado GR4.

JDAM

Although the EPW is now in service, the RAF still has a requirement for a precision-guided bomb (PGB) with 24-hour operation that can be used in all weather conditions. One proposal to the RAF requirement is a UK variant of the US JDAM. The Joint Direct Attack Munition (JDAM) is a low-cost guidance kit that converts existing unguided free-fall bombs into accurately guided "smart" weapons. The JDAM kit consists of a new tail section that contains an Inertial Navigation System/Global Positioning System. A contract decision on the PGB is expected during 2003.

Surface to Air Missiles

Details of the Rapier SAM are in the RAF Regiment section.

Rockets
CVR-7

This is an air-to-air and air-to-surface rocket system. Each rocket pod, weighing 240 kg, carries 19 rockets. The HE warhead is designed for use against light armour, vehicles, small vessels and helicopters. Deployed on the Jaguar and Harrier.

Freefall bombs

Conventional 1,000 lb (454 kg) bombs are still in service, as are Mark 1 and Mark 2 bombs weighing 570 lb (260 kg). By adding the Hunting 118 retarding tail, the weight of the latter is increased to 670 lb (304 kg).

Anti-ship missile
Harpoon

Length 3.84m: Diameter 0.34m: Span 0.91m: Total Weight 526kg: Warhead Weight 225kg: Range 110km. Guidance Sea-skimming cruise monitored by radar altimeter, active radar terminal homing.

The US-designed Harpoon is an extremely powerful anti-ship missile that is carried in the bomb bay of the Nimrod MR2. The air to sea version of the missile has extremely sophisticated Electronic Counter Measures (ECM), and the ability to fly a sea-skimming course on a dog-leg path through three pre-programmed way-points. The warhead is extremely powerful and a hit from Harpoon is almost certain to result in the destruction or disablement of a major surface vessel.

Air-launched Torpedo
Stingray

Length 2.6m; Diameter 0.34m; Weight 267 kg; Warhead 45 kg of HE in a shaped charge; Speed 45 knots; Range 8-11km; Depth 800m; Propulsion magnesium/silver-chloride seawater battery (Pump-jet); Guidance active/passive sonar.

Stingray is a lightweight homing torpedo that is carried in the bomb bay of the Nimrod MR2. The torpedo is fully programmable, with a number of search options and has been designed to destroy submarines. The torpedo seeker can either home in on the sound of the submarine or detect and track the target using its own sonar. From 2003, Stingray is to be upgraded to Mod 1 standard. The upgrade includes new digital homing, guidance and control systems and the torpedo is planned to enter service in 2006.

Ballistic Missile Defence

In 2002, the unilateral withdrawal of the United States from the 1972 Anti-Ballistic Missile Treaty with the then Soviet Union opened the way for the deployment of limited national and theatre ballistic missile defence (BMD) systems. In early 2003, the UK government agreed to a US government request to upgrade BMEWS system at RAF Fylingdales for BMD applications.

The UK MoD has been conducting studies on BMD - probably a Theatre High-Altitude Area Defence (THAAD) system - to defend the UK against incoming missiles. The MOD appears to be interested in creating a layered anti-missile defence, capable of multiple attempts at hitting targets at ranges of over 100 miles at heights of over 100,000 feet, to shorter-range systems such as the US Patriot that could hit targets at much closer range. Recent fears of nuclear proliferation, and the problems of nuclear-capable delivery systems such as the former Soviet Scud missile and derivative missiles being used by nations who hitherto have not been able to mount a credible threat to the UK, have forced the MoD to look at the options offered by adopting a high-level missile defence. Any UK programme in BMD would be collaborative, given the huge cost involved.

RAF Regiment

The need to raise a dedicated specialist force to protect air installations became apparent during WWII when unprotected aircraft on the ground were vulnerable to enemy air and ground attack. Consequently, the RAF Regiment was raised on 1 February 1942 by a Royal Warrant of King George VI. At the end of WWII, there were over 85,000 personnel serving in the RAF Regiment manning 240 operational squadrons. As of 2003, the strength of the RAF Regiment is around some 3,000, including some 300 officers and 500 part-time reservists. The Regiment is generally formed into Squadrons of 100 to 150 personnel. Currently the RAF Regiment exists to provide ground and short- range air defence for RAF installations, and to train all the RAF's combatant personnel to enable them to contribute to the defence of their units. RAF Regiment units are under the operational command of No 2 Group. As of 1 April 2003, RAF Regiment units are as follows:

Field Squadrons

No 1 Squadron	St Mawgan	Field Squadron
No 2 Squadron	Honington	Field /Para Sqn
No 3 Squadron	Aldergrove	Field Squadron
No 34 Squadron	Leeming	Field Squadron
No 51 Squadron	Lossiemouth	Field Squadron
No 63 (QCS)	Uxbridge	Ceremonial /Field Sqn

Air Defence

No 15 Squadron	Honington	6 x Rapier

No 16 Squadron	Honington	6 x Rapier
No 26 Squadron	Waddington	6 x Rapier
No 37 Squadron	Honington	6 x Rapier
Joint Rapier Training Unit	Honington	2 x Rapier
RAF Regiment Depot	Honington	
No 1 RAF STO HQ*	RAF Wittering	
No 2 RAF STO HQ	RAF Leeming	
No 3 RAF STO HQ	RAF Marham	
No 4 RAF STO HQ	RAF Honington	

* STO - Tactical Survive to Operate HQ

The RAF Regiment also provides some of the 244 personnel of the Joint NBC Regiment alongside two squadrons of the Royal Tank Regiment all of whom are stationed at Honington. Specialist RAF Regiment training for gunners is given at the RAF Regiment Depot at Honington. On completion of training at the RAF College Cranwell officers also undergo further specialist training at RAF Honington and, in some cases, the School of Infantry at Warminster in Wiltshire or the Royal School of Artillery at Larkhill. The RAF Regiment also mans the Queen's Colour Squadron (QCS) which undertakes all major ceremonial duties for the Royal Air Force. These duties involve mounting the Guard at Buckingham Palace on an occasional basis, and providing Guards of Honour for visiting Heads of State. The Queen's Colour Squadron also has a war role as a field squadron. The regiment is not alone in defending any RAF station. Every airman based at a station has a ground defence role and is trained to defend his place of work against ground attack and attack by NBC weapons. Training for this is given by RAF Regiment instructors who provide courses at station level for all personnel on various aspects of ground defence. There are now two basic RAF Regiment squadron organisations - the field squadron organised for ground defence against possible enemy ground action and the rapier squadron organised for defence against low-flying enemy aircraft.

Rapier Squadron-Possible Organisation

```
                      Sqn HQ & Headquarter Flight
        ┌──────────────────┬──────────────────┬──────────────────┐
   Rapier Flight      Rapier Flight       Rapier Flight    Engineering Flight
    2 x Rapier         2 x Rapier          2 x Rapier
```

Rapier Characteristics - Guidance Semi-Automatic to Command Line of Sight (SACLOS); Missile Diameter 13.3 cm; Missile Length 2.24m; Rocket Solid Fuelled; Warhead High Explosive; Launch Weight 42kg; Speed Mach 2+; Ceiling 3,000m; Maximum Range 6,800m; Fire Unit Weight 1,227kg; Radar Height (in action) 3.37m; Radar Weight 1,186kg; Optical Tracker Height 1.54m; Optical Tracker Weight 119kg; Generator Weight 243kg; Generator Height 0.91m.

The Rapier system provides area, Low Level Air Defence (LLAD) over the area around the airbase to be defended. It consists of an Optical Tracker, a Fire Unit, a Radar and a Generator. The into-action time of the system is thought to be about 15 minutes and the radar is believed to scan out to 12 km. Each fire unit can therefore cover an Air Defence Area (ADA) of about 100 km. Having discharged the 4 missiles on a Fire Unit, 2 men are thought to be able to carry out a reload in about 3 minutes. During the Falklands Campaign, Rapier was credited with 14 kills and 6 probables from a total of 24 missiles fired.

Rapier in service with the RAF Regiment has been upgraded from Field Standard B1(M) to Field Standard C (Rapier 2000). Rapier FSC offers significant enhancements to performance. The towed system launcher mounts eight missiles (able to fire two simultaneously at two separate targets) and is manufactured in two warhead versions. One of these warheads is armour piercing and able to deal with fixed-wing targets, while the other is a fragmentation warhead for the engagement of cruise missiles and RPVs. Rapier 2000 has the Darkfire tracker and a tailor-made 3-dimensional radar system for target acquisition. A Joint Service Rapier FSC OCU was formed at RAF Honington to oversee both the RAF's and Army's conversion to the new system.

Rapier has now been sold to the armed forces of at least 14 nations. We believe that sales have amounted to over 25,000 missiles, 600 launchers and 350 Blindfire radars.

Royal Auxiliary Air Force Regiment (RAuxAF Regt)
Airfield defence is further enhanced by squadrons of the RAuxAF Regt who are recruited locally and whose role is the ground defence of the airfield and its associated outlying installations. A RAuxAF Regiment Squadron has an all-up strength of about 120 personnel and costs approximately £500,000 a year to keep in service. As a general rule, a squadron has a headquarters flight, two mobile flights mounted in Land Rovers and two flights for static guard duties. RAuxAF Regt squadrons are as follows:

2503 Sqn RAuxAF Regt	RAF Waddington	Ground Defence
2622 Sqn RAuxAF Regt	RAF Lossiemouth	Ground Defence
2623 Sqn RauxAF Regt	RAF Honington	Rapier Squadron
2625 Sqn RAuxAF Regt	RAF St Mawgan	Ground Defence

RAF Reserves
The reserve component of the Royal Air Force on 1 April 2003 was as follows:

RAuxAF & RAFVR Reserves	-	1,600
Royal Air Force Reserve	-	12,700
Individuals liable to recall	-	27,600*
Total	-	41,900

* This number includes some 600 reserve officers. Aircrew who have served on Short Service Commissions have a mandatory reserve liability of four years.

The Controller Reserve Forces (RAF) is located at RAF Innsworth as part of RAF PTC. He is responsible for all of the non-operational aspects of reserve forces policy and co-ordination, ranging from recruitment, through training, promotions and welfare to future planning. The following are the formed Reserve Units (RAuxAF Regt Squadrons are listed in the preceding RAF Regiment section).

Royal Auxiliary Air Force

No 1 Maritime HQ	Northwood (London)	
No 2 Maritime HQ	Pitrivie (Scotland)	
No 3 Maritime HQ	RAF St Mawgan	
3 Sqn	RAF Henlow	Tactical Provost Wing

501 Sqn	RAF Brize Norton	Operations Support Squadron
504 Sqn	RAF Cottesmore	Harrier Support Sqn
600 Sqn	RAF Northolt	HQ Augmentation Unit
603 Sqn	Edinburgh	Operations Support Squadron
606 Sqn	RAF Benson	Helicopter Support Squadron
609 Sqn	RAF Leeming	Operations Support Squadron
612 Sqn	RAF Leuchars	Air Transportable Surgical Squadron
2620 Sqn	RAF Marham	Operations Support Squadron
2624 Sqn	RAF Brize Norton	Operations Support Squadron
4624 Sqn	RAF Brize Norton	Operations Support Squadron
4626 Sqn	RAF Lyneham	Aeromedical Evacuation Unit
7006 Flight	RAF High Wycombe	Intelligence Squadron
7010 Flight	RAF High Wycombe	Photographic Interpretation Squadron
7630 Flight	DISC Chicksands	Intelligence Squadron
7644 Flight	RAF High Wycombe	Public Relations Squadron
Mobile Met Unit	RAF Benson	Meteorological Services
Marham Support Flight	RAF Marham	Ground Crew
1359 Flight	RAF Lyneham	Hercules Reserve Flight personnel
TSS	RAF Shawbury	Training & Standardisation Sqn

Royal Auxiliary Air Force Defence Force Flights

RAuxAF Defence Force Flight	RAF Brampton
RAuxAF Defence Force Flight	RAF High Wycombe
RAuxAF Defence Force Flight	RAF Lyneham
RAuxAF Defence Force Flight	RAF St Athan

In war, these four flights would provide specialist assistance in public relations, foreign language interrogation, photographic interpretation and intelligence support.

Note: The RauxAF and the RAFVR were amalgamated on 5 April 1997.

Chapter 5 – MISCELLANEOUS

The MoD's Civilian Staff

The three uniformed services are supported by the civilian staff of the MoD. On the 1st April 2002 some approximately 105,000 civilian personnel (90,600 in the UK and 14,100 overseas-locally engaged) were employed by the MoD. This figure has fallen from 316,700 civilian personnel in 1980. UK based civilians are employed in the following areas:

Navy Operational Areas	-	4,000
Army Operational Areas	-	9,900
Air Forces Operational Areas	-	5,600
Service Personnel Commands	-	12,400
Defence Logistics	-	22,600
MoD Head Office, HQ Procurement	-	14,900
Defence Evaluation & Research Agency	-	15,100
UK Hydrographic Office	-	800
Chief of Joint Operations	-	400
Meteorological Office	-	2,100

In a recent clear and unambiguous statement the UK MoD stated that " The Department remains committed to a process of civilianisation. Increasingly, it makes no sense to employ expensively trained and highly professional military personnel in jobs which civilians could do equally well. Civilians are generally cheaper than their military counterparts and as they often remain longer in post, can provide greater continuity. For these reasons, it is our long-standing policy to civilianise posts and so release valuable military resources to the front line whenever it makes operational and economic sense to do so".

In addition to the permanent UK based civilians there were approximately 14,744 locally entered civilian personnel distributed around the following locations:

Continental Europe	-	7,944(1)
Gibraltar	-	987
Malta	-	5
Cyprus	-	2,384
Brunei	-	293
Nepal	-	359
Elsewhere	-	22
Other Areas	-	2,122(2)

Notes

(1) The overwhelming majority of this figure are locally entered civilians supporting BFG (British Forces Germany).

(2) In the main this figure represents locally employed personnel in Bosnia and Kosovo.

In general MoD Civil Servants work in a parallel stream with their respective uniformed counterparts. There are some "stand alone" civilian agencies of which the QinetiQ is probably the largest.

QinetiQ
(Formerly known as the Defence Evaluation & Research Agency)

From 1 April 1995, the Defence Evaluation & Research Agency (DERA) assumed the responsibilities of its predecessor the Defence Research Agency (DRA). DERA changed its title to QinetiQ on 2 July 2001. The new company has been set up as a PPP (Public Private Partnership).

The name QinetiQ was derived from the scientific term, kinetic (phonetic: ki'ne tik), which means 'relating to or caused by motion'. This in turncomes from the Greek, kinetikos based on 'kineo' which means 'to move'.

A quarter of QinetiQ is to be retained within the MoD as the Defence Science and Technology Laboratory (DSTL) to manage the research programme and the International Research Collaboration, along with other sensitive areas such as CBD (Chemical & Biological Defence), Porton Down.

It is planned that the remaining three-quarters will become a wholly government owned plc as a precursor to eventual flotation. A period of shadow trading is under way to ensure robustness of the two new organisations and their supporting infrastructure.
The UK Ministry of Defence (MoD) announced on 6 March 2002 that QinetiQ would not be floated on the stock exchange until 2004-2005 and that a 'strategic partner' for the company would be sought.

Under the old system, DERA combined the activities of a number of research and evaluation agencies under the umbrella of a top level budget holder.

Agencies such as the Directorate General of Test and Evaluation, the Chemical and Biological Defence Establishment and the Defence Operational Analysis Centre were grouped together in the new agency with a staff strength of some 11,100 people and an operational budget of just over £529 million (2001 figure). DERA was organised into four major operational divisions and during 2002 we believe that QinetiQ remains organised in a similar fashion.

DRA Division - Includes all except two of the old DRA's scientific business operations.
DTEO - The Defence Test and Evaluation Organisation consists of the Director General of Tests and Evaluation plus some other smaller elements operating in the DTEO sector from the old DRA.
CBDE - This division combines the activities of the old Chemical and Biological Defence Establishment at Porton Down in Wiltshire with the old DRA's Chemical and Electronics department.
CDA - Centre for Defence Analysis combines the activities of the old Defence Operational Analysis Centre and the DRAs Operational Studies Department.

Priorities
The current priorities of QinetiQ as described by the UK MoD are:
a. To keep the armed forces well equipped with modern capable equipment.
b. To support mobile and flexible response forces.
c. Support the procurement of military equipment which is sustainable, has high reliability and availability, and gives good value for money.

d. Ensure that the research programme reflects the changing international situation and defence objectives.
e. Maintain the longer-term research programme to sustain the science and technology base.
f. Place greater emphasis on research programmes aimed at reducing 'through life' costs.
g. Encourage the greatest possible industrial participation in maintaining the technological base and exploit academic expertise.
h. Maintain the longer-term research programme to sustain the science and technology base.
i. Encourage the greatest possible industrial participation in maintaining the technological base and exploit academic expertise.

The United Kingdom Defence Industry

Despite the demise of the Warsaw Pact, uncertainties over our future defence strategy and substantial cuts in defence spending, the United Kingdom's Defence Industry has proved to be a remarkably resilient and successful element of our national manufacturing base.

In the early 1990's defence related production accounted for some 11% of manufactured output in the United Kingdom. Coincidentally, defence work also provided employment for just under 10% of our manufacturing workforce employing 410,000 individuals in 1991. Despite the rationalisation which is still taking place within the defence sector, it is generally accepted that defence employment still puts around £6 billion annually into the broader UK economy via salaries paid throughout the supply chain.

Historically, the UK defence industry has possessed the capability and competence to provide a wide range of advanced systems and equipment to support our own Armed Forces. This capability, matched with their competitiveness, has enabled UK companies to command a sizeable share of those overseas markets for which export licence approvals are available. At home, UK industry has consistently provided some 75% by value of the equipment requirements of The Ministry of Defence. In simple terms, in recent years our industry has supplied £9 - £10 billion worth of goods and services for our Armed Forces annually while a further £3 -5 billion worth of business has accrued to the UK defence industry from sales to approved overseas customers. The spread of overheads resulting from export sales has also benefited The Ministry of Defence to the extent of approximately £350 million per annum.

The United Kingdom's defence companies are justifiably proud of their record in recent years in the face of fierce overseas competition. Reductions in the UK's Armed Forces and the heavy demands on our remaining Service personnel, who face an unpredictable international security environment, make it inevitable that considerable reliance will be placed upon the support and surge capacity offered by our comprehensive indigenous defence industrial base. Without this effective industrial base, the ability of the UK to exert independence of action or influence over collective security arrangements would be constrained. It is essential that government policies ensure that industry retains the necessary capabilities to support our forces in a changing world.

Up until now the United Kingdom's defence industry has been highly successful in supporting the United Kingdom's Armed Forces with high quality equipment and it has also made a significant contribution to our balance of payments. As a strategic resource it is vitally important that it should attract the appropriate levels of research and development funding to maintain the necessary technical excellence and production facilities to meet the needs of the future.

As importantly, the defence industry is not only a major employer but it is also the generator of high technology that is readily adaptable to civilian use in fields such as avionics and engine technology. The future of the UK's defence industry will almost certainly have to be property planned if it is to remain an efficient and essential national support organisation in times of crisis. A look at MoD payments to contractors during 2001-2002 identifies some of the larger manufacturers.

Major Contractors Listing

Contractors paid more than £250 million by the UK MoD during FY 2001-2002
AWE Management Ltd
BAE Systems (Operations) Ltd
BAE Systems Electronics Ltd
British Telecommunications PLC
DARA
Defence Science & Technology Laboratory
Devonport Royal Dockyard
MBDA UK Ltd
NETMA
QinetiQ Ltd
Rolls Royce PLC
Westland Group PLC

Contractors paid between £100 million and £250 million during FY 2001-2002
Annington Receivables Ltd
Alenia Marconi Systems Ltd
Babcock Support Services Ltd
BAE Systems Avionics Ltd
BAE Systems Marine Ltd
BFS Group
EDS Defence Ltd
IBM UK Holdings Ltd
ICL PLC
Interserve (Defence) Ltd
Lockheed Martin Corporation
Other UK Government Departments
Pricewaterhousecoopers
Royal Ordnance PLC
Serco Group PLC
WS Atkins

Contractors paid between £50 million and £100 million during FY 2001-2002
BAE Systems (Defence Systems) Ltd
British Aerospace Aircraft Group
Cap Gemini Ernst & Young UK PLC

Civil Aviation Authority
Cobham PLC
Compass Services (UK) Ltd
Esso UK PLC
Flagship Training Ltd
Fleet Support Ltd
General Dynamics UK Ltd
GKN PLC
John Mowlem & Co PLC
Meteorological Office
Sodexho Ltd
Thales Air Defence Ltd
Thales Defence Ltd
The British Petroleum Company Ltd
Vickers Engineering PLC

Another 38 organisations were paid between £25 million and £50 million during FY 2001 - 2002.

The Services Hierarchy
Officer Ranks

Army	Navy	Air Force
Field Marshal	Admiral of the Fleet	Marshal of the Royal Air Force
General	Admiral	Air Chief Marshal
Lieutenant-General	Vice-Admiral	Air Marshal
Major-General	Rear-Admiral	Air Vice Marshal
Brigadier	Commodore	Air Commodore
Colonel	Captain	Group Captain
Lieutenant-Colonel	Commander	Wing Commander
Major	Lieutenant-Commander	Squadron Leader
Captain	Lieutenant	Flight-Lieutenant
Lieutenant	Sub-Lieutenant	Flying Officer
Second Lieutenant	Midshipman	Pilot Officer

Non Commissioned Ranks

Army	Navy	Air Force
Warrant Officer 1/2	Warrant Officer	Warant Officer
Staff/Colour Sergeant	Chief Petty Officer	Flight Sergeant
Sergeant	Petty Officer	Sergeant
Corporal	Leading Rate	Corporal
Lance Corporal	Able Rate	Senior Aircraftsman
Private	Ordinary Rate	Leading Aircraftsman

Note: In general terms the rank shown in each column equates to the other service ranks in the columns alongside.

Pay Scales (From 1 April 2003)

The following are a selection from the Army pay scales relevant from 1 April 2003. Approximate scales for the other two services can be identified by using the previous table of of commissioned and non-commissioned ranks. Pay scales apply to both males and females.

Officers

Rank	Level		Daily	Annual
Brigadier	+4	Level 5	217.37	79,340.05
	+3	Level 4	215.14	78,526.10
	+2	Level 3	212.92	77,715.80
	+1	Level 2	210.70	76,905.50
	OA	Level 1	208.48	76,095.20
Colonel	+8	Level 9	192.11	70,120.15
	+7	Level 8	188.82	68,919.30
	+6	Level 7	187.52	68,444.80
	+5	Level 6	185.24	67,612.60
	+4	Level 5	182.96	67,875.40
	+3	Level 4	180.67	65,944.55
	+2	Level 3	178.39	65,112.35
	+1	Level 2	176.10	64,276.65
	OA	Level 1	173.81	63,440.65
Lt Colonel	+8	Level 9	165.91	60,557.15
	+7	Level 8	163.92	59,830.80
	+6	Level 7	161.96	59,115.40
	+5	Level 6	159.97	58,389.05
	+4	Level 5	158.00	57,670.00
	+3	Level 4	156.02	56,947.30
	+2	Level 3	154.06	56,231.90
	+1	Level 2	152.08	55,509.20
	OA	Level 1	150.09	54,782.85
Major	+8	Level 9	128.07	46,745.55
	+7	Level 8	125.43	45,781.95
	+6	Level 7	122.79	44,818.35
	+5	Level 6	120.15	43,854.75
	+4	Level 5	117.50	42,887.50
	+3	Level 4	114.86	41,923.90
	+2	Level 3	112.21	40,956.65
	+1	Level 2	109.58	39,996.70
	OA	Level 1	106.94	39,033.10
Captain	+8	Level 9	100.96	36,850.40
	+7	Level 8	99.82	36,434.30
	+6	Level 7	98.66	36,010.90
	+5	Level 6	96.37	35,175.05
	+4	Level 5	94.07	34,335.55
	+3	Level 4	91.78	33,499.70
	+2	Level 3	89.47	32,656.55
	+1	Level 2	87.17	31,817.05
	OA	Level 1	84.49	30,838.85

Lieutenant				
2nd Lieutenant	+4	Level 10	73.22	26,725.53
	+3	Level 9	71.48	26,090.20
	+2	Level 8	69.74	25,455.10
	+1	Level 7	68.00	24,820.00
	OA	Level 6	66.25	24,181.25
	2Lt	Level 5	55.12	21,118.80
University Cadet				
Entrants	+3	Level 4	38.84	14,176.60
	+2	Level 3	35.57	12,983.05
	+1	Level 2	31.68	11,563.20
	OA	Level 1	27.60	10,074.00

Warrant Officers, Non Commissioned Officers and Soldiers

Rank	Range 5	Higher Range		Lower Range	
		Daily	Annual	Daily	Annual
Warrant	Level 7	104.68	38,208.20	98.78	36,025.50
Officer 1	Level 6	103.10	37,631,50	96.08	35,069.20
	Level 5	101.30	36,974.50	93.45	34,109.25
	Level 4	99.52	36,324.80	91.66	33,455.90
	Level 3	97.73	35,671.45	89.88	32,806.20
	Level 2	96.08	35,069.20	88.10	32,156.50
	Level 1	94.22	34,390.30	86.42	31,543.30
	Range 4				
Warrant	Level 9	96.84	35,346.60	88.73	32,386.45
Officer 2	Level 8	95.49	34,853.85	86.76	31,667.40
Levels 5 - 9 only	Level 7	94.14	34,361.10	85.66	31,265.90
	Level 6	92.80	33,872.00	84.37	30,795.05
Staff Sergeant	Level 5	90.80	33,142.00	80.72	29,462.80
Levels 1 - 7 only	Level 4	88.77	32,401.05	79.63	29,064.95
	Level 3	86.76	31,667.40	77.81	28,400.65
	Level 2	84.75	30,933.75	75.37	27,510.05
	Level 1	82.74	30,200.10	74.40	27,156.00
	Range 3				
Sergeant	Level 7	82.68	30,178.20	76.37	27,875.05
	Level 6	81.17	29,627.05	75.80	27,667.00
	Level 5	79.64	29,068.60	73.27	26,743.55
	Level 4	78.12	28,513.80	71.41	26,064.65
	Level 3	77.15	28,159.75	70.69	25,801.85
	Level 2	75.24	27,462.60	68.96	25,170.40
	Level 1	73.35	26,772.75	67.21	24,531.65
	Range 2				
Corporal	Level 7	74.30	27,119.50	66.82	24,389.30
	Level 6	72.71	26,539.15	66.32	24,206.80
	Level 5	71.24	26,002.60	65.81	24,020.65
	Level 4	69.55	25,385.75	65.30	23,834.50

	Level 3	67.97	24,809.05	64.80	23,652.00
	Level 2	64.80	23,652.00	61.78	22,549.70
	Level 1	61.78	22,549.70	59.12	21,578.80
	Range 1				
Lance Corporal	Level 9	64.80	23,652.00	53.89	19,669.85
Levels 5 - 9 only	Level 8	61.78	22,549.70	52.01	18,983.65
	Level 7	59.12	21,578.80	49.73	18,151.45
Private	Level 6	56.53	20.669.95	47.68	17,403.20
Levels 1 - 7 only	Level 5	53.91	19,677.15	45.77	16,706.05
	Level 4	48.75	17,793.75	43.44	15,855.60
	Level 3	45.34	16,549.10	39.93	14,574.45
	Level 2	41.07	14,990.55	37.84	13,811.60
	Level 1	35.74	13,045.10	35.74	13,045.10
New Entrant Rate				30.47	11,121.55

Notes:
(1) Pay scales apply to both males and females. (2) These rates only show the most common basic pay rates. (3) From 1991 all recruits have been enlisted on an Open Engagement. The Open Engagement is for a period of 22 years service from the age of 18 or the date of enlistment whichever is the later. Subject to giving 12 months notice, and any time bar that may be in force, all soldiers have the right to leave on the completion of three years reckonable service from the age of 18.

Codewords and Nicknames

A Codeword is a single word used to provide security cover for reference to a particular classified matter, eg "Corporate" was the Codeword for the recovery of the Falklands in 1982. In 1997 "Bolton" was used to refer to operations during the reinfocement of Kuwait and Op Grapple was used operations in support of the UN in the former Yugoslavia. A Nickname consists of two words and may be used for reference to an unclassified matter, eg "Lean Look" referred to an investigation into various military organisations in order to identify savings in manpower.

Dates and Timings

When referring to timings the Armed Forces use the 24 hour clock. This means that 2015 hours, pronounced twenty fifteen hours, is in fact 8.15pm. Soldiers usually avoid midnight and refer to 2359 or 0001 hours. Time zones present plenty of scope for confusion! Exercise and Operational times are expressed in Greenwich Mean Time (GMT) which may differ from the local time. The suffix Z (Zulu) denotes GMT and A (Alpha) GMT + 1 hour. B (Bravo) means GMT + 2 hours and so on.

The Date Time Group or DTG can be seen on military documents and is a point of further confusion for many. Using the military DTG 1030 GMT on 20th April 2003 is written as 201030Z APR 03. When the Armed Forces relate days and hours to operations a simple system is used:

a. D Day is the day an operation begins.
b. H Hour is the hour a specific operation begins.
c. Days and hours can be represented by numbers plus or minus of D Day

Therefore if D Day is 20 Mar 03, D-2 is the 18 Mar 03 and D + 2 is the 22 Mar 03. If H Hour is 0600hrs then H+2 is 0800 hours.

Phonetic Alphabet

To ensure minimum confusion during radio or telephone conversations difficult words or names are spelt out letter by letter using the following NATO standard phonetic alphabet.

ALPHA - BRAVO - CHARLIE - DELTA - ECHO - FOXTROT - GOLF - HOTEL - INDIA - JULIET - KILO - LIMA - MIKE - NOVEMBER - OSCAR - PAPA - QUEBEC - ROMEO - SIERRA - TANGO - UNIFORM - VICTOR - WHISKEY - X RAY - YANKEE - ZULU

Useful Quotations

There are two groups - Military and General.

Military Quotes

"It is foolish to hunt the tiger when there are plenty of sheep around."
Al Qaeda Training Manual 2002

"Information is something that you do something with. Data is something that just makes officers feel good! I keep telling them but nobody listens to me."
US Army Intelligence specialist - CENTCOM Qatar 2003

"If you can keep your head when all about you are losing theirs and blaming it on you - you'll be a man my son".
Rudyard Kipling

"If you can keep your head when all about you are losing theirs - you may have missed something very important".
Royal Marine - Bagram Airfield 2002

Mrs Saatchi explained her 12 month silence after her husband started living with Nigela Lawson by quoting Napoleon's dictum

"Never disturb your enemy while he is making a mistake"

"We trained very hard, but it seemed that every time we were beginning to form up in teams, we would be reorganised. I was to learn in later life that we tend to meet any new situation by reorganising, and a wonderful method it can be for creating an illusion of progress, while producing confusion, inefficiency and demoralisation".
Caius Petronius 66 AD

"All through my service I have tried to stand between my superiors and my men. If things went wrong, I considered that I, and I only, was to blame".
Major General Sir Digby Raven 1915-2001.

"The only time in his life that he ever put up a fight was when we asked for his resignation."
A comment from one of his staff officers following French General Joffre's resignation in 1916.

"A few honest men are better than numbers."
Oliver Cromwell

"There has to be a beginning to every great undertaking"
Sir Francis Drake

"I do not know what effect these men will have on the enemy, but by God they frighten me".
The Duke of Wellingtom

"The beatings will continue until morale improves."
Attributed to the Commander of the Japanese Submarine Fleet 1945

"Take Risks - A ship in port is safe, but that is not what ships are for. Sail out to sea and do new things".
Rear Admiral Grace Hopper USN (died 1992)

"Take short views, hope for the best and trust in God."
Sir Sydney Smith

"Nothing is so good for the morale of the troops as occasionally to see a dead general".
Field Marshal Slim

"It makes no difference which side the general is on".
Unknown British Soldier

"There is no beating these troops in spite of their generals. I always thought them bad soldiers, now I am sure of it. I turned their right, pierced their centre, broke them everywhere; the day was mine, and yet they did not know it and would not run.
Regarding the British Infantry - French Marshal Soult - Albuhera 1811

"Confusion in battle is what pain is in childbirth - the natural order of things".
General Maurice Tugwell

"In war the outcome corresponds to expectations less than in any other activity".
Titus Livy

" This is just something to be got around - like a bit of flak on the way to the target".
Group Captain Leonard Cheshire VC - Speaking of his incurable illness in the week before he died.

"Pale Ebenezer thought it wrong to fight,
But roaring Bill, who killed him, thought it right".
Hillare Belloc

"Everyone wants peace - and they will fight the most terrible war to get it".
Miles Kington - BBC Radio 4th February 1995

"Having lost sight of our objectives we need to redouble our efforts".
Anon

"The military value of a partisan's work is not measured by the amount of property destroyed, or the number of men killed or captured, but the number he keeps watching."
John Singleton Mosby - Confederate Cavalry Leader (1833-1916)

During the Second World War Bomber Harris was well known for his glorious capacity for rudeness, particularly to bureaucrats. "What are you doing to retard the war effort today" was his standard greeting to senior civil servants.
Air Marshal Sir Arthur (Bomber) Harris

"What all the wise men promised has not happened and what all the dammed fools said would happen has come to pass".
Lord Melbourne

Admiral King commanded the US Navy during the Second World War. His daughter wrote:

"He was the most even tempered man I ever met - he was always in a rage. In addition, he believed that civilians should be told nothing about a war until it was over and then only who won. Nothing more!"

CIVILIAN

Homer Simpson's advice to his son Bart:

Homer to Bart: "These three little sentences will get you through life:

Number 1: (whispers) Cover for me.
Number 2: Oh, good idea boss.
Number 3: It was like that when I got here.

"Whenever I hear about a wave of public indignation I am filled with a massive calm".
Matthew Parris - The Times 24th October 1994

"They say hard work never hurt anybody, but I figured why take the chance".
Ronald Regan

"The primary function of management is to create the chaos that only management can sort out. A secondary function is the expensive redecoration and refurnishing of offices, especially in times of the utmost financial stringency".
Theodore Dalrymple "The Spectator" 6 November 1993.

"To applaud as loudly as that for so stupid a proposal means that you are just trying to fill that gap between your ears".
David Starkey - BBC (4 Feb 95)

"Its always best on these occasions to do what the mob do".
"But suppose that there are two mobs?" suggested Mr Snodgrass.
"Shout with the largest" replied Mr Pickwick.
Pickwick Papers Chapter 13.

"Success is generally 90% persistence".
Anon.

"I'm always there when I need me"
Kenny Everitt

"Every bumptious idiot thinks himself a leader of men."
George Bernard Shaw

"He knows nothing and thinks that he knows everything. That points to a political career."
George Bernard Shaw

"The men who really believe in themselves are all in lunatic asylums."
GK Chesterton

"Ah, these diplomats! What chatterboxes! There's only one way to shut them up - cut them down with machine guns. Bulganin, go and get me one!"
Joseph Stalin - As reported by De Gaulle

"Politics is war without bloodshed."
Mao Tse Tung

"It is only worthless men who seek to excuse the deterioration of their character by pleading neglect in their early years".
Plutarch - Life of Coriolanus - Approx A.D. 80

Despotism tempered by assassination.
Lord Reith's (former govenor of the BBC) idea of the best form of government.

You Liberals think that goats are just sheep from broken homes.
Anon

"Once the people begin to reason all is lost."
Voltaire

"I consider myself to be the most important figure in the world."
His Royal Highness - Field Marshal Idi Amin Dada.

"The only thing necessary for the triumph of evil is for good men to do nothing."
Edmund Burke.

"Fanaticism consists of redoubling your efforts when you have forgotten your aim."
Santayana - The Life of Reason.

City Financial Analayst - My best estimate is 44 per cent (plus or minus a few percentage points)
This is the figure you use when you are faced with a difficult question for which you do not have the answer. In general there are very few people who will argue with 44 per cent - not too much and not too little.

Extracts from Officer's Annual Confidential Reports

"Works well when under constant supervision and cornered like a rat in a trap."

"He has the wisdom of youth, and the energy of old age."

"This Officer should go far - and the sooner he starts, the better."

"This officer is depriving a village somewhere of its idiot."

"Only occasionally wets himself under pressure."

"This Officer is really not so much of a has-been, but more of a definitely won't-be."

"When she opens her mouth, it seems that this is only to change whichever foot was previously in there."

"He has carried out each and every one of his duties to his entire satisfaction."

"He would be out of his depth in a car park puddle."

"Technically sound, but socially impossible."

"This Officer reminds me very much of a gyroscope - always spinning around at a frantic pace, but not really going anywhere."

"This young man has delusions of adequacy."

"When he joined my ship, this Officer was something of a granny; since then he has aged considerably."

"This Medical Officer has used my ship to carry his genitals from port to port, and my officers to carry him from bar to bar."

"Since my last report he has reached rock bottom, and has started to dig."

"She sets low personal standards and then consistently fails to achieve them."

"His men would follow him anywhere, but only out of curiosity."

"I would not breed from this Officer."

"This officer has the astonishing ability to provoke something close to a mutiny every time he opens his mouth".

Abbreviations

The following is a selection from the list of standard military abbreviations and should assist users of this handbook.

AAC	Army Air Corps
AAR	Air to Air Refuelling
AAAW	Advanced Anti-Armour Weapon
AAW	Anti-Air Warfare
AB	Airborne
ABLE	Automotive Bridge Launching Equipment
ac	Aircraft
accn	Accommodation
ACE	Allied Command Europe
ACLANT	Allied Command North Atlantic
ACOS	Assistant Chief of Staff
ACV	Armoured Command Vehicle
AD	Air Defence/Air Dispatch/Army Department
ADA	Air Defended Area
ADA	Air Defence Alerting Device
Adjt	Adjutant
admin	Administration

admin O	Administrative Order
ADP	Automatic Data Processing
ADR	Airfield Damage Repair
AEW	Airborne Early Warning
AFCENT	Allied Forces Central European Theatre
AFNORTHWEST	Allied Forces Northwestern Europe
AFSOUTH	Allied Forces Southern Europe
AFV	Armoured Fighting Vehicle
AGC	Adjutant General's Corps
AGLS	Autonomous Navigation And Gun Laying System
AHQ	Air Headquarters
AIFV	Armoured Infantry Fighting Vehicle
AIRCENT	Allied Air Forces Central Europe
Airmob	Airmobile
ALARM	Air Launched Anti Radiation Missile
AMF(L)	Allied Mobile Force (Land Element)
AMRAAM	Advanced Medium Range Air-to-Air Missile
AOC	Air Officer Commanding
AP	Armour Piercing/Ammunition Point/Air Publication
APC	Armoured Personnel Carrier
APDS	Armour Piercing Discarding Sabot
APO	Army Post Office
ARBS	Angle Rate Bombing System
armd	Armoured
armr	Armour
ARRC	Allied Rapid Reaction Corps
ARRF	Allied Rapid Reaction Forces
arty	Artillery
ARV	Armoured Recover Vehicle
ASRAAM	Advanced Short-Range Air-to-Air Missile
ASTOVL	Advanced Short Take Off and Vertical Landing
ASW	Anti Submarine Warning
ATAF	Allied Tactical Air Force
ATGW	Anti-Tank Guided Weapon
att	Attached
ATWM	Army Transition to War Measure
AVLB	Armoured Vehicle Launched Bridge
AWC	Air Warfare Centre
AWOL	Absent without leave
BALTAP	Baltic Approaches
BAOR	British Army of the Rhine
BC	Battery Commander
Bde	Brigade
BE	Belgium (Belgian)
BFG	British Forces Germany
BFPO	British Forces Post Office

BG	Battle Group
BGHQ	Battlegroup Headquarters
BK	Battery Captain
BMA	Battery Manoeuvre Area
BMEWS	Ballistic Missile Early Warning System
BMH	British Military Hospital
Bn	Battalion
Bty	Battery
c sups	Combat Supplies
C3I	Command, Control, Communications & Intelligence
CAD	Central Ammunition Depot
cam	Camouflaged
CAP	Combat Air Patrol
cas	Casualty
CASEVAC	Casualty Evacuation
CASOM	Conventional Attack Stand-Off Missile
CASTOR	Corps Airborne Stand Off-Radar
cat	Catering
CATO	Civilian Air Traffic Operation
CCM	Counter Counter Measure
CCP	Casualty Collecting Point
CCS	Casualty Clearing Station
Cdo	Commando
CDS	Chief of the Defence Staff
CEP	Circular Error Probable/Central Engineer Park
CEPS	Central European Pipeline System
CET	Combat Engineer Tractor
CGRM	Commander General Royal Marines
CGS	Chief of the General Staff
CinC	Commander in Chief
CINCENT	Commander in Chief Central European Theatre
CINCUKAIR	Commander in Chief UK Air
civ	Civilian
CJO	Chief of Joint Operations
CJRDFO	Chief of the Joint Rapid Deployment Force Operations
Cmdt	Commandant
CO	Commanding Officer
COBRA	Counter Battery Radar
Col GS	Colonel General Staff
comd	Command/Commander
comp rat	Composite Ration (Compo)
COMRFA	Commander Royal Fleet Auxiliary
COMSEN	Communications Centre
coord	Co-ordinate
COS	Chief of Staff
coy	Company

CP	Close Protection/Command Post
CPO	Command Pay Office/Chief Petty Officer
CQMS	Company Quartermaster Sergeant
CRC	Control Reporting Centre
CRP	Control Reporting Point
CTOL	Conventional Take off and Landing
CTTO	Central Trials and Tactics Organisation
CUP	Capability Upgrade Period
CV	Combat Vehicle
CVD	Central Vehicle Depot
CVR(T)	Combat Vehicle Reconnaissance Tracked
CVR (W)	Combat Vehicle Reconnaissance Wheeled
CW	Chemical warfare
DAA	Divisional Administrative Area
DAG	Divisional Artillery Group
DASS	Defensive Aids Sub-System
DAW	Department of Air Warfare
def	Defence
DERA	Defence Evaluation & Research Agency
det	Detached/Detachment
DF	Defensive Fire
DHFS	Defence Helicopter Flying School
DISTAFF	Directing Staff (DS)
Div	Division
DK	Denmark
DMA	Divisional Maintenance Area
dml	Demolition
DMR	Daily Messing Rate
DRA	Defence Research Agency
DROPS	Demountable Rack Off Loading & Pick Up System
DS	Direct Support/Dressing Station
DTG	Date Time Group
ech	Echelon
ECM	Electronic Counter Measure
EDP	Emergency Defence Plan
emb	Embarkation
EME	Electrical and Mechanical Engineers
EMP	Electro Magnetic Pulse
en	Enemy
engr	Engineer
EOD	Explosive Ordnance Disposal
eqpt	Equipment
ETA	Estimated Time of Arrival
EW	Early warning/Electronic Warfare
EWOSE	Electronic Warfare Operational Support Establishment
ex	Exercise

FAC	Forward Air Controller
Fd Amb	Field Ambulance
Fd	Field
FEBA	Forward Edge of the Battle Area
FFR	Fitted for Radio
FGA	Fighter Ground Attack
FLA	Future Large Aircraft
FLET	Forward Location Enemy Troops
FLIR	Forward Looking Infrared
FLOT	Forward Location Own Troops
fmm	Formation
FOC	First of Class
FONA	Flag Officer Naval Aviation
FOO	Forward Observation Officer
FOSF	Flag Officer Surface Fleet
FOSM	Flag Officer Submarines
FOST	Flag Officer Sea Training
FR	France (French)
FRG	Federal Republic of Germany/Forward Repair Group
FRT	Forward Repair Team
FTS	Flying Training School
FUP	Forming Up Place/Forming Up Point
FWAM	Full Width Attack Mine
Fy	Financial Year
GDP	General Defence Plan/Gross Domestic Product
GE	German (Germany)
GOC	General Officer Commanding
GPMG	General Purpose Machine Gun
GPWS	Ground Proximity Warning System
GR	Greece (Greek)
GRSC	Ground Radio Servicing Centre
HAS	Hardened Aircraft Shelter
HE	High Explosive
HEAT	High Explosive Anti-Tank
hel	Helicopter
Hesh	High Explosive Squash Head
HOTAS	Hands on Throttle and Stick
HV	Hyper Velocity
HVM	Hyper Velocity Missile
Hy	Heavy
ICCS	Integrated Command & Control System
IFF	Indentification Friend or Foe
IFOR	Implementation Force
II	Image Intensifier
illum	Illuminating
Inf	Infantry

INTSUM	Intelligence Summary
IO	Intelligence Officer
IRF	Immediate Reaction Forces
IRG	Immediate Replenishment Group
IS	Internal Security
ISD	In Service Data
IT	Italy (Italian)
ITS	Inshore Training Squadron
IUR	Immediate Use Reserve
IW	Individual Weapon
JFHQ	Joint Force Headquarters
JHQ	Joint Headquarters
JRC	Joint Regional Command
JRDF	Joint Rapid Deployment Force
JSRC	Joint Sub-Regional Command
JSSU	Joint Services Signals Unit
KFOR	Kosovo Force
L of C	Lines of Communication
LAD	Light Aid Detachment (REME)
LANDCENT	Commander Allied Land Forces Central Europe
LGB	Laser Guided Bomb
LLAD	Low-Level Air Defence
LML	Lightweight Multiple Launcher
LO	Liaison Officer
Loc	Locating
Log	Logistic
LPH	Landing Platform Helicopter
LRATGW	Long-Range Anti-Tank Guided Weapons
LSL	Landing Ships Logistic
LSW	Light Support Weapon
LTW	Lyneham Training Wing
maint	Maintain
MAMBA	Mobile Artillery Monitoring Battlefield Radar
MAMS	Mobile Air Movement Squadron
MAOT	Mobile Air Operations Team
MATO	Military Air Traffic Operations
mat	Material
MBT	Main Battle Tank
MCM	Mine Countermeasures
MCMV	Mine Countermeasures Vessels
mech	Mechanised
med	Medical
MFC	Mortar Fire Controller
MG	Machine Gun
MIRV	Multiple Independently Targeted Re-entry Vehicle
MLRS	Multi-Launched Rocket System

MLU	Mid-life update
MNAD	Multi-National Airmobile Division
MND	Multi-National Division
MO	Medical Officer
mob	Mobilisation
MoD	Ministry of Defence
MoU	Memorandum of Understanding
MP	Military Police
MRG	Medium Repair Group
MRV	Multiple Re-entry Vehicle
msl	missile
MU	Maintenance Unit
NAAFI	Navy, Army and Air Force Institutes
NADGE	NATO Air Defence Ground Environment
NAEW-F	NATO Airborne Early Warning Forces
NATO	North Atlantic Treaty Organisation
NATS	National Air Traffic Services
NBC	Nuclear, Biological and Chemical Warfare
NCO	Non-Commissioned Officer
nec	Necessary
NGFSO	Naval Gunfire Support Officer
ni	Night
NL	Netherlands
NO	Norway (Norwegian)
NOK	Next of Kin
NORTHAG	Northern Army Group
NTR	Nothing to Report
NYK	Not Yet Known
OC	Officer Commanding
OCU	Operational Conversion Unit (RAF)
OEU	Operational Evaluation Unit
OIC	Officer in Charge
OOTW	Operations other than war
OP	Observation Post
opO	Operation Order
ORB	Omni-Radio Beacon
ORBAT	Order of Battle
P info	Public Information
pax	Passengers
PJHQ	Permanent Joint Headquarters
Pl	Platoon
PO	Portugal (Portuguese)
POL	Petrol, Oil and Lubrication
Pro	Provost
PTC	Personnel and Training Command
QCS	Queen's Colour Squadron

QM	Quartermaster
R & D	Research and Development
RA	Royal Artillery
RAC	Royal Armoured Corps
RAFASUPU	RAF Armament Support Unit
RAMC	Royal Army Medical Corps
RAP	Rocket-Assisted Projectile/Regiment Aid Post
RCMDS	Remote-Control Mine Disposal System
RCZ	Rear Control Zone
RE	Royal Engineers
rebro	Rebroadcast
rec	Recovery
recce	reconnaissance
Regt	Regiment
REME	Royal Electrical and Mechanical Engineers
RFA	Royal Fleet Auxiliary
rft	Reinforcement
RGJ	Royal Green Jackets
RHA	Royal Horse Artillery
RHQ	Regimental Headquarters
RLC	Royal Logistic Corps
RM	Royal Marines
RMA	Rear Maintenance Area/Royal Military Academy
RMAS	Royal Military Academy Sandhurst
RMP	Royal Military Police
RN	Royal Navy
RNMC	Royal Netherlands Marine Corps
RO	Retired Officer
Ro-Ro	Roll On-Roll Off
RP	Reporting Point
RPV	Remotely Piloted Vehicle
RRF	Royal Regiment of Fusiliers/Rapid Reaction Forces
RSA	Royal School of Artillery
RSME	Royal School of Mechanical Engineering
RSS	Royal School of Signals
RTM	Ready to Move
RTU	Return to Unit
SACLOS	Semi Automatic to Command Line of Sight
SACEUR	Supreme Allied Commander Europe
SAM	Surface-to-Air Missile
SAR	Search and Rescue
SAS	Special Air Service
SBS	Special Boat Service
SDR	Strategic Defence Review
Sect	Section
SH	Support Helicopters

SHAPE	Supreme Headquarters Allied Powers Europe
SIB	Special Investigation Branch
Sig	Signals
sit	Situation
SITREP	Situation Report
SLBM	Submarine-Launched Ballistic Missiles
SMG	Sub-Machine Gun
smk	Smoke
SNCO	Senior Non-Commissioned Officer
SOC	Sector Operations Centre
SP	Self Propelled/Start Point
SPS	Staff and Personnel Support
Sqn	Squadron
SSBN	Nuclear Powered Ballistic Missile Submarine
SSK	Single shot to kill
SSM	Surface-to-Surface Missile
SSN	Nuclear-Powered Attack Submarine
SSVC	Services Sound and Cinema Corporation
STC	Strike Command
STOBAR	Short Take-Off and Arrested Recovery
STOL	Short Take-Off and Landing
STOVL	Short Take-Off and Vertical Landing
TA	Territorial Army
tac	Tactical
TBT	Tank Bridge Transporter
TCC	Turret Control Computer
TCP	Traffic Control Post
TCV	Troop Carrying Vehicle
tgt	Target
THAAD	Theatre High-Altitude Area Defence
TIALD	Thermal Imaging Airborne Laser Designator
tk	Tank
TLAM	Tactical Land Attack Missile
TLAM-C	Tactical Land Attack Missile - Conventional
TLB	Top Level Budget
TMA	Troop Manoeuvre Area
TOT	Time on Target
tp	Troop
tpt	Transport
TTTE	Tri-National Tornado Training Establishment
TU	Turkish (Turkey)
TUL	Truck Utility Light
TUM	Truck Utility Medium
UAV	Unmanned Aerial Vehicle
U/S	Unserviceable
UK	United Kingdom

UKADGE	United Kingdom Air Defence Ground Environment
UKADR	United Kingdom Air Defence Region
UKMF	United Kingdom Mobile Force
UKSC (G)	United Kingdom Support Command (Germany)
UN	United Nations
UNFICYP	United Nations Forces in Cyprus
UNCLASS	Unclassified
US	United States
UXB	Unexploded Bomb
veh	Vehicle
VOR	Vehicle off the Road
WE	War Establishment
wh	Wheeled
WIMP	Whingeing Incompetent Malingering Person
wksp	Workshop
WMR	War Maintenance Reserve
WO	Warrant Officer
X	Crossing (as in roads or rivers)

This publication was produced by R&F (Defence) Publications.
Editorial Office 01743-235079: Fax 01743 241962
E Mail: Cheyman@Interramp.co.uk

The other publications in this series are:

The Royal Air Force Pocket Guide 1994-95
The Armed Forces of the United Kingdom 2001-2002 (Fourth Edition)
The British Army Pocket Guide 2002-2003 (Ninth Edition)

Visit the website www.armedforces.co.uk

Further copies can be obtained from :

Pen & Sword Books Ltd
47 Church Street
Barnsley S70 2AS

Telephone: 01226-734222   Fax: 01226-734438
(Major credit cards accepted)

Fifth Edition - October 2003